LEE'S YOUNG ARTILLERIST
WILLIAM R. J. PEGRAM

A NATION DIVIDED
NEW STUDIES IN CIVIL WAR HISTORY

James I. Robertson, Editor

LEE'S YOUNG ARTILLERIST
WILLIAM R. J. PEGRAM

PETER S. CARMICHAEL

UNIVERSITY PRESS OF VIRGINIA

CHARLOTTESVILLE AND LONDON

THE UNIVERSITY PRESS OF VIRGINIA
Copyright © 1995 by the Rector and Visitors
of the University of Virginia

First published 1995
First paperback edition 1998

Library of Congress Cataloging-in-Publication Data
Carmichael, Peter S.
  Lee's young artillerist: William R. J. Pegram / Peter S.
Carmichael.
      p.   cm.—(A nation divided)
  Includes bibliographical reference and index.
  ISBN 0-8139-1611-9 (cloth)
  ISBN 0-8139-1828-6 (paper)
  1. Pegram, William Ransom Johnson, 1841–1865.   2. Confederate
States of America. Army of Northern Virginia, 3rd Corps—
Biography.   3. Virginia—History—Civil War, 1861–1865—Religious
aspects.   4. Virginia—History—Civil War, 1861–1865—Artillery
operations, Confederate.   5. United States—History—Civil War,
1861–1865—Religious aspects.   6. United States—History—Civil
War, 1861–1865—Artillery operations, Confederate.   7. Soldiers—
Virginia—Biography   I. Title.   II. Series.
E547.N7P444   1995
973.7'455'092—dc20
[B]   94-48140
                                                              CIP

Printed in the United States of America

FOR MY PARENTS,

Lowell Gene and Charlotte Ann Carmichael,

whose love and support have given my life meaning and hope

CONTENTS

ILLUSTRATIONS

FIGURES

MAPS

ACKNOWLEDGMENTS

TEN YEARS HAVE PASSED SINCE I FIRST EXAMINED THE LETTERS OF WILLIAM R. J. Pegram at the Virginia Historical Society in Richmond. Since then, many people have assisted me along the way. I am deeply indebted to my mentor, Gary W. Gallagher, of Pennsylvania State University. He painstakingly read every draft of the manuscript and urged me to examine Pegram from a generational perspective. Without his friendship and advice I could never have finished the project. Nor could a work on any subject relating to the Army of Northern Virginia be completed without the help of Robert K. Krick. Bob provided countless references to obscure sources, scrutinized the entire manuscript, and offered valuable advice. James I. Robertson, Jr., of the Virginia Polytechnic Institute, encouraged me to submit my manuscript to the University Press of Virginia, and his suggestions have been critical to its completion. My good friend Robert E. L. Krick cheerfully tracked down a number of leads and raised important questions concerning Pegram's military career.

Theodore P. Savas, of *Civil War Regiments*, completed the maps for this book against a brutal deadline. His work is superb, and I am extremely appreciative of his efforts. Portions of three chapters benefited greatly from the critical reading of Carol Reardon. Nan Elizabeth Woodruff created a stimulating atmosphere in which to discuss the antebellum South in her seminars at Penn State. Her influence has been far greater than she can imagine. I also profited from long discussions with William A. Blair, whose work on the Virginia home front challenged many of my assumptions about Confederate nationalism and wartime dissent. My thanks as well to Keith S. Bohannon, who patiently listened to my ideas about college life in the 1850s and offered valuable comparisons to the intellectual environment at universities in Georgia on the eve of the Civil War.

I was fortunate to receive excellent training at Indiana University and Purdue University at Indianapolis. The professors were accessible and demonstrated genuine concern for the students' intellectual development. John K. Stevens guided my initial work on Pegram and gave more of his time than I had any reasonable right to expect. Peter J. Sehlinger, Monroe H. Little, Jr., Sabine Jessner, and Ralph D. Gray all insisted that I become familiar with the historiography of their respective periods and were instrumental in my decision to enter graduate school.

Pegram's descendants have not only enthusiastically supported this project but have led me to arcane sources that I could never have found on my own. I extend my heartfelt thanks to Virginia B. Maloney, Peter W. W. Powell and Ethel B. Powell, William Pegram Johnson III, the late J. Rieman McIntosh, and Robert E. Lee Pegram. My good friends and colleagues at the National Park

Service generously gave their assistance as well. My thanks, then, to Mike Andrus, Chris Calkins, Noel G. Harrison, Ian Lowe, Theodore C. Mahr, Gregory A. Mertz, James H. Ogden III, Frank A. O'Reilly, David R. Ruth, and Mac Wyckoff. I also wish to extend my gratitude to Stephen Belcher, James Chalker, Al Harris, Jon Lowry, Richard S. Skidmore and Wilda Skidmore, Dale S. Snair, James A. Trulock and the late Alice R. Trulock, Larry Williford, and the members of the Indianapolis Civil War Round Table.

It has been a pleasure to work with Richard Holway of the University Press of Virginia and the staff of the press, all of whom have proved patient and encouraging, as well as committed to this book. Pamela McFarland Holway, my editor, deserves special recognition for her efforts. She is all that anyone could ever want in an editor. In addition, a number of archivists have been especially helpful. I wish to record my gratitude to Richard J. Sommers, of the United States Army Military History Institute, Carlisle Barracks; Richard A. Shrader, of the Southern Historical Collection, Wilson Library, University of North Carolina; Michael Plunkett, of the Special Collections Department, University of Virginia Library; and Guy Swanson, of the Eleanor Brockenbrough Library, Museum of the Confederacy. More generally, my thanks go to the many helpful individuals I encountered at the William R. Perkins Library, Duke University; the Virginia State Library; the National Archives; and the William L. Clements Library, University of Michigan. E. Lee Shepard and his incomparable staff at the Virginia Historical Society deserve special recognition: their professionalism and friendliness remains unmatched. I cannot think of a finer institution in which to study Virginia history.

My two research assistants, Calbert and Lancelot, routinely terrorized my office, scattered papers across my desk, and failed to demonstrate the appropriate regard for my work. I am, of course, very grateful: their antics were welcome interruptions from the tedium of writing. Lloyd and Wilma Tomlinson helped me appreciate history by allowing their grandson to tag along on vacations, although I am sorry that Grandma Tomlinson and my grandparents William and Elva Carmichael did not live to see the publication of this book. I am indebted as well to the Carmichael clan of Brown County, Indiana, who have accepted me as one of their own. Ruth Donelson has patiently endured my childish pranks over the years. She is a wonderful woman. I am equally grateful to Robert L. Walter and Lynne P. Walter, who proved to be stalwart battlefield companions and equally stalwart supporters of this project, and to my good friend, Joseph S. Podeswa, whose wonderful stories brightened many a walk. Tara Michelle Walter, the granddaughter of Joseph and Angeline Podeswa, is my best friend, whose love and understanding helped me believe in myself when I thought I would never finish this project. I am both fortunate and grateful to have her in my life.

Peter S. Carmichael

LEE'S YOUNG ARTILLERIST

WILLIAM R. J. PEGRAM

INTRODUCTION

WILLIAM RANSOM JOHNSON PEGRAM FORGED A RECORD AS ONE OF THE most prominent and efficient artillerists in the Army of Northern Virginia. Rising from sergeant to full colonel in less than four years, he earned an enviable reputation by using his cannon as offensive weapons. Battle transformed the normally mild-mannered Willy Pegram into a bold and effective military leader. Calm, focused, and self-possessed in combat, he inspired his men to perform their duty even in the most desperate situations. Always eager to engage the enemy, Pegram participated in every major battle fought by the Army of Northern Virginia. He sought combat not for martial glory but because he considered the battlefield a place where he could demonstrate to God, his family, and his community devotion to ideas he had cherished long before the war.

A slaveholder and devout Episcopalian, Pegram understood his world through a religious framework. As Donald Mathews has pointed out, the Episcopal church in Virginia was strongly influenced by evangelical Protestantism, which prescribed a rigid code of behavior that Pegram tried to observe throughout his life.[1] Religion also gave Pegram a sense of belonging to a Christian community, committed to slavery as an institution and to its attendant hierarchical social relations. Indeed, broad interdenominational agreement existed on social questions in the Old South: differences over Calvinist doctrine mattered little when it came to the defense of slavery. Intolerance and bigotry existed among all denominations, but Southerners nonetheless firmly believed they belonged to a Christian community.[2]

While Methodists, Baptists, Presbyterians, and Episcopalians disagreed about critical theological matters, they all stressed the original sin of man, the need for reliance upon Providence's will, and the importance of the conversion experience followed by "a life of discipline and devotion."[3] Southern Evangelicalism also called for moral regeneration through the power of individual action—not as isolated displays of piety but as public behavior subject to community scrutiny. For Southern men like Pegram, duty to church extended beyond personal concerns to include protection of family and friends from physical harm and from insult.

Pegram's view of the Old South and the Confederacy as a religious society reflects his allegiance to the ethos of the planter class. Prominent theologians and secular thinkers alike had constructed a Christian defense of slavery as an extension of the master class's ideology. Religious leaders offered a broader scriptural interpretation of society that emphasized human inequality between master and slave as part of a greater social hierarchy visible among all people—parent and child, man and woman, rich and poor. Support of slavery was thus viewed as a Christian duty for all white Southerners, and slaveholders duly used this Christian philosophy to justify governing their inferiors on the theory of mutual obligation.[4]

Not surprisingly, theologians and ministers exerted a tremendous influence on the everyday lives of Southerners. Even members of the intellectual community took their religion seriously and recognized the importance of interpreting the South as a divinely sanctioned society. Professors, college presidents, academy principals, and teachers offered a defense of slavery and the South's social relations that transcended class and religious divisions among Southerners.

As part of the last generation of antebellum slaveholders, William Pegram spent his formative years during the 1850s, a time when the ideological explanation of the South's way of life had fully matured.[5] Southern divines and moral and social philosophers defended slavery in terms of an ideological war with the North. The religious instruction he received from Charles F. E. Minnigerode at Saint Paul's Episcopal Church in Richmond, coupled with the teachings of Albert T. Bledsoe and James P. Holcombe at the University of Virginia, influential defenders of slavery who warned of the evils of free labor and the rise of bourgeois democracy, must have contributed to Pegram's hierarchical worldview and his belief in the moral superiority of his society.[6]

In short, William Pegram believed he lived in a Christian society. He entered Confederate service to defend a way of life ordained by God. Although Pegram was hardly given to introspective or intellectual discussions, his letters reflect the profound influence of the secular and divine explanations of slavery and the social relations of the Old South. Claiming Southerners as God's chosen people, Pegram saw the South as engaged in a war to preserve the home of Christian civilization from the ungodly North, although his condemnation of the North and of the Republican party is best interpreted as a rejection of free labor ideology. Pegram looked upon the sizeable immigrant population in the North with disgust, fearing they had attained too much influence within the political system. As his letters strongly suggest, Pegram not only accepted the hierarchical view of Southern social relations but also considered rapid social mobility among the lower classes a threat to an orderly society. His fears surfaced during the war when he blamed parvenus in Richmond for demoralizing society's respectable classes.[7]

Neither zealot nor fanatic, Pegram articulated a view that almost certainly reflected the basic assumptions of many men of his class and generation. His attitudes toward secession, Northerners, the Confederacy, and God were shared by many well-educated white Southerners connected to the slaveholding class who served in the Confederate army. Ardently nationalistic, these men believed they fought for the survival of a Christian civilization founded upon hierarchy, with biblically sanctioned slavery at its center.

Religion thus formed the cornerstone of Pegram's nationalistic convictions. Although personally reluctant to leave the Union, he believed that Northerners and Southerners had evolved into two different races. Foreigners had polluted the North, Pegram claimed, and were ruled by men who represented ideas antithetical to the Southern way of life. After the Republicans seized the presidency in 1860, for example, Pegram described the vice president-elect, Hannibal Hamlin, as half-black and Congress as a body ruled by Germans. Although he probably did not mean these comments literally, his characterization of the country's leaders underscores his view of the North as an alien land.[8]

While the South considered reform movements and all the various "isms" that surfaced during the antebellum period as a threat to the social order, Northern reformers as well as more moderate Republicans elevated the individual as the locus of power and promised social mobility for anybody, regardless of family background or previous standing in society.[9] Slaveholders like Pegram shuddered at the prospect of the masses attaining prominence and power in their society. After all, God assigned men and women specific stations in life. Tampering with this delicate arrangement constituted a direct challenge to God's preordained world. Pegram accordingly saw the Republican party a menace to Southern rights and considered their designs against slavery in the territories as promoting radical change in the social, political, and moral order of the country.[10]

The son of a staunch Whig, Pegram must have viewed the South as a "progressive" society mercifully free of the besetting evils of free labor. Whiggish slaveholders, like Pegram's father, favored economic development and saw no conflict between cultivating economic relations with the North and their cherished belief in a social hierarchy resulting from the natural differences in men. Pegram probably welcomed the material prosperity of the 1850s, when railroads, turnpikes, and light industries increasingly brought Virginia into market relations with the North. Accepting these improvements, however, did not quell slaveholders' fears over who would receive the benefits of progress and the dangerous possibility that such progress might alter the traditional class structure.[11]

The birth of the Confederacy offered Pegram an opportunity to support a Christian society that would ensure the continued existence of slavery and hierarchy. Pegram demonstrated his deep nationalistic convictions by fighting recklessly on the battlefield. He firmly believed in a religion of action, not just of prayer. As Drew Gilpin Faust has correctly pointed out, Confederate ideology "transformed God himself into a nationalist and made war for political independence into a crusade." Because God had ordained this crusade, Pegram and his men were obligated to do everything in their power to defeat the enemy. Pegram repeatedly assured his family that Providence protected Christian soldiers in combat. Should God suddenly lift his shield, Pegram harbored no fear because heaven awaited all Southerners who gave their lives in this holy war.[12]

Contrary to what many historians have argued about a waning Confederate will to resist, Pegram's determination to create an independent nation never wavered.[13] He equated losing faith in the Confederacy with abandoning God, family, and community—in short, the entire world into which he had been born. He could not conceive of defeat at the hands of ungodly Northerners: setbacks might occur, he admitted, but only as temporary aberrations in God's plan. Pegram saw no connection between reversals in Confederate fortunes and the existence of slavery or some other national sin. Rather, defeats resulted when people back home lost faith in God and/or when cowardly profiteers challenged the antebellum social order. These people, in effect, had become as degenerate as the enemy. If the Southern people would just trust in God, Pegram earnestly believed victory would be theirs.

Pegram was well educated, receiving his training as part of the last generation of antebellum Southern men. His formative years fell at a time of sectional fervor in the South. Planters and politicians concerned themselves with justifying slavery as a positive moral good, while Southern schools stressed the region's superior way of life. Like others of his generation, Pegram developed little attachment to the Union: this was a time when Southern leadership had passed from those who favored strong ties to Union to those committed to Southern rights.[14] He shared the values of young Confederate officers such as John Hampden Chamberlayne, Greenlee Davidson, Charles Colcock Jones, Jr., William Gordon McCabe, James Drayton Nance, William Dorsey Pender, Stephen Dodson Ramseur, and John C. C. Sanders. Either members of or tied closely to the South's ruling elite, these men matured in a highly charged atmosphere that emphasized Southern distinctiveness. Born into slaveholding families, they enjoyed a good education and were at least moderately religious. Their faith in God infused them with a powerful sense of nationalism. Whenever Southern armies encountered setbacks, they encouraged the people back home to trust that God would see the nation through its dark times.[15]

Military experience reinforced nationalistic sentiments and forged a common bond among soldiers.[16] Not only did these Southerners witness the sacrifices of their comrades, but they also saw the Yankees becoming more ungodly as the war progressed, engaging in acts of terror against civilians and even going so far as to employ black soldiers. These crimes validated existing assumptions about the "inherent nature" of the people above the Mason-Dixon Line. From their experience in the Confederate army, these men increasingly believed they would triumph because the depredations of the Federal army inevitably would put God on the Confederate side. Moreover, Robert E. Lee emerged as a figure embodying the virtues of the Confederacy and gave determined Southern soldiers reason for fighting even when the cause seemed hopeless to civilians. Pegram himself pointed out in one of his letters that God would never abandon "his people," who had made such tremendous sacrifices to preserve a way of life that they believed to be moral and good.[17]

Southern officers such as Pegram proved their loyalty and devotion to the Confederacy throughout the war. Aggressively fighting the enemy, they repeatedly exposed themselves under fire, displaying not the slightest concern for personal safety. When Confederate forces fled in a blind panic at the Battle of Third Winchester on September 19, 1864, for example, Stephen Dodson Ramseur grabbed a musket, rode to the "foremost," and "knocked every man on the head who refused to halt and by this means . . . got the div'n again in line."[18] Ramseur's brazen disregard for his own life typified the conduct of these Southern officers in combat. Although camaraderie based on shared experiences in the army undoubtedly motivated them in part, the belief that Southern independence must be achieved at any cost also prompted them to risk their lives. Surrender would be worse than defeat.

What distinguished Pegram from several other such officers was the extent to which he saw the world through a prism of Christian duty. Once Pegram enlisted in the army, he believed that he had made a contract not only with the Confederacy but also with God. Duty to God equaled duty to nation. This was a covenant that could not easily be compromised or abandoned, especially when God seemed to be testing his people with misfortune on the battlefield. Pegram's eagerness to risk his own life and those of his men by no means indicated that he desired promotion or enjoyed the excitement of battle. In his eyes, he was simply trying to fulfill his obligations. Ambition, Pegram declared, undermined Christian character. If he carried out his duty, God would reward him, either on earth or in heaven.[19]

Pegram and other young Confederate officers thus stand as testimony against current wisdom concerning Confederate nationalism and morale. Many historians portray a Confederacy unable to forge a nation or withstand the sacrifices necessary for modern war. In seeking an explanation for this lack of will or failure to persevere, some scholars have pointed to guilt over slavery that bred an almost unconscious desire for a Northern victory, which would free Southern whites of their moral burden. Others have argued that the pressures of war forced many Southerners to confront conflicts that always had existed between slaveholders and nonslaveholders, planters and yeomen, rich and poor, black and white. While the thesis of weak Confederate nationalism and morale might accurately describe certain elements in the South, it obscures the fact that thousands of Southern men were willing to die for a cause that, by 1863, appeared doomed to many outsiders.[20]

Without further research into this area, one can only speculate as to how the religious framework of the Old South shaped the thinking of Southerners who at least initially supported the Confederacy. Religion did not make all

Southerners uniformly nationalistic. Pegram's experience does, however, offer a signpost to guide further inquiry, for it introduces the possibility that many slaveholders and nonslaveholders interpreted their world through a similar religious prism—one that gave Pegram and thousands of other young Confederates just cause and comfort for which to die.

ONE

"THE GOD OF ALL NATIONS"
WILL DIRECT ALL THINGS FOR THE BEST

ON THE EVE OF THE AMERICAN REVOLUTION, PRISTINE FORESTS stretched endlessly below Petersburg, Virginia. The trees were big and sturdy, and loblolly pines predominated. In 1752, 329,000 acres of this densely wooded terrain became Dinwiddie County, but even with legal organization the land remained a virtual wilderness. Settlement of the area always had been slow. Most roads resembled roughly hewn paths, having changed little since they were blazed by Native Americans. Access to navigable waterways, such as the James and Appomattox Rivers, proved difficult. Transporting goods and crops across this rugged landscape deterred most coastal farmers from leaving their plantations.

Beginning in the 1750s, however, the situation altered dramatically. Virginia's cash crop, tobacco, had exhausted most of the farmland in the tidewater region. When they were obliged to look westward, the rich soil of Dinwiddie enticed planters to leave their homes. Yet plantation life in tidewater Virginia could not be recreated in Dinwiddie County. Heavy timber in the area generally limited the size of farms to fewer than 350 acres. The homes were simple, and few slaves tilled the fields. But abundant streams provided water for mills to grind corn and flour, and farms quickly became self-sufficient enterprises. The growth of Petersburg near the end of the eighteenth century provided Dinwiddie residents with a readily available commercial center in which to sell their tobacco. Prosperity blessed the community, as plantations increased in size and number.[1]

One of the most successful planters in the county was General John Pegram, whose father Edward had moved to the area in the 1750s after fulfilling his obligations as an indentured servant. The elder Pegram amassed a sizeable estate of land and slaves before he died in 1795. John Pegram built upon his father's wealth, expanding his holdings during the early 1800s and becoming a prominent figure in the community's political affairs. He was a gentleman justice of Dinwiddie, sheriff of the county between 1763 and 1772, and a member of the Virginia House of Delegates from 1797 to 1801 and of the Virginia Senate from 1804 to 1808. During James Monroe's tenure as president (1817–25) John Pegram received the appointment as United States marshal for the Eastern District of Virginia, partly because his service in the War of 1812 had already given him lasting fame. A brigadier general in the Virginia militia before the conflict, he rose to the rank of major general before hostilities ended. Pegram's military exploits left his family with a proud martial legacy that his descendants strove to emulate.[2]

On his estate Bonneville, John Pegram and his second wife, Martha Ward Gregory, reared twelve children, including William R. J. Pegram's father, James West. Born on January 22, 1804, James West Pegram received his education at home from some of the finest tutors in the area. He possessed a "natural fondness" for literature and language, which prompted him to pursue law, but his father apparently could not afford to send him away to school. Undaunted, James West diligently saved his earnings while he worked as a deputy marshal under his father. After accumulating sufficient funds, the younger Pegram entered Harvard and studied law under Joseph Story. Returning to Petersburg in the 1820s, Pegram attracted many clients.[3]

James West also continued his father's tradition of fulfilling civic duty. Some time between 1830 and 1844, he received appointments as colonel and then brigadier general in the Virginia militia. He also climbed the ranks of the Whig party, a vibrant organization in the Petersburg-Dinwiddie area that drew its strength from the planter class. The party's economic policy, which supported new banks, paper currency, and the creation of new corporations, must have appealed to James West's interests, given that he entered banking in the 1830s. An orator of "striking abilities," Pegram frequently advocated Whig policies at political rallies and public meetings. Although he remained a firm supporter of Southern rights and slavery, he preached moderation on sectional issues.[4]

James West Pegram married Virginia Johnson of Chesterfield County in 1829. Her father, William Ransom Johnson, ranked among the region's wealthiest planters, whose fortune and reputation were based on his abilities as a horse breeder and racer. He was known as the "Napoleon of the Turf" and considered by some to be the "leviathan of the betting ring" because he wagered enormous sums of money on his horses. Johnson also played a role in politics. He supported the Whig platform while serving in the state senate from 1822 to 1826 and in the lower house from 1828 to 1838, and he entertained Henry Clay at his home.[5]

William Johnson pressured his daughter and son-in-law to reside at his estate, Oakland, after their wedding. Within a year or two, however, James West felt constrained and isolated on the plantation. He was eighteen miles from Petersburg and twenty-two from Richmond. The sedate life at Oakland simply did not satisfy his ambitions. Anxious to start their own life, Pegram and his wife returned to Petersburg in 1831–32, where Pegram became head of the bar and was elected cashier to the local branch of the Bank of Virginia. He quickly established himself throughout the state "as a lawyer and able financier." The marriage of Virginia Johnson to James West Pegram, though clearly founded upon romantic love, also strengthened the ties between old planter families and the financiers in the city, whose wealth had been acquired relatively re-

Figure 1. William Ransom Johnson, "The Napoleon of the Turf," Willy's grandfather. (Photograph courtesy of the Virginia Historical Society)

cently. James West Pegram adopted the assumptions of the ruling elite as espoused by the dominant planter class. Like most merchants and financiers, he desired membership in the aristocracy. He eventually acquired interests in two Mississippi plantations; however, he never owned more than eight slaves at his Virginia residence.[6]

The Southern upper class was committed to a hierarchical society, the culture, politics, and economy of which were defined by slavery as a system of labor. Southern values emphasized family, a code of honor, and an aristocratic spirit that called for men to aspire to a life of ease. The accumulation of land, slaves, military titles, and political honors satisfied the acquisitive nature of most Southerners. James West Pegram and Virginia Johnson ascribed to these beliefs: they accepted not only the material aspirations and ideological interests of the planter class but also the social relations characteristic of a slave society—relations governed by paternalism. This social code imbued Southerners with a sense of communal responsibility, and it made community standards of acceptable behavior paramount in their lives. The historical context of the antebellum South that shaped the attitudes of James and Virginia Pegram also molded the ideology of their children. All three of their sons would eventually go to war to preserve this way of life.

Stockholders from the Bank of Virginia in Richmond quickly recognized James Pegram's talents. When the institution suffered a serious defalcation in 1840, amounting to a loss of more than $500,000, bank officials offered him a position as cashier of the main branch. The incident had created a lingering controversy and shaken the people's faith in the financial system. Nevertheless, Pegram accepted the offer and moved to Richmond with his wife and children, ten-year-old Mary Evans, eight-year-old John, and James West, Jr., who was less than a year old. The Pegrams occupied a home on Main Street next to the bank and near the center of town. Not long after the removal of the family to Richmond, on June 29, 1841, Virginia gave birth to her third son, who was named William Ransom Johnson. Family members and close acquaintances called him "Willy." [7]

Less than two years after Willy's birth, James West was appointed president of the Bank of Virginia, replacing the well-known Dr. John Brockenbrough, who had controlled the office for thirty-eight years. Brockenbrough had been much admired, and news of Pegram's advancement caused heated debate in some corners—but he seems to have ignored his critics. He fulfilled his duties capably, with the result that his new position brought additional financial rewards and prestige. The Pegram home attracted people from some of the most prominent circles in the city. Among the noteworthy visitors was General Winfield Scott, an associate of Pegram's father during the War of 1812. His responsibilities at the bank were demanding, but even so James West spent most of his free time with his family. He often assisted his older children, Mary and John, with their studies or read stories to James West, Jr., and Willy. If any of the children fell ill, Pegram exhibited "womanly tenderness" in nursing them, including the most recent addition to his family, a baby girl born two years after Willy, on July 15, 1843, and named Virginia Johnson. [8]

When Willy was about three years old, his father returned from work with a hobbyhorse that he presented to his youngest son. He also had a small scooter for James, Jr. Both boys scurried to the garden to test their new toys. The wheels on the scooter allowed Jimmy to ride circles around his younger brother. As Jimmy sailed "gayly and triumphantly around the garden," Mary Pegram recalled, "poor little Willy" whipped and scolded his wooden horse for not keeping pace with his brother's mechanical toy. Willy had a terrible lisp as a small child. His father overheard him say: "I won't have this old horst that can't do anything but stand still; I want one like Jimmy's that can go everywhere." Impressed by his son's spirit, James West exchanged the hobbyhorse for "the kind that could go." Interestingly, Mary Pegram believed that ultimately this was Willy's only memory of his father. [9]

Because power and status in the South depended almost entirely upon ownership of slaves and land, James West Pegram's ambitions required that he expand his chattel holdings. His desire to become a planter became reality when he purchased a share of a large cotton operation in Mississippi. In October 1844 Pegram started for the Deep South to settle the details of the transaction. He arrived at Louisville, Kentucky, on October 22 and that evening delivered a fiery speech to a crowded assembly hall. Henry Clay later learned from a member of the audience that Pegram "ably and eloquently" expounded Whig principles.[10]

The next day James West boarded the *Lucy Walker,* a craft destined for New Orleans. As the afternoon sun dipped in front of the boat, the vessel stalled in the middle of the Ohio River about four or five miles below New Albany, Indiana, where it sat helplessly for some five minutes. Suddenly, a blast from the boiler room rocked the ship. Fragments of machinery, wood, and human beings shot straight into the air. One passenger descended with such force that his limp body crashed through the upper deck. Fire quickly erupted, as the vessel began to sink into the river. Within fifteen minutes the ladies' cabin was completely submerged, and screams of the surviving women echoed along the shore. Pegram, who had not been injured by the initial explosion, made his way through the wreckage, trying to locate a woman who had been placed under his care by some friends in Louisville. (As it turned out, the woman already had secured her safety.) When the list of passengers was finally read, no one answered to the name James West Pegram. The Ohio River never yielded his body.[11]

News of Pegram's death shocked the people of Richmond. "Rarely has a community been more sadly impressed by any similar event than this," stated the *Richmond Whig and Public Advertiser.* The same tribute pronounced James West one of the finest examples "of the Virginia gentleman of the olden time" and "a superior model of what a son, a father, a husband, a friend or a citizen ought to be." Members of Richmond's city council and Bank of Virginia employees resolved to wear the "usual badge of mourning" for thirty days. The bank's board of directors also offered "our most sincere condolements to his widow and family on an occurrence which has so unexpectedly embittered their happiness." Henry Clay found the death of James West Pegram particularly disturbing: "Having long and well known him, I have rarely been so much affected by the loss of any friend," he wrote, adding that Pegram was a "distinguished champion" of the Whig cause. Sentiments of consolation did little to relieve the sadness that overwhelmed Virginia Johnson and her five children. A neighbor in Richmond recalled that the wife's grief did not subside until many years after her husband's death.[12]

Nor did Virginia Pegram have much time to recover emotionally from this trauma before financial troubles began to besiege her household. When James West drowned in the Ohio, he had on his person and in his trunks "a large sum of money in Bank notes, and sundry valuable papers, all of which were irretrievably lost." Not only did this disaster make it difficult for Virginia Pegram to provide the material comforts to which her family had grown accustomed, but she also found she could not meet her husband's business obligations. Fragmentary records suggest he owed a modest sum of $482 to a furniture merchant in Baltimore, in addition to which he may have had outstanding debts to another businessman in Baltimore. Whatever the extent of his debts, it is clear that the sinking of the *Lucy Walker* had greatly diminished James West Pegram's estate. "Poor Mrs. Pegram has gone to her father's place in the country," a family friend wrote shortly after Pegram's death. The friend also had heard that "it is doubtful she will have anything left after her husband's debts are all paid. Poor woman, what a change in her condition. From prosperity and happiness to poverty and misery. From the 'head of society' in Richmond to profound retirement in the country." This may have overstated the matter, but Virginia's daughter Mary later recalled that the financial situation immediately after her father's death "led to serious embarrassments" for the family.[13]

Yet Virginia and her five children were by no means destitute. Her father, William Johnson, cushioned the economic and emotional blow by inviting them to stay at his estate, Oakland. It is difficult to determine when and for how long Virginia and her children lived at her father's home, but in all likelihood the Pegrams shuttled between Richmond and Johnson's plantation. Not until Virginia established a women's school in Richmond in 1855 did the family reside in the city on a more permanent basis.[14]

Oakland proved a veritable paradise for a young boy like Willy. Rolling fields interspersed with patches of timber could be explored during long summer afternoons, or a relaxing day might be spent fishing along the banks of the Appomattox River. Riding horses must have been a favorite family pastime, considering Johnson's proclivity for racing horses and his elaborate training facilities. He had constructed a two-mile track that ran perfectly straight so that he could keep an eye on his thoroughbreds even while entertaining guests in his eighteen-room mansion. A sign over the main entrance of the plantation read: "There is nothing so good for the inside of a man as the outside of a horse." Though surrounded by some of the finest animals in the South, Willy never fully mastered the art of horsemanship. As a comrade in the Army of Northern Virginia would later recall, Pegram was not only a "poor horseman" but could "hardly distinguish the horse he rode for years from any other" because he was so nearsighted.[15]

Without a father figure in the house (William Johnson frequently left his plantation on business), Willy's older brother John assumed the patriarchal role in the family. Willy looked at his brother with admiring eyes, wanting very much to be like him. In his estimation, John's character and conduct were beyond reproach, and he eagerly sought his brother's counsel and approval. John's departure for the United States Military Academy in 1850 left a vacuum in Willy's life that could not be filled. A letter written by James West, Jr., in 1860 illustrates John's exalted position in the family. "Brother has at last reached home," he observed of John, "and of course all of the Pegrams are delighted at having their idol at home again," to which he added that "you never saw anything like the fuss that they all make up at home over him and the funniest thing of all is that they say I do not care at all about him because I do not fall down and worship him too." James West thought "they treat him more like a god than a human being and I confess I can not keep up to them in this." [16]

As was the case with most Southerners, family remained a central part of Willy Pegram's life. He was especially close to his sisters and mother and disliked separation from them. Mary Evans Pegram, his older sister, was one of the "most noted conversationalist[s] of her day." Well educated and articulate, she deported herself in an aristocratic but "affable" manner. Willy's younger sister, Virginia Johnson, exhibited similar traits. Called Jennie by her intimates, she was a legendary beauty who inspired rumors about jilted beaux "rising disconsolate from her feet." And yet she was more reserved than Mary and was never "disparaged as a coquette." Pegram's other brother, James West, Jr., or Jimmy, had a sharp tongue and a quick wit, but he lacked purpose and direction, often embarking on business ventures that left him frustrated and plagued by doubts about any ultimate success. In 1860 Jimmy wrote a friend: "Oh Ellis if I were just worth about a hundred thousand dollars I would shut up and never utter a complaint again about being poor." He hoped "before very long to be able to give up this single and miserable way of living." [17] As for Willy's own letters, they were consistently filled with sentiments of concern, respect, and genuine love for his family.

While his brothers and sisters obviously helped to shape Willy's personality, it was his mother who most influenced him. A neighbor described Mrs. Pegram as possessing "one of the loveliest characters it has ever been my fortune to know." Charitable, gentle, and deeply religious, she was "so spiritual," never breathing "a word against a human being." Willy's acquaintances described him in similar language: one of his soldiers later said that Pegram "had the voice and manners of a school girl." But, while "kind and gentle to his men," he was "still a stern disciplinarian, requiring every one to do his whole duty." [18] In social affairs, Pegram bore himself with refined manners and extreme politeness. He embodied the aristocratic formality that had governed the conduct of his ancestors and seldom addressed even close friends by their first names.

Handicapped by the financial restraints placed on a widow in the nineteenth century, Virginia Pegram struggled to maintain a style of life commensurate with the family's social distinction. A neighbor recollected that Virginia "made brave and persistent efforts" to overcome the obstacles facing a widowed mother "without however accomplishing all that she desired." Watching her

Figure 2. Mary Evans Pegram Anderson (1830–1911). Willy promised his oldest sister in 1864 that once the war was over they would visit Europe together. "Cheer up! & do not despair," he told her, because "our time will come yet." (Photograph courtesy of the Virginia Historical Society)

Figure 3. Virginia Johnson Pegram McIntosh (1843–1920). On her twenty-first birthday, Willy congratulated his sister on obtaining her "majority" and "freedom from all restraint" because "so many young ladies cut themselves off before they attain it, by getting married." (Photograph courtesy of the Virginia Historical Society)

labor tirelessly for the well-being of his brothers and sisters gave Pegram a serious, almost grave outlook on life. Virginia also infused her youngest son with a deep commitment to God, family, and duty that Willy's close associates often mentioned. John Cheves Haskell, a fellow artillery officer in the Army of Northern Virginia, thought Pegram "one of the most earnest Christians I ever met" and marveled at Pegram's ability to overcome any obstacle. Haskell attributed Willy's success to his "character and will that were grand, a sense of duty, never surpassed, and a determination to do his best, utterly regardless of his own safety or comfort." Another Confederate comrade compared Pegram to Thomas J. Jackson because Willy "combined the strongest Christian faith and the deepest spirituality with the most intense spirit of fight." [19]

Religion in the antebellum South emphasized personal salvation and individual morality rather than the need to improve society so popular among Northern Evangelicals. Northern reformers challenged God's sovereignty, most Southerners maintained, by trying to ameliorate the human condition. They were radicals who had abandoned Providence's preordained way of life. Like most Southerners, who did not question seriously the moral condition of their society and accepted God's immutable laws, Pegram believed he lived within a Christian community. His religious background made it virtually impossible for him to contest Southern institutions and the worldview of the planter class.

Figure 4. James West Pegram, Jr. (1839–1881). Just before Willy entered the University of Virginia in 1860, James West wrote that his little brother was "perfectly charmed at the idea of going to the University . . . and I think he will do well at it." (Photograph courtesy of the Virginia Historical Society)

In Pegram's mind, Providence ordered the South's way of life, thereby making slavery and the hierarchical structure of society divinely ordained. To condemn the South as a godless land because of its system of labor or some other moral crime would have forced Pegram to condemn his own family and friends.[20]

Information regarding Pegram's youth is sketchy. According to the noted Virginia biographer, Samuel Bassett French, Willy attended "the best schools in his native city." He might have been a pupil at the famous Hanover Academy. It is also quite possible that Pegram received a good deal of his formal instruction from his mother and oldest sister—both of whom enjoyed solid reputations as educators. As he neared the end of adolescence, Pegram retained his boyish features and form. His face was smooth and round, with a noticeable dimple on his chin that set off his small mouth and thin lips. He parted his hair on the left side and allowed it to grow bushy around the ears. Gold-rimmed spectacles were usually perched on his nose. Without them, he was virtually helpless. Pegram's severe nearsightedness and his small body, which gave him an awkward appearance, probably contributed to his extreme self-consciousness and painful degree of shyness. He could seem almost distant with strangers. One of his contemporaries noted that Willy "had always been such a modest, self-contained and almost shrinking youth."[21]

Sad news reached Pegram and the rest of his family in February 1849. During a visit to Mobile, Alabama, grandfather William Johnson had died, albeit from natural causes. To offset unpaid bills in both Mobile and New Orleans, Johnson's only asset was a champion racehorse, rather ironically named "Revenue." As his lack of collateral suggests, financial difficulties plagued Johnson's last years—and doubtless his fondness for gambling and wild speculation on horses explains in part his diminished estate. Johnson's children, including Virginia Pegram, stared at a ledger that tallied debts of over $58,000 and another $13,000 in litigation fees. One source valued his landholdings throughout the South at an estimated $200,000, yet another assessment of his property showed a value of only $40,000. Unfortunately, the difference between these two figures is impossible to reconcile on the basis of the available records. It is clear, however, that the fortunes of William Johnson had been on the decline for some time.[22]

Virginia and her children apparently received a paltry inheritance from Johnson's will. Since 1850 Virginia Pegram had overseen the dormitories and taught music at the Southern Female Institute in Richmond, an occupation that hardly befitted her social standing and yet afforded a modest income. Then, in 1855, she accepted a "helping hand" from an unidentified friend. This assistance came in the form of a loan that enabled her to open a women's school in her home on Linden Row, where the Pegrams now occupied the buildings at 106–108 Franklin, having moved from Main Street after James West's death. Advertisements soon appeared in the newspapers, and applications for admission quickly followed.[23]

With the help of her oldest daughter, Mary, Virginia Pegram created one of the most reputable institutions for women in Richmond. The curriculum was rigid and the work demanding. Classes began at eight in the morning and officially ended at two in the afternoon, although they were followed by a late afternoon session of French conversation. The girls' daily routine also included mandatory study periods. The school required literature, spelling, the classics, music, art, and even algebra—one student complaining to her mother: "Ma *please, please,* let me stop Algebra. . . . I do despise it." Adjustment to the school's strict discipline also proved difficult for many women. After having been denied permission to visit a friend in Richmond, another student exclaimed: "Mrs. P. will not rule me always. I am so glad that I can stay two weeks at home."[24]

William Pegram's reaction to the waves of young women who washed in and out of his home is not known. It was a predicament that undoubtedly placed him in an enviable position with the neighborhood boys. His family's residence on Franklin Street, according to a neighbor, radiated an aura of "elegant refinement." Boarders made the premises seem cramped and crowded, however, since Virginia Pegram usually took in more students than she could accommodate comfortably. "Mother has her house as full of young ladies as it can hold," James West, Jr., wrote in 1859. "Consequently the house is very gay,

Figure 5. Linden Row, the antebellum and wartime residence of the Pegram family. (Author's photograph)

and I may say most too much so for a young man who wants a quiet place to study in. . . . But they are the best looking and most aristocratic looking set in the City." If Willy wanted relief from the ceaseless chatter of schoolgirls, Richmond offered ample avenues of escape.[25]

Richmond came to maturity in the 1850s, during which the population topped thirty thousand. This increase was accompanied by a dramatic rise in the value of railroad stock and the number of mills, ironworks, warehouses, markets, and tobacco factories. By no means an industrial metropolis, Richmond had nevertheless become a major commercial center of the South. The James River and Kanawha Canal flowed nearby; five railroads emanated from the city in all directions. Because of its excellent transportation network, Richmond proved a popular market for the crops from the state's tidewater and piedmont districts. But even with all this economic development, Richmond retained its charm and Southern flavor. "The city follows the curve of the river, seated on amphitheatric hills, retreating from its banks," noted one observer. "No city of the South has [a] grander or more picturesque approach."[26]

Pegram and his family lived a good distance from the manufacturing district of the city. Franklin Street was located in one of the most exclusive sections of town; acceptance into this neighborhood rested on one's wealth, name, or occupation, or a mixture of the three. Since their home was physically close to the heart of the city, the Pegrams must have attended the theater, a form of entertainment that thrived in Richmond. Lectures, concerts, farming exhibitions, and circuses were also popular diversions. Richmonders frequently visited the Haymarket Garden, with its terraced slopes and beautiful flowers. On summer evenings vendors strolled across the lawns there, selling cakes and lemonade, while throngs of people watched fireworks. Sundays found the Pegram carriage parked outside Saint Paul's Episcopal Church on Grace Street, of which James West Pegram had been a founding member. His wife continued the family's association with Saint Paul's after his death, and Willy apparently received his first communion there.[27]

Continuing the tradition established by his father and grandfather, William Pegram joined a militia company in 1858. He was about sixteen when he entered the ranks of F Company, an elite unit reserved for the "best men" of Richmond. The members of this crack outfit wore cadet-gray uniforms lined with "fire-gilt" Virginia buttons. They carried knapsacks, imported from Paris, made of "hairy calfskin" painted red and white. Pegram relished the opportunity to don his military attire and participate in the company's encampments.[28]

While Willy enjoyed a romantic view of soldiering, his oldest brother experienced the harsh reality of army life on the western frontier. Graduating tenth in West Point's class of 1854, which included James E. B. "Jeb" Stuart, John Pegram had entered the famous First United States Cavalry. His assignments in the West, as well as a two-year stint as an observer of the 1859 war between

Austria and Italy, left his family in emotional turmoil. John's absences especially affected his mother's nerves. When he left Richmond for New Mexico in 1860, Virginia Pegram "went to bed and was not seen for a few days." James West, Jr., later wrote: "I wish that brother was out of the Army and settled down here in some good business, for mother will never be contented as long as he remains in the Army."[29]

If the safety of his brother troubled William Pegram during the 1850s, the future of his country also proved worrisome. Harmonious relations between North and South no longer seemed possible. The antagonism inherent between a free labor society and a slave labor society had surfaced in the western territories. Violence in Kansas, acrimonious debates in Congress over the expansion of slavery, the 1856 assault on Charles Sumner in the United States Senate shortly after his famous attack on slavery, and the emergence of a Republican presidential candidate that same year forced Pegram to evaluate the South's place in the Union. The rise of the Republican party was particularly disturbing. Its support for social mobility, equal opportunity in the marketplace, and the right of people to enjoy the fruits of their own labor conflicted with Southern values and the hierarchical structure of Southern society. If this sectional party were to capture the federal government, reasoned Pegram and many other Southerners, even the Constitution could not protect their region from perfidious Republican policies. Under Republican control, the South's way of life would eventually unravel, and with this the power of the planter class would also dissolve.[30]

On October 16, 1859, John Brown led a band of twenty-one men into Harpers Ferry, Virginia, at the confluence of the Potomac and Shenandoah Rivers, and captured the United States arsenal there. The group's hope was to spark a slave insurrection that would spread across the countryside. Marines under Colonel Robert E. Lee crushed the incipient rebellion within two days, but before the insurrection was quelled word of Brown's actions had reached Richmond. As fear seized the hearts and minds of most Richmonders, Governor Henry A. Wise called F Company to the scene. Sixty members of the unit boarded trains, but they reached Harpers Ferry after the crisis had passed; by October 19 they were back in Richmond. It is impossible to determine whether Pegram participated in this expedition, although he did accompany F Company and six other militia companies to witness the execution of John Brown at Charlestown on December 2. Willy left no written impressions of the event, even though it was a most solemn occasion in the view of most observers. Indeed, his only reference to the hanging is extremely oblique: "I had intended writing you immediately on my return from Charlestown," he wrote to his brother John on January 23, 1860, "but as I was absent from the office two weeks, my work got so much behind and that I could not find time to do so."[31]

But if he never felt the need to record his reaction to Brown's execution, the militant spirit that swept the South after John Brown's raid clearly impressed Pegram. "You never saw anything like the military and patriotic feeling now existing at the South," he explained to his brother in the same letter. "Before the Harpers Ferry outbreak this Regiment could not muster over three hundred and fifty men; now we have about seven hundred and fifty." When he looked at the First Regiment, he saw men who "were never seen in any ranks" before. In his eyes, no stronger evidence demonstrated the South's determination to protect its way of life. Although he acknowledged that "the excitement has very much died out in this State now," he was quick to add, "but the people are very firm, and the southern trade hereafter will depend much more on the Southerners than on the Northerners." [32]

In the commercial center of Richmond, Pegram had witnessed the dependence of Southern farmers on Northern facilities for the transportation and final production of their goods. Rising charges by middlemen had drained the South's capital, which prevented reinvestment, stalled attempts at diversifying the economy, and limited the development of a home market. Pegram wanted his section of the country to strive toward a more autonomous economic position. The people below the Mason-Dixon Line, in his estimation, had developed into a separate entity within the country. Not only were their financial interests at odds with those of the North, but their values, social system, culture, and political system also had forged a civilization superior to that of the Yankees, for whom crass materialism and radical individualism dictated human relations. [33]

Before entering the University of Virginia as a law student in the fall of 1860, Pegram worked as a clerk for Richmond's circuit court. He was not on the city's official payroll but received his salary on a fee basis that varied according to the demands of the court. But when not in his office, Pegram centered his recreational time around F Company. He drew much satisfaction from the unit's musters. One of the most celebrated events of 1860 was Washington's birthday, on February 22. "Dark and portentous clouds" hovered over the city on this important day, and soon sheets of heavy rain turned the clay roads into pools of red mire. The semi-weekly *Richmond Enquirer* reported that "the adhesive mud around the walks of the capitol was over shoe-tops . . . and in all, it was most disfiguring to military neatness on a gala day." Willy admitted that it "was a very bad day with us," although he went on to declare that "nevertheless we had a very fine military parade." "But I paid very dearly for my fun," he remarked to his cousin John Combe Pegram, "for I have been very unwell ever since and am now confined to the house." Two months later he had to retire to Petersburg "for his health." Plagued by a weak constitution, Pegram often fell ill, a pattern repeated during the war. [34]

Sickness, routine work, and the country's dangerous political situation failed to dampen Pegram's enthusiasm about entering the University of Virginia in

Figure 6. William Ransom Johnson Pegram (1841–1865). Probably taken in the fall of 1860, before he entered the University of Virginia, this is the earliest known photograph of Willy. (Courtesy of Dale S. Snair)

the fall of 1860. The previous spring he had been "very anxious" to see his brother John to "talk about the University." His older brother, James West, Jr., commented that Willy was "perfectly charmed at the idea of going to the University in the Fall, and I hope he will not be disappointed after he gets there." He had never seen anyone "in all my life so bent upon anything as he is upon law, and I think he will do well at it." Still, leaving his family for Charlottesville must have been difficult for Pegram. He also was leaving the company of a Miss Annie Claybrooke, a young woman who had captured his heart but apparently did not return his affections. "I still teaze him a good deal," James West, Jr., told a friend on May 21, 1860. "He is very much in love with her," he added; "I thought that lately his affection had cooled off but I do not believe it has." [35]

Economic activity in Charlottesville mirrored that in Richmond, albeit on a much smaller scale. The construction of turnpikes, canals, and railroads between 1830 and 1850 had turned what was once a hamlet into a bustling market-place. The university, designed and founded by Thomas Jefferson, stood a mile west of town on 390 acres of land. Its center was known as the Academical

Village, a large rectangular collection of red brick buildings highlighted by white trim. The village included the housing for faculty, students, and staff. Interspersed among the student quarters were classrooms. The nine dormitories also provided sheltered walkways that allowed students to attend class regardless of the weather. In the middle of the rectangle was a large expanse of grass known as the Lawn, which served as the focal point of the village, stretching for six hundred yards and marked at its northern tip by a particularly elegant building, the Rotunda. Modelled after the Pantheon in Rome, this impressive structure housed the school's library of thirty thousand volumes. The southern portico of the Rotunda offered a spectacular view of the surrounding mountains and of Jefferson's own home, Monticello. The students referred to the entire area as "the grounds." All in all, it was a serene place for reflection or serious studying.[36]

Pegram approached his work with Spartan discipline. He declined, for example, an invitation to a party at a Mr. Minor's near the beginning of the term. Sounds of laughter and idle chatter from the gathering drifted past his room, but Pegram "managed to study through the whole of it." Nineteen years old when he entered the university, Pegram remained uncomfortable and self-conscious. William Gordon McCabe, a friend at the university and his adjutant near the end of the war, recalled that Pegram was "reserved almost to shyness . . . partly [due] to his extreme near-sightedness, partly to the modesty of his nature." At the same time, he was "gracious" and exhibited "much of the charm of an old-fashioned politeness." Pegram's "keen sense of humor" surprised many students who were not his intimates, who often remarked with amazement that a singularly "quiet, sober-looking lad" could possess such a quick but delicate wit.[37]

Attending the University of Virginia was an expensive venture. Each class cost twenty-five dollars, and a student had to attend at least three, on top of which additional money went to the library and for infirmary, contingencies, boarding, washing, and fuel. Total costs for the nine-month session amounted to $423.50. Only affluent families could afford higher education for their sons, and sending Willy to the university must have strained the Pegrams' budget. In return for this hefty financial commitment, he received rigorous training. There were nine lectures a week, accompanied by daily examinations. Attendance was mandatory. Pegram spent most of his time listening to Professor James P. Holcombe, who taught civil, constitutional, and international law. Holcombe frequently delivered persuasive lectures regarding the South's right to secede from the Union. One of his pupils recalled that other students cut their assigned classes and filled Holcombe's lecture hall in order to hear his stirring addresses, noting that "they heard eloquent discourses which, if they did not excite, certainly did not check their secession tendencies."[38]

Pegram has left no written impressions of Holcombe, but he did regard

some of his classmates as "stuck-up." This opinion appears to have had its gene-
sis in a confrontation Pegram had one day with a third-year student. Willy's
correction of this individual's grammar initiated a heated "discussion on the
subject," but Pegram ultimately demonstrated the correctness of his argument.
At this point, the other man said that "he had been at college three years, and
ought to know." With obvious disbelief, Pegram concluded that "this is considered to be a very smart fellow."[39]

During the 1860–61 term, 604 students walked the halls of the University of
Virginia, only three of whom hailed from above the Mason-Dixon line. More
than half of the students lived in the Old Dominion itself. Strict regulations
governed their behavior. Gambling, carrying firearms, making boisterous
noises, drinking excessive amounts of alcohol, and exhibiting disrespect to faculty members might result in expulsion. Pegram's mother received a monthly
notice of her son's academic performance, conduct, and attendance. At the
same time, cricket, horse racing, dances, or short jaunts into the countryside
interrupted the grinding monotony of studying and classes. Students eagerly
anticipated laughing-gas day. Under the "vigilant eye of the professor of chemis-
try," the chosen subject inhaled a potent dose of nitrous oxide gas on the Lawn
while surrounded by his classmates. The victim then "fell into the strangest
contortions, and burst into peals of hysterical laughter." A number of students
also resorted to alcohol to achieve a similar mind-numbing state, and charges
of drunkenness were not uncommon. Usually, such repeatedly tipsy students
were given a choice between joining the Temperance Society and leaving
school.[40]

But students pursued amusements with less than the usual vigor in the fall
of 1860. The grave political situation had created a serious, almost somber outlook, for many of the students were greatly distressed at the prospect of the
Republican party seizing the White House. Most Southerners interpreted
Abraham Lincoln's stand on the expansion of slavery as a direct attack against
their institution at home. Then, on November 6, the prairie lawyer from Illinois
was elected sixteenth president of the United States. News of Lincoln's victory
immediately divided the student body. Acrimonious debates filled the dining
areas, classrooms, and residence halls. One student overheard supporters of the
Southern Democratic candidate John C. Breckinridge taunt admirers of the
Constitutional Unionist candidate John Bell: "You are a traitor to the South,
and we'll hang every one of you old Whigs." Bell's advocates replied: "You are
a traitor to the South, the North, and the whole country. We'll hang every
one [of] you disunionists." Shortly after the election, a student from Tennessee
remarked that disunionists and supporters of Bell frequently used the word
"traitor" to describe each other, "all of which seems to be taken in good part,"
he added. But he could recognize that, "when not in each others' company that
they are in earnest about it."[41]

In Pegram's eyes the triumph of a Republican portended a dark future for the South. An advocate of Whig principles, as his father and grandfathers had been, he felt an attachment to the Union and consequently supported presidential candidate John Bell and Edward Everett, both of the Constitutional Union party, who carried Virginia by a narrow margin. "Although I think we have great cause to boast of Mr. Bell's majorities," Pegram wrote his youngest sister a few days later, "I have not done so, because I am so much concerned about Lincoln's election." In Willy's estimation, the lanky Republican and his party embodied the very worst of Northern society. "On the one side we have a President, opposed to us in every way," Pegram asserted, "and a vice-President, who is to preside over that august body, the Senate of the United States, a half-negro [body]; and the Germans for our *masters;* while on the other side, we have disunion, and the greatest of all evils, '*a civil war*' staring us in the face." "Isn't this perfectly dreadful," he stated. "But this is a time when we ought to be thinking seriously about it," Pegram added, referring to the political situation. "This is not a mere Jno. Brown raid." [42]

Although Pegram hesitated to advocate secession, he could not submit to rule by a party that had attacked slavery in the territories and criticized the institution in existing slave states. Accepting the Lincoln administration would force Pegram to dismiss insults leveled against a way of life he believed sanctioned by God. His allusion to the United States Senate as a refuge for men sympathetic to blacks and Germans sounded a common theme among Southerners, as well as reflecting his broader view of the North and the Republican party. In Pegram's estimation, Southerners constituted a distinct and superior people, whereas Northerners had become polluted by foreigners, abolitionists, and Republican rhetoric that encouraged lower-class whites to climb the social ladder. Compared to the conservative South, thought Pegram, Northern society lacked respect for order and inherent social hierarchy. Pegram's fears over the incumbent Republican administration, if biased, were far from irrational. He well understood that Lincoln's victory, unlike John Brown's raid, represented more than an isolated incident. The ascendancy of the Republican party in 1860 not only marked a shift in national sentiment but also offered its members the opportunity to implement ideas that Pegram found abominable. In his mind, disunion would now be difficult to avoid. [43]

When Pegram returned from his morning class on November 10, he discovered a package on his mantlepiece that contained some slippers handmade by his sister Jennie. Willy wrote her a short letter to say "how nice I consider them, and how highly I shall prize them." He worried, however, that "I will not have much time to wear them." Disunion and conflict approached, and he "wouldn't be surprised if I were ordered away at any time." If the governor suddenly activated the militia, he wanted his brother Jimmy to "get all my uniform together, and telegraph me immediately." "In case of war," he suspected that the "faculty will suspend lectures, and pay the students back their money for the time over which they have not gone." The thought of prematurely ending his studies at the university saddened Pegram, who hoped to follow his father's example and become a lawyer. "It seems as if there was bound to be some fatality attending my course at the University," Willy wrote despairingly. "But I hope that I will not have to leave." Typically, Pegram resigned his fate to the will of Providence: "All we can do is to hope that 'The God of all nations' will direct all things for the best."[44]

As the leaves fell from the trees and winter drew near, the country moved closer to civil war. South Carolina left the Union on December 20, followed by Mississippi, Florida, Alabama, Georgia, and Louisiana in January, and Texas on February 1. With seven states out of the Union, sentiment among the students crystallized in favor of secession. One young man observed on January 20 that "the feeling amongst the students here now is almost, though not quite, unanimous in favor of immediate secession." Being of the same mind, the faculty nullified the school's ban on student-sponsored militia companies, whereupon two units quickly sprang into existence. Pegram actively promoted one of the organizations—the Southern Guard—and received the rank of second sergeant for his efforts. Pegram's comrades, who wore distinctive blue pantaloons, cap, and shirt, drilled on the Lawn or on Carr's Hill. Martial fever also intoxicated the professors, who formed their own company. They presented an awkward appearance and "wisely" practiced inside a private room. But it was not long before they "grew bold enough to appear on the Lawn to the boundless amusement of the better drilled students."[45]

Support for the nascent Confederacy grew increasingly more brazen at the university. Near the end of February two students made a perilous night climb to the top of the Rotunda and attached the banner of the rebellious states to the flag pole. When the morning sun revealed the act, the students and faculty worked themselves into such a frenzy that lectures and recitations were suspended for the rest of the day. The chairman of the university stated that he would not take action against the men involved if they lowered the flag. Another band of students took it down, only to raise it above Carr's Hill a few days later. Pegram, however, seemed more concerned about Congressional attempts to placate the secessionist South than about the political sentiment of the students. Unsatisfied with Northern efforts at compromise, Willy probably referred to the Crittenden Compromise when he wrote: "As far as I can see, it is no improvement whatever on the Constitution. And to read the Constitution one would think that we had every guarantee in the world." Although Pegram did not specify how the Constitution should be altered, he stated clearly that the South could not withstand Republican encroachments without firm and explicit protection of Southern rights by the federal government. In short, he saw his way of life at the mercy of the Lincoln administration.[46]

While compromise and political discourse broke down in Washington, tension thickened in South Carolina, where the Union garrison at Fort Sumter in Charleston harbor had been cut off. Confederate officials demanded its surrender and would not allow the Northern bastion to receive supplies. As Major Robert Anderson steadfastly refused to evacuate the fort, during the early morning hours of April 12 Southern batteries arced their shells toward the Union post. After a thirty-four-hour bombardment, the garrison finally submitted. News of Anderson's surrender galvanized the South. The Southern Guard performed an afternoon review on the Lawn late that day. Drawn up in battlelines, the students watched a messenger hand one of their officers a telegram that read: "Fort Sumter has surrendered and the Palmetto flag now floats over its wall." Jubilant shouts echoed across the grounds. Although classes were not canceled, most of the students, including Pegram, headed home anyway. With Jefferson's beloved Monticello hovering in the background, Willy left Charlottesville to join F Company in Richmond.[47]

TWO

WE ARE GOING TO HAVE A TERRIBLE WAR

ON APRIL 18, 1861, PEGRAM DASHED OFF A LETTER TO CHARLES ELLIS Munford, an old friend from Richmond and classmate at the University of Virginia. From the future capital of the Confederacy he informed Ellis that "Virginia has seceded, and we are now out of the old government—in the new." Expecting "to be ordered to Norfolk" at any moment, he warned that "we are going to have a terrible war." Pegram invited Munford and anyone else at the university to "hurry down" and enlist in F Company. "There are about forty vacancies," he reported, "as the Gov. has allowed us to take about a hundred and fifty men in the Company."[1]

Willy's uncle, Robert Baker Pegram, had been made commander-in-chief of the naval forces of Virginia. Pegram understood through his relative that a number of prominent men "have been trying to get Gov. Letcher to send forces to take the Navy Yard out of the hands of the black republicans." He had also learned about the seditious activity of John Snyder Carlile, a vociferous supporter of the Union at the Virginia Secession Convention. His views earned him expulsion from the assembly, unkind words from the *Richmond Enquirer,* and threats of bodily harm. After the delegates had secretly cast the state's lot with the Confederacy, Carlile headed straight for the telegraph office, where he tried to warn the Lincoln administration about the Old Dominion's withdrawal from the Union by recommending that Federal forces be sent immediately to crush Virginia's rebellious movement. "Fortunately," Pegram noted, "the telegraphic wires are in the possession of the state authorities, and the operator carried the dispatch to Gov. Letcher instead of sending it on."[2]

"The second Arnold," as Pegram called Carlile, was arrested in Fredericksburg and incarcerated at Richmond. "I suppose he will be tried as a traitor & hung," he added. It is significant that Pegram would describe Carlile as a second Benedict Arnold. Like many Southerners, Pegram drew upon America's revolutionary heritage to legitimize the creation of the Confederacy. Southerners commonly argued that far from rejecting the ideas of the founding fathers, they had elected to secede in order to reaffirm those principles, which had been desecrated and abandoned by the North. Writing in a more emotive style than Pegram, Charles Colcock Jones, Jr., perhaps captured best the attitude of his generation. "The dissolution of this Union cannot silence those consecrated voices of the past," he asserted. "Nor can it rob us of the relationship which we bear to, or of the veneration which we shall ever cherish for, the virtues and the great deeds of the Father of our Country. He was of us."[3]

Richmond bustled with excitement on April 21, when rumors flew about the whereabouts of the Northern gunboat *Pawnee*. The Union vessel was supposedly sneaking up the James River to bombard the city into submission. As the armory bell near the state capitol rang its distinctive warning, most Richmonders sat in church, although it is impossible to say whether Pegram and his family attended service at Saint Paul's Episcopal Church that day. Pegram, however, apparently donned his cadet-gray frock coat and his kepi with the letter F embossed on top. After Captain R. Milton Cary assembled F Company, Pegram and his comrades tramped past Rocketts, a riverside sector of Richmond, amid cheering civilians waving white handkerchiefs. The entire area was "alive with human beings," remembered John H. Worsham, who served in the ranks with Pegram. A few zealous patriots in the crowd shouted at Cary's men that they would resort to throwing stones at the Union vessel if it dared to enter Richmond's harbor.

As the sun crept behind the steeples of the city, F Company had marched a little more than five miles to the Wilton plantation, located across the river from Drewry's Bluff. Cary placed a thin picket line along the steep banks of the James and instructed the men to fire on the *Pawnee* as soon as it came within shooting range. Most of the soldiers in Cary's command, though, enjoyed a more comfortable evening back in camp, dining on cooked ham and fresh bread delivered by wagon from Richmond, their laughter and conversation drifting through the night air. Festivities continued without interruption until F Company returned to the city on two barges the next day without having spotted any sign of the *Pawnee*. Heralded nonetheless as the saviors of Richmond, the men received a continuous ovation as they marched from the docks up the cobblestone streets to their quarters on Main Street. The "Pawnee War" had come to a close.[4]

But Pegram did not have to store his uniform for long. Almost immediately after the *Pawnee* incident, news flashed through Richmond that Federals had landed at the mouth of Aquia Creek on the Potomac River, not far from Fredericksburg. Early on April 24 Cary's men, together with the Richmond Light Infantry Blues, filed into the cars waiting in the gray dawn at the railway depot. They headed north to Fredericksburg, where they disembarked for the courthouse. Pegram and the rest of Cary's men received royal treatment from the citizens of Fredericksburg, who sent benches and straw to the Richmonders—arrangements that normally would have afforded a pleasant night's sleep had it not been for some of Pegram's more unruly comrades. One man blasted a horn, only to be answered by another soldier who drew a high-pitched shrill from his whistle. The revelers continued until their lips finally grew numb, leaving them no choice but to put away their instruments.[5]

The next morning F Company headed toward Fredericksburg's fairgrounds, later called Camp Mercer, where they bivouacked in horse stables. Cary's soldiers spent little time in their quarters for the rest of the month, as they frequently found themselves shoulder to shoulder drilling on the parade grounds.

The *Fredericksburg News* observed on May 3 that F Company handled itself with "dexterity and celerity" while performing the Zouave drill. The townspeople who sauntered out to camp every evening lauded the men's professionalism. The Fredericksburg paper assured its readers that Cary's company, because of its soldierly bearing on the drilling field, would doubtless play an important role in the destruction of the "Black Republican dynasty."[6]

At the beginning of May a new six-gun battery called the Purcell Artillery arrived at Camp Mercer. The unit was composed of Richmonders and commanded by Captain Reuben Lindsay Walker, but it lacked well-trained officers. Walker needed assistance in transforming his awkward band of civilians into soldiers, and Pegram responded to his call for help. Temporarily assigned to the position of drillmaster in the battery, Willy discharged his duties so efficiently that the men elected him to the position of second lieutenant.[7]

At the same time, the sedentary routine of camp disgusted Pegram. "There has been no change in our situation since I wrote," he complained to Mary Pegram on May 3, "and from what I can hear there is not any probability of there being any for some time." Worst of all, pangs of homesickness undercut Pegram's spirits. He had hoped to return to Richmond "for a day or two" but now realized that this was an impossibility. Concerned that his mother and two sisters might worry unnecessarily while he was away, he wrote that "I would like very much to be at home with you all now, but hope, as I can't be there, you will not be uneasy." Briefly adopting a more optimistic stance, Pegram noted he had heard that "it is more pleasant being in this encampment than in the one at Richmond." The secession of Tennessee also buoyed his spirits, as he had "always liked that state."[8]

Pegram's new unit entered active service on May 20, and three days later the *Richmond Dispatch* reported that the Purcell Artillery was "one of the first companies who went into service from this city." "Should the enemy conclude to land at Aquia Creek," the paper added, "they are the very boys to meet him and rebuke his presumption in a most effective and convincing way." The *Dispatch* called on its readers not to worry about enemy columns swarming through the city because "the company is armed with the deadly Parrott rifled cannon, which they know how to handle."[9]

At the end of May the Purcell Artillery left Camp Mercer for the Aquia Creek district, an area threatened by Federal steamers that prowled the Potomac River. The battery unlimbered its guns at Pratt Point, overlooking the juncture of the Potomac River and Potomac Creek. Despite Pegram's best efforts, Walker's men—who now found themselves thrust into an area where the enemy's vessels frequently made their presence known—were still not well prepared for combat. On May 22 Daniel Ruggles complained to the adjutant general of Virginia forces that the Purcell Artillery has not "been put in readiness for the field, being deficient in men and equipments." Because Walker's guns made up the only field battery in the department, Ruggles warned, a possible Federal landing would inevitably require the evacuation of Fredericksburg.[10]

Four Union ships tested Ruggles's prophecy on May 31. While the vessels chugged toward a southern position at the mouth of Aquia Creek, Pegram and his comrades were lounging on the banks of their new encampment at Marlboro Point. Alerted to the approaching danger, the untested cannoneers "promptly responded," according to the *Richmond Dispatch*. From two and a half miles away, they raced to the scene, and after pushing their artillery pieces up a steep hill, they opened fire. It is unlikely that shells from Walker's company could have had any severe effect at that great distance, but the Northern commander of the flotilla insisted that the Confederates dropped "shot on board and about us like hail for nearly an hour." The *Dispatch* also claimed that a number of the battery's rounds "badly injured" one of the ships.[11]

The manner in which the men of the Purcell Artillery handled their weapons impressed Ruggles, whose official report complimented the battery for its "skillfully directed" fire. The Federal ships withdrew from the fight late in the afternoon. Pegram and his comrades had fired one hundred and fifty missiles, most of which fell harmlessly into the murky waters of the Potomac. General Robert E. Lee chastised Ruggles for this wasteful pyrotechnic display—a bloodless initiation into combat that no doubt deluded a few of Pegram's comrades into claiming veteran status.[12]

Pegram and the other men in the Purcell Artillery returned to their posts the next day when "the 'Enemy,' in the shape of the *Pawnee, Anacosta, Philadelphia* and *James Guy* commenced a most severe and active bombardment." Watching from a neighboring bluff, a regiment of Tennessee volunteers cheered Walker's gunners. The *Fredericksburg News* reported that the *Pawnee* spewed "her iron tempest" upon the Richmond battery, the Northern rounds falling through a curtain of smoke that poured from a burning dock the Confederates had purposely ignited. The *News* added of the *Pawnee* that "it was fearful at first to think she might even from her cowardly distance strike down some man." But the only damage to the Confederate side, according to one civilian observer, "was the death of a chicken, though a stray ball killed a horse on the opposite side of the creek."[13]

The Fredericksburg paper overlooked the fact that at that "cowardly" range, the Purcell Artillery was equally ineffective. The commander of the *Pawnee* reported that his ship received the brunt of the enemy's fire and was "struck nine times during the bombardment" while most of the Confederate "rifled shot" passed "over and around us." Even so, the *Richmond Dispatch* still found reason to compliment the cannoneers of Walker's Battery: "Our men were as cool as icebergs, every one exhibiting a bravery and determination that would have done credit to veteran soldiers." Veteran soldiers, however, would not have burned precious ammunition to no purpose.[14]

For the rest of June, the Purcell Artillery shuttled between Marlboro Point, Brooke's Station, and Pratt Point. The cannoneers frequently spotted Northern ships prowling near the shore as they sat on the banks of the Potomac River, prohibited from training their sights on the enemy's vessels. Frustrated by the brazen Federal disregard of the Confederate presence in the Aquia Creek district, General Theophilus H. Holmes wrote: "I could use the rifled 6-pounders that I now have in Walker's battery to annoy the enemy's commerce; but we have not the ammunition to spare." [15]

A month later disaster struck not only the Confederacy but also the Pegram family. At Rich Mountain in western Virginia, John Pegram of the Twentieth Virginia commanded Camp Garnett, a post located eight miles west of Beverly near Buckhannon Gap. Confident that the enemy could not assail him in such tangled country, Pegram allowed the Federals to envelop his left flank. They captured the road and the mountain pass behind Camp Garnett, forcing Pegram to surrender 553 soldiers two days later. Everyone but Pegram received a parole. Previous service in the United States Army placed him in an ambiguous situation. After much debate Union authorities decided to hold him as a prisoner of war, not as an officer in rebellion. John's incarceration and his uncertain future must surely have played upon the nerves of Willy and the rest of the family. On top of this the debacle at Rich Mountain also provoked considerable criticism of General Pegram across the South. John would remain in Federal hands until the spring of 1862. [16]

The danger at Rich Mountain, however, paled in comparison to the Federal threat that materialized north of Manassas during the middle of July. Led by Union General Irvin McDowell, a force of 35,000 men crawled toward a smaller Confederate army under General P. G. T. Beauregard. When the clouds of dust raised by tramping feet signaled the enemy's approach, Beauregard retired behind the banks of Bull Run Creek and wired for reinforcements. Answering the call on July 18, the Purcell Artillery and Holmes's brigade hurried to the scene. After covering twenty-five miles in two days, Pegram and his comrades fell in line on the Confederate right near Camp Wigfall, a reserve position behind General Richard S. Ewell's brigade at Union Mills. [17]

An unmercifully hot sun greeted Walker's artillerists on the morning of July 21. The air was still, disturbed only occasionally by a nervous picket's cracking rifle. Hoping to strike McDowell's left before the Northerners launched an assault, Beauregard prepared his troops for a general advance. At dawn Walker's artillerists had been notified to take the offensive at a "moment's notice." Supporting Holmes's infantrymen, the cannoneers pulled their guns a little closer to Ewell's men at Union Mills. Ripples of musketry and blasts of artillery resounded from the Confederate left flank as the day wore on. McDowell had struck first, and the Federals plowed through the Southern line at Matthews Hill. Continuing the advance across the Warrenton Turnpike, they crossed

Young's Branch, pushed up Henry House Hill, and threatened to drive the Confederates from the field.

Stretched across Henry House Hill, the Southern line wavered in the face of McDowell's advancing battle lines. Beauregard bolstered his position by shifting troops from the right. At about two in the afternoon a staff officer galloped up to Holmes and instructed the North Carolinian to push his brigade and the Purcell Artillery toward the sound of the fighting. The battery immediately moved out. The artillerists lashed at their horses, the hooves of the animals kicking up dust as the men held on tightly to their caissons. It was not long before Pegram and his comrades witnessed the destructive hand of war. As they marched forward, they encountered horribly wounded soldiers who warned the cannoneers of the smoking inferno that awaited them.[18]

Sometime between 4:00 and 4:30 in the afternoon, Holmes's brigade and the Purcell Artillery arrived at General Joseph E. Johnston's headquarters at the Lewis House, better known as "Portici." At this point, Johnston halted the infantrymen because reinforcements from the Shenandoah Valley had already restored and then extended the Confederate left flank, allowing the Southerners to deliver a counterattack that swept McDowell's regiments backward. Fear seized the Federals, many of whom fled in a blind panic. Discarded knapsacks, wagons, canteens, and haversacks attested to their flight.

Even though Johnston did not use Holmes's infantry, the Purcell Artillery could still perform useful service. Holmes directed the battery to a knoll seven hundred yards northeast of Johnston's headquarters. There Walker's men unlimbered next to the famous Rockbridge Artillery and fired into a sea of frightened Federals streaming across Cub Run Bridge. With their jackets off as they rammed rounds of ammunition down the barrels of their guns, Walker's gunners impressed Beauregard with their marksmanship. The general's official report spoke of how "Walker's rifled guns . . . came up in time to be fired with precision and decided execution at the retreating enemy." Joseph Johnston also thought that Pegram and his comrades had worked their pieces "with great skill."[19]

While Walker's grimy cannoneers undoubtedly welcomed the accolades they received from their superiors, the enemy's knapsacks, wagons, and haversacks held treasures that offered a more satisfying reward. John McHenry Howard and two other friends from the University of Virginia serving in the First Maryland spotted Pegram after the battle, close to dusk. Although Pegram did not recognize them at first, he visited the Marylanders's camp later that evening. "Our meeting Pegram was a very good thing for us," recalled Howard, because Willy had gathered some "provender he had snugly stored away in a caisson." His former classmates also noted Pegram's annoyance that his unit did not "get up in time to take much part in the fight." As at Aquia Creek, the Purcell Artillery's exposure to combat at Manassas had been bloodless.[20]

After First Manassas, Pegram and his comrades returned to the Aquia district, where they bivouacked at Marlboro Point, an area opposite which enemy steamers frequently moved up and down the Potomac River. On the afternoon of August 23, Colonel R. Milton Cary of the Thirtieth Virginia spotted the Union vessels *Yankee* and *Release,* both of which had dropped anchor at the juncture of Potomac Creek and the Potomac River. Unable to resist this motionless target, Cary called on Walker to send a section of the battery to the extreme tip of Marlboro Point. But before Walker's men could wheel their two guns into position, the *Release* opened the duel. Northern shells exploded near Pegram and his comrades, but fortunately their sharp fragments injured no one in the battery. In a senseless use of ammunition, Walker allowed his men to lob "some twenty-five shot and shell" at the two boats, which eventually retired for more tranquil waters. According to Cary, Walker's men "behaved with proper coolness and deliberation," and he commended Pegram and two other officers in the battery for their gallant conduct under fire.[21]

Walker's men remained in the Aquia district until September 13, when the company reinforced General Isaac R. Trimble's command at Evansport, located southeast of Dumfries at the mouth of Quantico Creek. There the battery occasionally engaged Federal ships that passed along the Potomac, but these interludes did little to interrupt the humdrum existence of camp life, which probably taxed Pegram's patience. During the month of November, Walker's men constructed their winter quarters at a place called "Cross Roads," probably located somewhere between Evansport and Marlboro Point. The cannoneers left their cozy shelters in January for a new set of winter cabins at Camp Price, a move that doubtless caused great displeasure among Pegram and the other cannoneers.[22]

Early in 1862 Pegram and his comrades were still housed in their winter quarters at Camp Price. By this time, news of Confederate defeats in the West had lowered the men's spirits and spread gloom throughout the South. "We are all very much depressed by the news from Tennessee and North Carolina," Pegram wrote his brother John on February 11, 1862. "The surrender of Fort Henry was a very cowardly thing," he added, for the incident indicated that "the people in that direction do not seem to fight so well, as in every other." Though it looked "very badly that we should allow the enemy to get ahead of us at any point," Pegram recognized that "these defeats seem to be having a very good effect on the men, in making them reenlist." Nearly every man in Pegram's district planned to offer his services to the Confederacy for an additional term, and rumors suggested "that this is pretty much the case at Manassas & on the Peninsula." In the same letter, Pegram indicated his approval of a bill passed by the Virginia legislature making the militia subject to state service. "It was very natural that those men who had already served twelve months should not wish to see the militiamen staying at home," Pegram observed, "and now that this evil is remedied, there will be no difficulty." Two months later, his views had grown yet stronger: he refused to "sympathize with any coward, who wants to be drafted in the militia"—sentiments with which volunteers on both sides doubtless agreed. As the war progressed, Pegram continued to favor stronger measures from the Confederate government to improve the army's strength and efficiency. His resentment also increased toward such laggardly patriots who tried to evade active service.[23]

Pegram also worried about his brother John, who was still being held at Fort Monroe as a prisoner of war because a proper exchange could not be arranged. "I am very much distressed to hear that you have to return to Fortress Monroe," Pegram told his brother, but "I trust that you will soon be able to return." Recent Southern disasters had nonetheless left Willy feeling uneasy about John's future: "I fear that after their three recent victories, the Yankees will not be so willing to let you return." If John had the time, Pegram wanted him to write as soon as possible about his chances "for a speedy return" to the army, adding: "I pray God that it may be very soon, that you may again be enabled to take up arms in defence of our beloved country, against this ungodly, fanatical, depraved Yankee race."[24]

Possibly, the simple fact of his brother's captivity largely explains this outburst of anger, easily Pegram's most acrimonious statement against Northerners. And yet, far from making him an extremist, Pegram's perception of the North reflected an attitude common among Southerners: that the South and North had developed into two separate societies whose values were not merely different but outright antagonistic. Pegram's characterization of Northerners as an "ungodly" and "depraved Yankee race" clearly reveals his conviction that those in the North were inherently different from Southern whites because they had turned against God. The prospect of Southern independence had reinforced a belief in Pegram that the Confederates were responsible for protecting Christian civilization, an idea that legitimized the Confederacy in his eyes and formed the cornerstone of his nationalistic beliefs. Stephen Dodson Ramseur, a North Carolinian born in 1837, expressed a similar view: "Oh! I do pray that we may be established as an independent people," he wrote, "a people known and recognized as God's Peculiar People."[25]

Recent Northern victories also troubled Lindsay Walker, who decided to raise another battalion of artillery. He apparently assigned his first and second lieutenants to this new organization, leaving Pegram second-in-command of the Purcell Artillery. Then, on March 20, Walker was promoted to major and left the ranks of the battery altogether, elevating the twenty-year-old Pegram to command of the company. Taking charge of a six-gun battery might give pause to any man, regardless of age, and the task presented a thorough challenge to Pegram. Under his watchful eye were roughly one hundred horses and "a hundred & fifty as high spirited, respectable, able-bodied men" as could

Figure 7. Reuben Lindsay
Walker (1827–1890). It was
Walker who first noticed
Willy's leadership abilities,
and he continued to play a
crucial role in Pegram's rise
through the ranks. (Photo-
graph from *The Long Arm of
Lee,* by Jennings Cropper
Wise, Bell Co., 1915)

be found. Willy's duties consumed all of his energy; he found little time to write
home since "my election to the captaincy." "My hands are full," he bluntly told
his youngest sister from Fredericksburg on April 3, joking that he had "grown
six inches since my promotion" and "employed two barbers to keep my beard
in trim, for fear my friend[s] don't know me." At the same time, he realized
that he had a "great deal to be thankful for" and considered himself "very fortunate" when his commission as captain arrived on March 31. "The position is a
very responsible one," he added, "but I would not exchange places with anybody in the Confederacy." Unaccustomed at first to his new title, he sometimes
looked around for Lindsay Walker when addressed as captain. Though bur-
dened by his enlarged responsibilities, he was determined not "to allow anything, except my duties to God, [to] interfere with my duty to my country."[26]

Pegram longed for the company of his family during the spring of 1862. John
had been recently exchanged from Fort Monroe, but now, back in Richmond,
he refused to part from the stunning Hetty Cary of Baltimore. Disappointed,
Willy asked his younger sister to persuade his brother to "leave his 'Dulcinea
Del Baltimoriaso' for a day or two, and come up and see what a battery I have."
Because he was so "very anxious" to see John, Willy devised a plan that satisfied
all parties involved. If his brother "could not leave Miss Hettie any longer" than

Figure 8. William Ransom Johnson Pegram. This, the only wartime photograph of Pegram, was probably taken after the Seven Days campaign, while Willy was serving as a captain in the Purcell Artillery. (Courtesy of Mrs. Virginia B. Maloney)

a day, "he could leave Richmond at six o'clk, & get back by 2½,—spending an hour & a half with me. You could come with him." Pegram also hoped that the prospect of seeing "several of his old classmates" might lure John away from Richmond. It was out of the question for Willy to return home for a short visit, an especially discouraging circumstance because he wanted "very much to be with you all, particularly now whilst I am so near." [27]

Pegram moved closer to his family and Richmond on April 18. The Purcell Artillery, accompanying General Charles W. Field's Virginia brigade, evacuated the town of Fredericksburg when McDowell's forces appeared on the heights rising above the Rappahannock River, opposite the town. To slow the enemy's advance, Pegram's cannoneers and Field's infantrymen set their torches to the bridges spanning the river, the wharf, and the schooners and steamers docked near the shore. After burning everything of military value, Pegram's artillerists marched away from the river and through the dirt streets of Fredericksburg. "Amidst the smoke & flame & the tears & lamentations of the inhabitants we departed, in full view of the enemy on a retreat wh[ich] I think, was ill & hurriedly done," wrote John Hampden Chamberlayne, a friend and subordinate of Pegram's. Fountains of black smoke rising above the town saddened Chamberlayne, who wrote from the battery's new camp near Guinea Station: "The evacuation of Fredsbg went to my heart, it was [and] is one of the few places, one of the last abodes where lingers the old time spirit of Virginia gentry." [28]

On May 5 Pegram's cannoneers packed their personal belongings and marched toward a new bivouac along the banks of the Rappahannock River. Unlike most of the hikes Pegram's men would make during the war, this excursion actually rejuvenated their spirits, thanks to one small incident. As the battery passed by the house of a local resident, three ladies strolled out the front door. Chamberlayne immediately fastened his eyes upon one of them, whom he considered "a perfect wayside lily." Fortunately for Pegram's artillerists, the column had stalled, and Chamberlayne found it amusing to see "the rude soldiers gathered round her for the pleasure of being a moment in the sphere of gentleness refinement & beauty." The men directed question after question at the three women. With red cheeks, they smiled and answered the inquires, asking in turn "where we were going & how many we were & how far our guns would shoot." One of the women instructed a slave to go and get some water, and Chamberlayne noted, "such a thirsty set of souls as we suddenly became!" The sound of the bugle, however, shattered this idyllic scene. As Pegram's soldiers headed back for the road, Chamberlayne turned to his "wayside lily," took off his hat, and bowed. "I don't know her name & I shall never see her again," he wrote, "but I am indebted to her for much more than a cup of water." [29]

From the battery's new camp overlooking the Rappahannock, Pegram and his cannoneers could see the enemy's bivouac three and a half miles away. The

Confederates had set up their canvas shelters in a "broom straw old field" that assured them many restful evenings. The monotony of camp life quickly settled over the battery, and there was little for the men to do except sleep and lounge on the banks of the river. "It rains every other day generally," Chamberlayne noted on May 6, "but I suffer no inconvenience, & setting aside idleness & anxiety I am quite as comfortable & content as need be." Every day, Pegram drilled his men across the parade ground. After witnessing one of these sessions, Lieutenant John Tyler of the Letcher Artillery recorded in his diary on May 20 that "Willie Pegram['/s comp[an]y drill very well." Bureaucratic chores vied with drill for Pegram's attention. Maggie Tucker informed Pegram's friend, Charles Ellis Munford, that Pegram's sister "Jennie says she wrote to beg Capt Willie to come down, if it was only for one day, but he could not leave his Company."[30]

Fate, however, soon brought Willy to Richmond for a longer stay than either he or his family could have imagined. General Joseph E. Johnston's forces had moved back to the gates of the city by the end of May, pursued by McClellan's slow-moving Army of the Potomac. Under tremendous pressure from Confederate authorities, Johnston developed a plan to wrest the initiative from the Federal army. But before he could undertake this offensive, he called for reinforcements. General Joseph R. Anderson's command near Guinea Station, which included the Purcell Artillery, found itself marching for the capital of the Confederacy. The prospect of fighting near their homes in Richmond must have pleased Pegram and his men—though many probably wished in the end that they had remained at their old camps.

It rained without interruption from the moment the bugle sounded the advance on May 24 until the battery arrived in Richmond three days later. Because Anderson had failed to organize the march properly, there were numerous stops, which repeatedly caused the battery's guns to sink into the road. Pegram's cannoneers waded through the mud, cursing and complaining, until they liberated cannon and animals from the road's grip. A cannoneer from the Crenshaw Battery captured the men's frustration: "We was marching from Guinea's Depot for five days and three nights and I tell you it was very hard indeed. We marched through the mud up to the horses' knees and we had to stop and prize [sic] out many times. We did not have anything to eat for 48 hours and the Yankees was very near after us."[31]

Pegram and his bedraggled men finally reached the northeastern outskirts of Richmond on May 31, in time to hear blasts of musketry resounding from the Seven Pines battlefield. Amid dense vegetation and a driving rain, Johnston hurled his forces at the Federals in two days of combat. Uncoordinated Confederate assaults fell apart under a relentless fire, resulting in more than six thousand casualties, including the army's commander, who left the field after a piece of shell pierced his chest. Yet out of the confusion that enveloped the Southern army after Seven Pines emerged Robert E. Lee, who concentrated his forces around the defenses of the city and ordered the soldiers to strengthen their positions with picks and shovels. As the soldiers tossed dirt into the air, murmurs of discontent filled the ranks. Many believed that Lee lacked the resolve to launch an audacious stroke against McClellan.

Isolated north of the Chickahominy, the Union Fifth Corps provided Lee an offensive opportunity that quieted his critics. There, he assembled Jackson's Valley troops, along with A. P. Hill's division, for a turning movement on June 26. Unfortunately for Hill, "Stonewall" Jackson was unusually slow that day. Hill's "Light Division" had been ordered to hold its advance until Stonewall's troops opened the fighting. As the sun drifted to the west, Hill grew increasingly anxious, straining his ears to catch the battle cry of the Valley troops.[32] By now, he had relinquished all hope of seeing Jackson's men by three in the afternoon. He impetuously directed Field's brigade and the Purcell Artillery to lead the division's movement across the Chickahominy River.

Before the bugle sounded its call to the front, Pegram rode forward to "face his battalion." In a voice as "clear as a bell," he recited the following lines to his cannoneers:

To every man upon this earth
Death cometh soon or late;
And how can man die better
Than facing fearful odds
For the ashes of his fathers
And the temples of his Gods?

The drivers put their whips against the flanks of their horses "with a cheer." As the battery's caissons rumbled behind the Virginia infantrymen and the wheels of Pegram's six guns spun onto the Cold Harbor Road, a number of his artillerists joined in a chorus of "Maryland, My Maryland." After crossing the river and pushing through Mechanicsville, the battery ascended a steep hill that afforded some shelter from incoming Northern shells. Stubborn fighters of General George G. Meade's Pennsylvania Reserves awaited the Confederates behind freshly dug entrenchments beyond Beaver Dam Creek. Even though Pegram had told his men earlier in the day that there was no better way of dying than in front of "fearful odds," he scarcely could have imagined the seething cauldron his battery was about to enter.[33]

With the Purcell Artillery behind the middle of the brigade, Field's soldiers moved toward the center of the Federal position. Union artillery commanded their mile-long approach, ripping gaps in the advancing Confederate lines. Field thought it was the "most destructive cannonading I have yet known." He knew that he must rush his men across the exposed plain and engage the Union

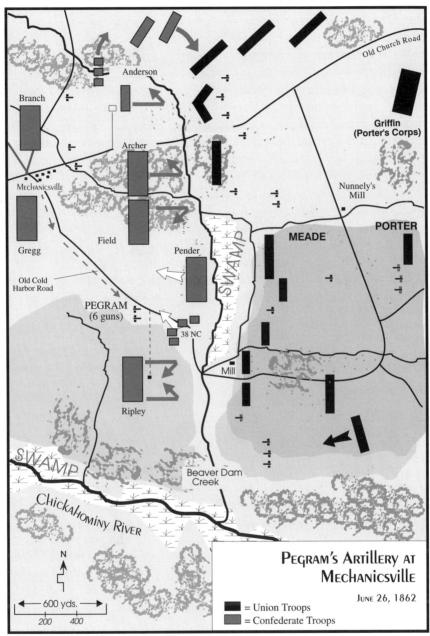

Old Church Road

Anderson

Branch

Griffin
(Porter's Corps)

Archer

Mechanicsville

Nunnely's
Mill

Field

PORTER

MEADE

Gregg

Pender

Old Cold
Harbor Road

PEGRAM
(6 guns)

38 NC

Mill

Ripley

Beaver Dam
Creek

SWAMP

CHICKAHOMINY RIVER

N

600 yds.

200   400

PEGRAM'S ARTILLERY AT
MECHANICSVILLE

JUNE 26, 1862

= Union Troops

= Confederate Troops

Theodore P. Savas

Map 1.

infantry at close quarters; Federal artillerists would then have to focus their sights elsewhere or risk hitting their own troops. Advancing at the double quick, Field's regiments veered to the left, off the Cold Harbor Road, and plunged straight into the boggy lowlands around the creek. The musketry intensified to an awful crescendo. As the Virginia infantrymen surged forward, Field directed Pegram to unlimber his pieces and open fire. The artillerists wheeled their guns into position about three-quarters of a mile from the Federal entrenchments. As the *Daily Richmond Examiner* subsequently reported, "No sooner had they got into position in this field than it was evident the battery had been drawn into an ambuscade." While rifle balls buzzed over their heads like gigantic horse flies, the artillerists struggled to get off a few rounds. Aware that his battery could not withstand the weight of Union ordnance, Pegram ordered his guns to the protection of a woodlot behind Field's brigade.[34]

For thirty minutes Pegram sheltered his battery in the timber. Then, after General James J. Archer rushed his troops to the left of Field's brigade, Pegram ran his battery forward just south of the Cold Harbor Road. Although the Federal artillery had a number of targets, it must have seemed to Pegram and his men that every Union cannon across Beaver Dam Creek was focused on them. Indeed, twenty-four Northern field pieces bombarded the Purcell Artillery. As General William Dorsey Pender's brigade passed to the right of Pegram's battery on its way to the front, the North Carolinian observed that Federal cannon played on the Virginia artillerists "with great effect." Amid the destruction, Pegram sat "motionless in his saddle, no more concerned at the shells which were ploughing up the dust about him than if he had been lounging on the porch in Franklin Street."[35]

Francis W. Dawson, an Englishman who later served on General James Longstreet's staff, informed his mother after the battle that he had acted as a volunteer for "a very dear friend of mine, Capt. Willie Pegram." Early in the fight a shell fragment partially shredded Dawson's trousers, "cutting a hole about 4 inches in length by 1 in. deep in the back of my leg." One of his comrades yelled out, "That Britisher has gone up at last." But, like a number of injured men in the Purcell Artillery, Dawson refused to leave his post. He recovered his "senses," tied a handkerchief around the bloody wound, and returned to his position to find that "our battery . . . had to bear the weight of the fire from the Yankee guns, which were so placed that they had a cross-fire upon us during the whole of the time."[36]

Enemy shells exacted a heavy toll among Pegram's cannoneers. Dawson recalled that "at each moment some poor fellow would fall, groaning, to the ground, there to lie for hours untended, and uncared for." "The carnage among our men was fearful," the *Examiner* recorded, "but manfully and coolly they stood to their posts." A single missile killed three horses and one man before tearing the leg and arm off another soldier. As the fighting wound down, Pegram, Dawson, and two other men worked one gun "instead of the complement of ten" men.[37]

Pegram's stoic behavior undoubtedly steadied the nerves of his men during their first real taste of combat. Seemingly oblivious to the fact that his command was being obliterated before his eyes, he refused to retire from the field. Only the benevolence of dusk saved his battery from total annihilation. Out of the ninety-two men who had galloped into action earlier in the day, forty-two lay wounded, one mortally wounded, and three dead. Four of Pegram's six guns had been disabled during the fight and more than a dozen battery horses killed—shocking figures that, in Dawson's estimation, spoke a "more eloquent" testament to the battery's courage "than words!" An artillerist from another Richmond company scribbled in his diary that evening that the Purcell Battery had "won an enviable fame."[38]

Undeniably, Pegram bore some responsibility for his company's staggering casualties. While inflicting little damage to the enemy, he had needlessly exposed his gunners to the powerful Federal artillery. Most of the responsibility for this disaster, however, rests with the organization of Lee's artillery, whereby one battery accompanied every infantry brigade. This system not only dispersed the Southern guns but also enabled the enemy to mass their firepower against scattered Confederate batteries. Moreover, Lee's artillery officers received their orders from brigade commanders, which had the unfortunate effect of preventing the men of Lee's "long arm" from acting independently and coordinating their fire. In his later years Dawson still lamented the fact that the organization of the army enabled the Federals virtually to blast the Purcell Artillery out of existence. "It was one of the greatest errors of the early days of the Confederacy," he wrote, "that batteries were allowed to be knocked to pieces in detail, when, by massing a dozen batteries, the enemy could have been knocked quickly out of time and many lives saved." Regarding the performance of the Southern artillery at Mechanicsville, Jennings C. Wise reached a similar conclusion in his thorough study of the Army of Northern Virginia's artillery. The gunners were not at fault, explained Wise: "The pernicious brigade distribution destroyed their power at the outset to cope with Porter's masses. They were but victims of a system."[39]

In his first battle as commander of the Purcell Battery, Pegram extinguished any doubts about his ability to command men. Facing overwhelming odds, he maintained his composure, leading by example as his ranks grew steadily thinner. Even his disregard for his men's safety (as well as his own) ultimately reflected Willy's belief that a soldier should willingly resort to any measure to defeat the enemy. That night, while his men slept on the field, Pegram tapped his apparently endless reservoir of energy and obtained "four splendid Napoleon guns" that had been captured from the Federals—efforts that did not go unnoticed by his superiors. A. P. Hill applauded the efforts of his young artillerist, stating in his official report that "Pegram, with indomitable energy and earnestness of purpose, though having lost 47 men and many horses at Mechanicsville, had put his battery in condition." [40]

The sun rose above a smoldering field on the morning of June 27. As the Confederates peered through the haze across Beaver Dam Creek, they could see abandoned Federal trenches. General Fitz John Porter had retired to a defensive line overlooking the lush vegetation of Boatswain Swamp near Gaines's Mill. Undaunted by his costly assaults the previous day, Lee pursued the retreating Federals with the Light Division in the van. Hill's troops collided with the enemy about mid-afternoon. As on the previous day, Hill imprudently flung his units piecemeal against Porter's force. While Hill's infantry struggled against a telling fire, Pegram's cannon raced past Gaines's Mill toward the front. About three hundred yards east of New Cold Harbor, the Purcell Artillery moved off the dusty road. While the battery awaited orders, a few shells exploded harmlessly nearby and stray bullets whined overhead. Hill's men started to give way about four o'clock. Stragglers scurried to the rear; other soldiers remained on the field, huddled together in the open but refusing to fire a shot.

When Hill called for reinforcements, Pegram rushed his fieldpieces to the garden of the New Cold Harbor Tavern near the center of the sagging Confederate line. Sighting the muzzles of his guns toward the southeast, he fired on Federal infantry located in a patch of timber. As his guns hurled shells into the bog around Boatswain Swamp, enemy sharpshooters hit a few of the battery's horses but claimed no human victims. Near dusk, Pegram and his gunners witnessed a magnificent assault by John Bell Hood's and Evander M. Law's brigades that swept across the meadow, scaled the Union works, and drove the enemy from the field. The Union line had finally been broken, but at a cost of more than eighty-five hundred Confederate casualties. Still, Porter's stand at Gaines's Mill allowed McClellan to continue his retreat toward the James River. Determined to destroy the Army of the Potomac, Lee stayed on McClellan's trail for the next three days. [41]

Pegram and his men rested under some trees near New Cold Harbor the next day. On June 29 they crossed the Chickahominy River at New Bridge and encamped at Piney Chapel on the Darbytown Road. Back on the road by ten o'clock the next morning, the cannoneers marched behind General James Longstreet's men. As the battery moved down the Long Bridge Road, the booming of cannon, followed by ripples of musketry, drifted from the front. Close to four in the afternoon, Longstreet's division attacked Porter's men near Frayser's farm. "Old Pete" soon called for Hill's division, located three-quarters of a mile behind the firing line, to support the assault.

Working his way down the clogged road, Pegram brought his company into position on Nathan Enroughty's pasture, better known as "Darby field." According to the *Examiner,* Northern projectiles fell around Pegram's men in "a perfect storm." One shell chipped the side of a caisson, sending splinters in every direction. "Had it struck a few inches lower," the *Examiner* observed, the caisson would have exploded with "frightful" results. To make matters worse, the ground chosen for Pegram's guns afforded no clear shot at the Federals. His men consequently stood at their posts "without firing a gun, and without the loss of man or horse" until darkness settled over the field.[42]

The heated exchange at Frayser's farm proved indecisive for Lee, the Union forces remaining intact. That evening the Northerners headed for a nearly perfect defensive position at Malvern Hill, a prominent rise that covered McClellan's retreat to the James. On July 1 the gray light of morning revealed that the Army of the Potomac held ground that would chasten even the most resolute fighter. Rows of Federal cannon crowned the hill, which rose some 150 feet, dominating the open fields below. Porter had arranged his infantry behind the Northern gunners, with a heavy skirmish line in front. In the words of Jennings C. Wise, "The setting was complete for a tremendous disaster."[43]

Because of illness, Lee exerted little authority on July 1, leaving most of the tactical arrangements to subordinates who botched their assignments: not until midday were the troops in position. Jackson's men occupied the left flank, General Daniel Harvey Hill's forces filled the center, and General John B. Magruder's troops anchored the right. Longstreet believed that Jackson's artillery stationed near the Poindexter farm and Magruder's guns on the right would produce a crippling converging fire, but he failed to organize his batteries in such a fashion. Without adequate artillery support, General Lewis A. Armistead pushed his Virginia brigade within a few hundred yards of the Union's left flank on the Crew farm, followed closely by General Ambrose R. Wright's Georgia brigade. Both officers then called for support. Two pieces of Grimes's Artillery hurried to the scene, only to receive fierce counterbattery fire from more than thirty Federal guns. To support this lone company, Moorman's Confederate Battery rushed forward, only to find one of Grimes's cannon disabled and the remaining gunners abandoning their posts.[44]

With the loss of Grimes's Artillery, Moorman's gun crews became the focal point of the enemy's metal. They could not hold on for long. Close to three o'clock, Pegram and his Purcell Artillery galloped up Carter's Farm Road to the Confederate right flank, where his men unhitched their horses and unlimbered their guns two hundred yards to the left of Moorman's company. As Pegram's men loaded their cannon, Moorman's artillerists withdrew from the field. Isolated and alone, Pegram's battery became the enemy's prime target. It was Mechanicsville all over again. Referring specifically to the Purcell Artillery, the *Examiner* reported: "This proved, by all odds, the fierescest [sic] fight our men had been engaged in." Only a half mile from the Unionists, Pegram could see their gunners loading their pieces. Federal missiles thundered down from the sky, plowing into the earth or spraying jagged metal in the air. A number

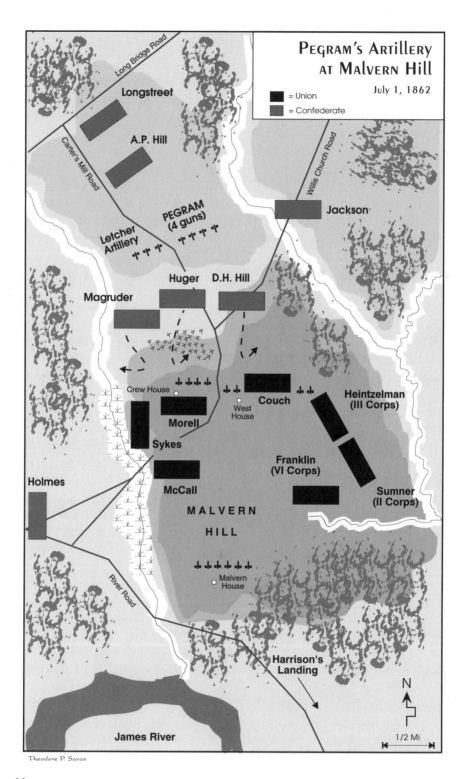

Map 2.

of Pegram's men fell to the ground in agonizing pain. Killed instantly was Charles B. Watkins, a nineteen-year-old private. His younger brother John, a sixteen-year-old who also served in the company, carried his brother's lifeless body off the field while his comrades continued their deadly work.[45]

General A. R. Wright observed that the Purcell Artillery had "opened a well-directed fire upon the enemy, which told with fearful effect upon them." But considering the overwhelming odds, it is difficult to imagine that Pegram's ordnance had the effect on Federal guns that Wright suggests. In fact, the outspoken General D. H. Hill called the efforts of the Confederate artillery at Malvern Hill "almost farcical." Armistead sought to even this unequal contest by demanding that Magruder and Longstreet forward additional batteries, but his requests fell on deaf ears.[46]

In the words of General Wright, Pegram's men "manfully" continued the struggle without additional support. Such were their losses that within an hour there remained only enough men to operate one cannon. With unshaken determination, Pegram's artillerists "firmly held their ground and continued to pour a deadly fire upon the enemy's line." "Seeing the utter hopelessness of the contest," Wright finally ordered Pegram to cease firing until more batteries could be brought into action. About four o'clock, the Letcher Artillery went into battery about three hundred yards to the right of Pegram's company. "Again the gallant Pegram opened with his single gun," Wright reported, while the Letcher Artillery also peppered the Federal line. In the ranks of this Virginia battery was Pegram's friend, Charles Ellis Munford. Engaged to Pegram's sister Jennie, Munford had been Willy's classmate at the University of Virginia. The day after Virginia seceded, Pegram had sent a missive to Munford, encouraging him to enlist and fight the "black Republicans." Now the two friends stood within sight of each other as they battled the Federals. Munford grabbed one of his men by the hand and told him: "I forgive you for past offences." Suddenly, a spherical shell exploded directly overhead, spewing musket balls in every direction. Three balls hit Munford. One passed through his eye, another through his head, and the last struck his thigh. He crumpled to the ground, his heart stopping instantly.[47] While the air shook with concussions from the enemy's shells, Pegram assisted his men in loading the battery's single gun. When not working the piece, he cheered on the remnant of his command, even though several of the cannoneers who "stuck to their posts" already had been wounded three times. The Examiner reported that "Pegram's courage and gallantry showed pre-eminent where all were brave." The Purcell Artillery's steadiness under fire also impressed Lewis Armistead, who wrote that "no men could have behaved better than Captain Pegram['s]."[48]

Shortly after five o'clock, Pegram's single gun and the Letcher Artillery supported the first wave of Confederate infantry assaults. Northern batteries concentrated on the charging infantry, giving the Southern artillerists a much-

Figure 9. Charles William Field (1828–1885), to whom Pegram's battery was first assigned. "I have taken occasion before to speak of the distinguished services of Pegram's battery," Field wrote of Cedar Mountain. "It is sufficient to say now that it fully sustained the reputation made on other fields." (Photograph courtesy of the Massachusetts Commandery Military Order of the Loyal Legion and the U.S. Army Military History Institute)

needed respite. Within minutes, however, the Confederate attackers stumbled back through the smoky haze that had engulfed the field. The day had been a perfect fiasco for Lee. More than five thousand wounded or dead Confederates littered the field. The Purcell Artillery had lost three of the company's four Napoleons; two men lay dead and another six wounded, and twenty horses had been cut down.[49] At about six o'clock, Pegram ordered his cannoneers to retire. Grimy and exhausted, they carried their lone piece onto a road jammed with vehicles and headed for the fairgrounds at Richmond to recover from their devastating losses during the Seven Days. Opening the campaign with some eighty to ninety men, at least fifty-seven members of the Purcell Artillery had been killed or wounded. No other Confederate artillery company during the Seven Days sustained heavier losses.[50]

The virtual destruction of Pegram's command might well suggest an inauspicious future for his career in the Army of Northern of Virginia. At this early stage of the war, however, officers who exhibited tenacity, aggressiveness, and audacity on the battlefield secured not only the admiration of their men but also the confidence of their superiors. Regardless of casualties inflicted or sustained, it was important for Civil War officers (as well as the enlisted men) to behave "manfully" under fire and to encourage their men by their calm example. Pegram's religious convictions inspired him to fight recklessly against a foe he considered immoral and subhuman. Willy saw godliness and courage as intimately connected and hoped he could inspire his men to similar behavior: they need only realize that heaven awaited those who died in battle. Indeed, many Confederate officers of his generation displayed an enthusiasm for battle comparable to Pegram's. William Dorsey Pender, a pious twenty-seven-year-old North Carolinian, informed his wife in 1861 that "the men seem to think that I am fond of fighting. They say I give them 'hell' out of the fight and the Yankees the same in it." Greenlee Davidson, a Virginian born in 1834, also thought it desirable to seek battle whenever possible. He welcomed his battery's assignment to a brigade that "is one of the best fighting commands in the army and is always sent in the advance."[51]

Even though Willy Pegram had led his battery to its virtual extinction during the Seven Days, the army applauded his lust for combat. Superiors pointed to the Purcell Artillery's long casualty list as proof of Pegram's competence and promise. Charles Field wrote glowingly in his official report that "the conduct of Captain Pegram's battery in the engagements excites my admiration. Always eager, always alert, Captain Pegram was in every action where opportunity offered, and always doing his duty, as the loss of every officer killed or wounded and 60 out of about 80 men, sadly attests." "I trust," concluded Field, "that the merits of this officer will not go unrewarded by the Department."[52]

THREE

WHAT HAVE I TO FEAR FROM
YANKEE BULLETS AND SHELLS?

THE SEVEN DAYS BATTLES DRAINED TWENTY THOUSAND MEN FROM THE army of Northern Virginia, but McClellan's forces were no longer within sight of Richmond's steeples. While the Union general imagined plots against him in Washington, his men sweltered along the James River. The people of Richmond rejoiced at the recent Confederate victories and heralded the accomplishments of their hometown Purcell Artillery and its bespectacled commander. On July 15, 1862, the *Daily Richmond Examiner* ran a front-page story covering the battery's exploits in the last campaign. If any details were omitted from this lengthy piece, the paper explained, it was because Pegram's men were "too busy to take note of anything but their guns and the enemy in their front." During a theatrical performance in the city, an actor brought cheers from the crowd when he declared that Pegram engaged the enemy at such close quarters "because he was too near-sighted to see a dozen yards." Veterans in the audience, many of them convalescents still wearing slings and bandages, rose to their feet and filled the air with lusty shouts of approval.[1]

But Pegram seemed decidedly uncomfortable with his sudden popularity and sought to avoid public attention. According to William Gordon McCabe, the captain rarely left the battery's camp outside Richmond, venturing into the city only to visit his immediate family. Pegram blushed "furiously" when anyone mentioned the excitement his gallantry had elicited during the recent fighting. Labeling "a laudatory paragraph about himself" in the papers "simply disgusting," he expressed a fear that "every man at the front will be laughing at it." Pegram's standing in social circles mattered less to him than the condition of his battery, which he labored hard to improve during July. Three new cannon gave the company four altogether, and a number of his injured men also returned to duty.[2] Like Pegram, Ham Chamberlayne viewed the "idleness of camp life" as a "great evil." As the army "sits quietly down," Chamberlayne postulated, the "guiding minds" of Lee's forces were "cutting out work for us." Even as Pegram refitted his battery, Chamberlayne complained on July 17 that "we are like a flight of locusts, leaving no green thing behind us. Our army treats Virginia as a conquered province."[3]

The "guiding minds" of the Army of Northern Virginia were, in fact, mapping out a new campaign. Lee worried not only about McClellan's force on the Peninsula but also about another enemy column pushing into north-central Virginia under the leadership of General John Pope. To meet the latter threat, Lee shifted Jackson's and Richard S. Ewell's divisions to Gordonsville on July 13.

While the two opposing forces cautiously shadowed each other, Pope's army swelled in strength to nearly 50,000 men. If Jackson had any chance of striking Pope before he consolidated his command with McClellan's, he required reinforcements immediately. Lee, however, concluded that Confederate forces faced no immediate danger, and so it was not until July 27 that Hill's Light Division of infantry boarded cars for the critical railhead at Gordonsville.[4]

Two days later, Hill's artillery abandoned its camps outside Richmond. The batteries rumbled down the city's cobblestone streets before moving along the James River to enter Goochland County. The third day of the march found the Purcell Artillery rolling across the luscious farmland in the Green Spring district, amidst scenery Chamberlayne described as "a beautiful country and rich as the richest." The crisp air and picturesque setting revived Pegram's morale and restored his fortitude, which had sagged after the Seven Days. "My health & spirits have improved very much since we came up here," he confided to his sister Mary. "You can't imagine how much I enjoy the pure air & fine scenery of the mountains." The invigorating environment had a desirable effect on Pegram's battery as well. "I have eighty-five men present," he added, "and not one on the sick list."[5]

The Purcell Artillery and Hill's other batteries reached Jackson's encampment below Gordonsville on August 1. As Pegram's cannoneers approached their destination, the welcome cadences of "Dixie" and "Maryland, My Maryland" drifted through the air, contending with the resounding cheers of Jackson's men. An artillerist in Hill's column scribbled in his diary that evening: "This is the gayest army I have seen yet. The men seem to have more life and spirit than any troops in service. They swear by Father Jackson, as they call him, and believe him to be the greatest general in the field." Pegram and his men relaxed in camp for the next few days, during which Chamberlayne found time to inform his mother on August 4 that Jackson's "force here is now about 25,000, of all arms; plenty, we think, to thrash Pope & his crew. Pope's men, by all accounts, are a dastard set."[6]

Pope's Army of Virginia had become a fixation for Jackson. Before the Union general could strike the Confederates near Gordonsville, Jackson set his troops in motion on August 7. But in the vicinity of the hamlet of Orange Court House their progress was slowed, and there they remained at nightfall. Pegram learned that evening that a few Northern prisoners had been captured while in the act of burning some mills. "I understand," he wrote, "that two of them were very obstreperous, & our men hung one, & killed the other."[7]

Confusion between Hill and Jackson over the order of march brought unnecessary delays the next day as well. Although the men shuffled a mere eight miles along the dusty road, Pegram seemed undisturbed by the grinding march. "We arrived at this point a few minutes ago," he reported in a letter to his sister at the end of the day, "and start early in the morning in pursuit of the enemy, who are falling back before us." Pegram complained that no letters from home had come recently. Nor did he have the time to send one to his family: "Since my last letter we have been so constantly on the march, that I have not had time to write. I have not heard a word from home since I left." Reluctantly, Willy accepted "the fact that I will hear very irregularly and seldom from home," which he considered "the only drawback to being with Jackson." He especially wondered when his mother and two sisters had left Richmond and was "anxious" about his mother because she had been unwell the last time he heard from home. The sun had almost vanished as he approached the end of his letter, making it virtually impossible for him to see the paper he was writing on. Before he put the letter aside, however, he assured his sister: "You cannot imagine how my heart yearns to be with you all, when I am away from you particularly now, that I cannot hear from you often." In the future he "would take every opportunity I can to write home." Willy closed "with the sincere prayer that God may ever protect and direct my dear Mother & Sisters." [8]

On August 9 Jackson pushed his troops northward up the Culpeper Road. The heat sapped the men's vitality; sporadic skirmish fire disturbed the morning. Enemy cavalry harassed the Confederates for most of the day before Jackson stumbled into the main body of General Nathaniel P. Banks's corps five miles south of Culpeper. Lacking proper reconnaissance of the area, Jackson swung his troops into battle along the Culpeper Road, a narrow approach bracketed by trees and choked with wagons, ambulances, and caissons. Southern units trickled to the front, preventing Stonewall from massing his brigades for one concentrated assault on the Federals. [9]

Pegram and his cannoneers remained at the back of Hill's column on the Culpeper Road while blasts of artillery resounded from the north. About three o'clock Hill directed Lindsay Walker to hurry his long-range guns to the front. Walker instantly called on Pegram's Purcell Artillery and the Middlesex Artillery, which was led by Lieutenant William B. Hardy. Both battery commanders struggled to move their pieces down a road clogged with vehicles, stragglers, and walking wounded, but they eventually managed to bring their batteries to the point where the Culpeper Road intersected the Crittenden Farm Lane. As Pegram and his men neared the intersection, Walker noticed that Federal fire was converging at that spot. Hoping to lead the two units past the dangerous area, he pointed rightward down the Crittenden Lane and ordered his artillerists to deploy just east of the dirt track in some corn fields near the center of Jackson's line. Unfortunately, Walker had not made a reconnaissance of the area. His instructions brought Pegram's and Hardy's guns "within 150 yards of the enemy's skirmishers." [10]

Pegram and Hardy wheeled their cannon into line and quickly opened fire on the Federal batteries opposite them. Pegram's section of guns, coupled with

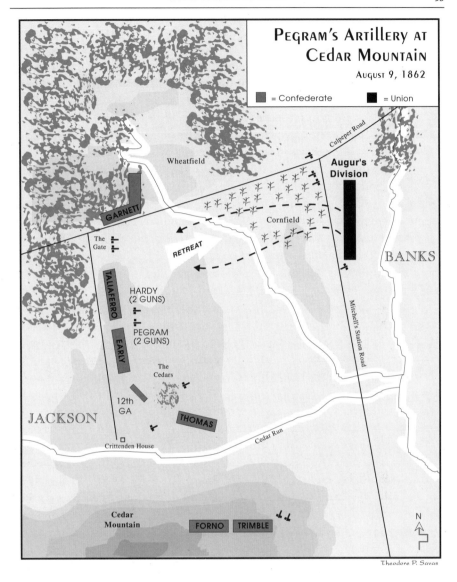

PEGRAM'S ARTILLERY AT CEDAR MOUNTAIN

AUGUST 9, 1862

■ = Confederate   ■ = Union

Map 3.

Hardy's two pieces, occupied the center of Jackson's wide artillery deployment. The other Southern batteries stood in three clusters parallel to the Crittenden Lane. Jackson had twenty-three cannon in all. Before Pegram and Hardy opened their duel with Banks's gunners, the counterbattery fire had raged for about an hour. A field of tall green corn in front of Pegram's position sheltered Federal sharpshooters. Somehow Willy had the presence of mind to tabulate the number of times they tried to place a mark on him. "One sharp shooter," he nonchalantly informed his youngest sister after the battle, "took deliberate aim at me eight or ten times and missed me." Pegram also cited "four bullet holes through the skirt of my coat" as proof that the Northerners lacked skilled riflemen. This seeming invulnerability to enemy missiles reinforced Pegram's belief that God's hand shielded him from destruction. "How is it possible," he asked Jennie, "to shew gratitude adequate to such divine mercy?"[11]

The duel between the artillery of Banks and Jackson sputtered along, subsiding at times into an uneasy silence punctuated by occasional cannon shots. The tall corn and the gentle folds in the terrain made it difficult to discern Banks's intentions, and the troops in the center of Jackson's line could not see as the enemy gathered for an assault. Employing the element of surprise, the three brigades of General Christopher C. Augur's Union division drove through the corn field and struck at the brigades of Jubal A. Early and William B. Taliaferro. Positioned on a little knoll with his two available pieces, Pegram "had a good opportunity of seeing all the infantry movements on both sides" while his guns fired on the Federals.

The sight was inspiring, but Pegram played the observer for only a few moments. The hard-charging Federals scattered portions of Early's and Taliaferro's brigades. Pegram thought the Confederate infantry "behaved badly," as he watched the Federals surge toward his guns. Keeping "a sharp lookout," he called for "double charges of canister." A mighty blast staggered the attackers momentarily, but they put their heads down and continued on toward their prospective trophies. "We fired round after round of shell and then canister," a private in Pegram's company recalled, "but still on they came in grand style."[12]

Northern skirmishers had almost reached Pegram's guns when Willy grabbed the company's flag and waved it, imploring his men to remain at their posts. "Don't let the enemy have these guns or this flag," he shouted over the violent crash of battle, "Go on, men; give it to them." His cannoneers jerked their lanyards, their guns rocked backward, and canister raked the Union lines. Although Walker thought Pegram's fire had inflicted "great loss on the enemy," the Federals pushed on. The battery continued its work "until the enemy were right at the guns," remembered one of Pegram's men. Fortunately for Pegram, Walker finally ordered the stubborn artillerist to retire.[13]

At Pegram's command, "Limber to the rear!" his two guns withdrew. The Union battle lines were less than a hundred yards away, and an enemy missile knocked one of the battery's horses to the ground, threatening the loss of a gun. Private Albert S. Drewry recalled wanting to desert the cannon, but Pegram "quickly gave the order: 'Action, front! Fire double charges of canister!'" One last time a shotgun-load of round balls slowed the Federals long enough for the drivers to unharness the dead animal. As the battery lumbered off the field, an enemy bullet dropped one of the drivers from his saddle. When another man hesitated to take the wounded soldier's place, Pegram brandished his saber and prepared to strike him. A third cannoneer jumped onto the lead team, enabling the battery to gallop rearward "barely in time to save the gun." Pegram left a caisson and three dead horses on the field, but he later reported to Jennie that "after we drove them back I got my caisson." Once safely behind the lines of friendly infantry, Pegram overheard some of his men discussing how they had nearly lost their guns to the enemy. "Men," he told them, "when the enemy takes a gun of my battery, look for my dead body in front of it." [14]

Having stabilized his line, Jackson launched a counterattack against the Federal right about seven o'clock. Outflanked and outnumbered, the exhausted Northerners grudgingly retired toward Culpeper. Jackson ordered A. P. Hill's command to pursue the Federals, hoping his infantry could reach the town by sunrise. Even though it was close to eight o'clock, the thermometer still read a sizzling 86°, and Hill's weary troops were disorganized and soaked with perspiration. They responded slowly, but, as the moon illuminated the steamy night air, Hill pushed his column up the Culpeper Road. His artillery companies splashed across Cedar Run near a church of the same name. Fearing an ambuscade in a woodlot above the church, the Confederate high command deployed Hill's artillery to flush out any remnants of Banks's rear guard that might be hiding in the forest of oaks and pines. Eighty yards from the woodlot, Pegram's four cannon (his second section had arrived on the field late in the day) and three other batteries opened what Stapleton Crutchfield, Jackson's chief of artillery, termed a "heavy fire . . . in various directions." [15]

Nonetheless, only a few Federals scattered from the woods. Just beyond these trees and an adjoining field lay the main Northern battle line. Jackson again relied on his artillery for reconnaissance, instructing Pegram to toss some shells from the edge of the Cedar Run Church woods into the field beyond. Willy later wrote that "the hottest time for me, was that night." He placed his four guns on a knoll at the edge of the woods just to the left of the road. Staring out into the darkness the officers in the company disagreed about the exact identity of their target. They could hear the idle chatter of men, the thud of soldiers' feet pounding the ground, and wagons creaking down the road. Determined to have a definitive answer, Pegram turned to one of his subordinates, Joseph McGraw, and said: "McGraw, I shall ride up close to these fellows; keep a sharp lookout, and if you see me wave my hat, open all the guns." Pegram then darted across the field, vanishing into the growing darkness. [16]

Pegram reined in his horse within a few yards of the Seventh Indiana's picket line. After the war, a member of that unit, W. S. Odell, offered a colorful account of his regiment's run-in with Pegram. Odell saw a young officer with a linen duster on his hat (a detail substantiated by a member of the Second Virginia Infantry). Looking down from his horse, Willy stated the obvious: "You look like Yankees." "And you must be a d—n Rebel," replied one of the Hoosiers. Odell, however, thought Pegram a member of McDowell's staff and told his comrade to control his tongue. They let Pegram ride away, despite the grumbling of Odell's comrade. As he crossed the field to rejoin his command, Pegram waved his hat back and forth. McGraw ignored the signal, waiting for his return before opening fire. With Jackson watching nearby, Pegram shouted: "Pitch in, men; General Jackson's looking at you!" The battery's missiles then streaked through the sky, exploding amid Pegram's new acquaintances in the Seventh Indiana.[17]

Chaos ensued among the Federals. Horses stampeded and men scrambled for safety as their officers tried to restore order. "There was a great deal of the enemy's infantry in the field," Pegram wrote, "and we could soon hear them in great confusion, the officers trying to make their men charge upon me, and the men running." Jackson also noted the early success of the Purcell Artillery, reporting that its "well-directed and unexpected fire produced much disorder and confusion among that portion of the Federal troops." But the tables quickly turned on Willy's battery. The enemy soon realized that Pegram's fire was a spectacular display of pyrotechnics that posed no serious threat, at which point three Union batteries supporting General James B. Rickett's division replied to Pegram's guns. At a distance of just four hundred yards, the shower of sparks spewing from Pegram's cannon provided a useful marker for Banks's gunners to gauge the range of their target. In fact, the Southern cannoneers were so close to the enemy they could hear the distinct accent of some New England artillerymen who served in a Maine Battery.[18]

Arrayed in a broad arc, the powerful Federal batteries soon launched their missiles toward the knoll where Pegram's battery remained helplessly exposed. The converging Union fire created the impression that Pegram's men were sur- rounded. One Southern gunner believed the battery received enemy rounds "obliquely" and from "our backs," concluding that "this was one of the hottest actions the battery was ever in for the short time we were engaged." Indeed, it was virtually impossible to escape the jagged pieces of Northern metal. Cais- sons exploded, shooting flames skyward, while the cries of wounded men and the shrieks of crippled battery horses rose above the din of battle. One shell decapitated Pegram's lieutenant, Mercer Featherstone; a Confederate cavalry- man standing next to the slain officer felt the force of the missile before it struck Featherstone. The shell "passed through one horse into the body of another, and then exploded, tearing him to atoms." The first animal had collapsed on top of Featherstone, and it was some time before the men could extricate his lifeless body from the bloodied beast. So unnerved was he by this gruesome scene that the cavalryman sought a more tranquil setting from which he could watch the duel—but before he could depart, three other men had fallen.[19]

Despite losses that made it impossible to work his cannon effectively, Pe- gram remained steadfast: his personal code of behavior prevented him from withdrawing from the knoll. Pegram's superiors must have thought that sending additional batteries to rescue him would have been pointless. After an hour of constant pounding by the enemy's four batteries, Pegram's guns fell silent. A defiant Pegram later maintained that "if they had brought another battery by me, we could have whipped them." Once Pegram's cannon began to cool, Confederate cavalry groped in the darkness for the enemy, but for all practical purposes Jackson had called off the pursuit of Banks. The Purcell Artillery, which had reached the farthest point of the Confederate advance, slept on the field. At the first glimmer of dawn the grimy cannoneers fell back, leaving three dead men and a number of horses on the field but carrying their twelve wounded to safety. The losses at Cedar Mountain understandably upset Pegram. "I had gotten a pretty large Company together," he wrote, "but this of course throws me back." Pegram assured his youngest sister, however, that "I still have as many men as I had when I left Richmond, and can do some pretty good work yet." [20]

Pegram's performance once again attracted the notice of his commanding officers. Lindsay Walker complimented Pegram and William Hardy because they "inflicted great loss on the enemy," adding that "their conduct, with that of the men under their command, cannot be too highly commended." Charles Field reserved his highest praise for Pegram and his battery. Field called Willy a "gallant officer" and declared: "I have taken occasion before to speak of the distinguished services of Pegram's battery. It is sufficient to say now that it fully sustained the reputation made on other fields." As on the Peninsula it was Pegram's absolute fearlessness in battle—rather than the degree of punishment actually inflicted on the enemy—that caught the eyes of his superiors. His comrades in the army began to see uncommon valor as a predictable pattern of behavior for Pegram. Ham Chamberlayne reflected this view shortly after the battle, writing that "Willy Pegram acted with his usual gallantry & also suffered in men & horses." [21]

After a refreshing thunderstorm on August 10, the temperature climbed back into the nineties as Jackson's command marched away from the battlefield toward Orange Court House the following day. The Confederates halted near Gordonsville. On August 14 Pegram, who knew his family must "be very uneasy about me," informed Jennie that he had survived the latest battle. "But I presume Mother's anxiety is relieved," he added, "by seeing that my name was not amongst the list of casualties, in the paper." Pegram admitted that he "again got in a very hot place . . . but an ever merciful God again took me under His protection and brought me safely through the fight." Emerging from Cedar Mountain without a scratch, Willy asked: "What have I to fear from Yankee bullets and shells, as long as I am under His protection?" He hoped Jennie would "ask Mother to cheer up, and remember that we are all under His protection." [22]

Pegram's faith that God shielded him from danger typified the thinking of those Confederates who believed that Providence ensured not only the safety of good soldiers but also the triumph of their righteous cause. "I have been again shielded in the day of battle," wrote a twenty-five-year-old South Carolinian, James Drayton Nance, in 1863: "I cannot sufficiently thank our good and merciful God for His loving kindness to me." Shortly after Gettysburg, Dodson Ramseur informed his wife that "my horse was shot & killed under me. I made many hairbreadth escapes—thanks to an all kind Father." For men like Pegram, Nance, and Ramseur, death in battle held no terror because they saw themselves engaged in a holy war: if they were killed by the Northern infidels, God's kingdom awaited them. Nance maintained that the "martyrs" of the cause "deserve the lasting gratitude of posterity for the noble part they have borne in this righteous struggle." "It is better to die the death of the righteous," he added. Military experience reinforced the antebellum idea that God intervened in human affairs for the benefit of his people. Men like Pegram accepted the loss of life, destruction of property, and all the civilian hardships as a test of faith. If the people of the South endured, God would reward them with independence.[23]

Proud of his battery's performance on August 9, Pegram promised to send the family an extract of Field's report that "was very complimentary and asked for my promotion, which I do want." A member of A. P. Hill's staff, in fact, had "hinted" that Willy would receive higher rank in the near future. There were "only two reasons" why he would accept it, Pegram informed his sister Jennie: "One is that it would not be right to keep the officers under me back, and the other is, the higher my position in this army, the higher it will be in the regular army." He warned his sister that "all this about promotion is entre nous, and must not be mentioned on any account." Pegram also noted that Longstreet's division had arrived, and that Lee was certainly on the way. "Hurrah!" he exclaimed. "On to Philadelphia! I'll get your shoes &c." Pegram closed with a request that Jennie write often to her "devoted brother."[24]

Though Jackson had checked Pope's southward progress at Cedar Mountain, the Federal army was receiving reinforcements daily, and it was clear that Pope soon would have his army back in motion. Determined to strike before Pope united his troops with McClellan's men from the Peninsula, Lee abandoned his position along the James and by August 16 consolidated his army around Gordonsville. He sent cavalry toward the Rapidan with instructions to cross at Morton's Ford, slide around the enemy's rear, and disrupt Pope's communications. Once Jeb Stuart had executed the first part of the plan, Lee's soldiers would cross the Rapidan at Raccoon and Somerville Fords and strike Pope's flank and rear. Pope, however, managed to evade the trap when he learned of the prospective Confederate movements from documents found on one of Stuart's aides. Soon the Federal army lay behind the protection of the Rappahannock River.[25]

By August 17 Pegram and his men had accompanied the rest of Jackson's command to the banks of the Rapidan. Behind the Confederates towered the area's most impressive topographical feature, Clark's Mountain, which afforded a commanding view of Virginia's piedmont region. In a letter to his mother describing the events from August 17 to September 7, Pegram endeavored "a full account of our adventures, in the form of a diary." On the first afternoon Pegram had "witnessed a military execution of three men, deserters from Jackson's division." Pegram considered the entire affair "a solemn and impressing sight"—an attitude at variance with the usual response to executions. For example, another artilleryman who saw the same deserters lose their lives on August 17 conceded that executions "keep the army together" but thought such punishment "a cold-blooded thing." Pegram's seemingly heartless attitude toward an act that sickened most men serves to underscore his conviction that soldiers must fulfill their duty under any circumstances—an extreme stance in 1862, when most civilian-soldiers had not grown accustomed to seeing comrades die as the result of the verdict of a military court. Pegram's views on military executions as the war progressed became more common, though, and many veterans favored purging the army of perfidious elements.[26]

In the letter to his mother, Pegram mistakenly stated that the army crossed the Rapidan River on August 18, when Lee actually pursued Pope's retreating army two days later. Before dawn on August 20, Pegram's cannoneers had boiled their coffee, rolled up their blankets, and harnessed their horses. Situated at the tail of Hill's division, they crossed the Rapidan at Somerville Ford, while James Longstreet's men waded the river at Raccoon Ford. The roads filled with dust as Longstreet marched to Kelly's Ford on the Rappahannock and Jackson followed a course through Stevensburg on the way to Rappahannock Station. Pegram's battery "bivouac'd in a very pretty grove" that evening.[27]

By August 22 Jackson had pushed his troops close to White Sulphur or Fauquier Springs. Leaving his right flank vulnerable, Pope massed most of his force directly opposite Longstreet, who held the Confederate right between Freeman's Ford and Rappahannock Station. When Pegram's battery and the rest of Hill's division arrived at the bluffs overlooking the springs, a violent thunderstorm erupted. "In the hardest rain & got the most severe ducking [I] ever saw," Pegram noted in the letter to his mother. Listless from hunger, his bedraggled cannoneers "drew rations" the next morning after positioning their cannon above the springs. Pegram considered his company to be "in a half starving situation."[28]

Hill's division and its artillery crowned the hills around the springs on August 24. Assigned to repel any Northern attempt to storm the bridge near the springs, Hill's troops watched General Franz Sigel's Federals stumble toward the river late in the afternoon. It had taken them the entire day to cover the six miles from Waterloo to the springs. Artillery exchanged fire for most of the day, while the Federals occasionally sent working parties to attempt to destroy

the wooden bridge. As the roar of the guns reverberated between the hills surrounding the springs, shells from the Confederate cannon quickly dispersed
the demolition crews. Henry Kyd Douglas of Jackson's staff thought it was the
"noisiest artillery duel I ever witnessed"; another Southern officer stated that
"the report of the shell and the whistling of the fragments was so deafening"
that it prohibited conversation. Near dusk, the Federals called off their feeble
attempts to destroy the bridge. Pegram reported to his mother that his company was "engaged the whole day with their batteries & skirmishers—Purcell
Battery very fortunate—Only one man killed." [29]

Because of Jeb Stuart's foray around Pope's right flank between August 22
and 23, Lee decided to send Jackson's force toward the Federal rear. Rapid
marching might enable Jackson's 22,000 men to sever the Federal supply line
along the Orange & Alexandria Railroad. As Jackson slashed around Pope's
flank, Longstreet would occupy the enemy's attention with heated demonstra-
tions near Warrenton Springs and Waterloo. During the evening of August 24,
Pegram's battery abandoned its position near the springs and moved to Jeffer-
sonton with the rest of Jackson's command, after which Longstreet's troops
occupied the spot vacated by Hill. [30]

Jackson embarked on his daring maneuver the next day. Ewell's division led,
followed by Hill's men. The troops moved briskly through the refreshing morning air, but crossing the Rappahannock proved difficult. Steep banks lined the
river, and one artillerist in Hill's division described the descent into the swirling
water as "terrible." To make it up the opposite bank, many batteries required
the assistance of black laborers. Still, Jackson's column managed to overcome
these natural obstacles, passed through the hamlet of Orleans, and bivouacked
a few miles from Salem on the Manassas Gap Railroad. In describing this
twenty-five-mile hike Pegram reported to his mother that the Confederates
"marched rapidly until midnight, making a flank movement & crossing the
Rappahannock above Warrenton, completely fooling the enemy, and getting
to their rear." But the march, while taxing, at least had a pleasant interlude for
Pegram when he crossed paths with Jeb Stuart, a West Point classmate of John,
"who inquired particularly after all the family." [31]

With aching feet and tight muscles, the Confederates returned to the road
early the next morning. Dust rose quickly on what promised to be another very
hot day. The soldiers trekked through the town of Haymarket before settling in
for the evening at Bristoe Station, where other Confederates had already destroyed some track and a number of engines and cars. Manassas Junction had
been captured as well that evening, although the bulk of Jackson's force did not
reach that important railhead until the next day. Ignoring the posted guards,
the men swarmed around Federal boxcars containing delectables worthy of a
French gourmet. Pegram thought the Union supply trains contained "everything that the human mind can imagine," estimating the value of the captured
goods "at several millions of dollars." Confederates stuffed canned lobster, con-

densed milk, candies, pickled oysters, and fruit into haversacks that previously had held only green corn. Pegram's close friend Ham Chamberlayne found the scene at the depot slightly comical: "To see a starving man eating lobster salad & drinking rhine wine, barefooted & in tatters was curious; the whole thing is indescribable." [32]

Following the example of his men, Pegram plunged into the crates. "I got the following articles," he proudly informed his mother: "A first-rate yankee horse, bridle & sabre, canteen, enough sugar & coffee to last [our] mess for six months, a small tent fly which accommodates two or three persons, & can be carried behind the saddle with the blankets, a dozen cakes of the nicest toilet soap & as many tooth brushes, which I hope to send home—also a good stationary [sic] . . . and various other small articles." Willy was thankful that Stonewall had led the army to the enemy's cornucopia. Without the captured rations, he noted, "we should have starved." [33]

A New Jersey brigade under the command of General George W. Taylor rudely interrupted the Confederate feast. Jackson invited Taylor to surrender peacefully, but when the Federals rejected his offer, he directed Lindsay Walker's battalion, including the Purcell Artillery, to the scene. Pegram placed his guns behind an old redoubt. "After some very pretty practicing" by his old company and the Pee Dee, Crenshaw, and Fredericksburg batteries, Walker reported, the enemy brigade was "put to flight." It was close to 11:00 P.M. when Pegram and his cannoneers returned to the depot, and an hour later they were back on the road with the rest of Hill's division. As the battery moved toward Centreville, flames shot into the black sky from fires set by Confederates at the depot. Pegram regretted that they "were forced to burn everything we could not carry off." [34]

The next morning, August 28, Jackson sent Hill's division to Centreville before he pushed his entire command down the Warrenton Turnpike. Eluding Pope, who was ignorant of Confederate whereabouts, Jackson settled his troops on a wooded ridge north of the turnpike on the old Manassas battlefield. A railroad cut that ran along the crest of the ridge strengthened a natural defensive position. Jackson launched an assault late in the afternoon when the Federals appeared near Groveton, but both sides refused to give ground and fought fiercely until dark. The engagement at Groveton captured Pope's attention. He decided to rally his forces against Jackson while ignoring Longstreet's troops, who had pushed through Thoroughfare Gap. For the next two days, Pegram wrote, the situation of the army "may be said to have been one of extreme hazard, and nothing but the most obstinate courage of our troops could have saved us." [35]

Sporadic picket fire broke out early on August 29. Posted on the ridges north of the Groveton-Sudley Road, Pegram's cannoneers waited with their guns behind Hill's infantry on Jackson's left. It is difficult to determine the exact disposition of the Purcell Artillery; however, the unit probably was near the center of

Jackson's line at the juncture of Hill's and Ewell's divisions. As the sun started to descend, Pope's troops assaulted Hill's position in piecemeal fashion. Amid increasingly intense musketry, Pegram wheeled two guns into the firing line. Even though thick white smoke hung in the woods, he spotted a Federal battery and ordered his cannoneers to silence the Union guns. His men worked their pieces at a feverish pace until a shell burst "right in the midst of one of my gun's crew." The destructiveness of the missile shocked Pegram, who told his mother that it killed a pair of "my best men," wounded two others, stunned the remainder of the crew, as well as killing three horses and "disabling a wheel & cutting through a tree." "It was," he said, "the worst shot I ever saw." One of the fatalities in Pegram's battery was William P. Fassett, whom Willy considered a noble soldier. "It seems such a pity," wrote Pegram, that "Fassett could not have lived to see Maryland." The Purcell Artillery limped off the field shortly after the mercilessly well-directed shell devastated the company, but Jackson's line held firm for the rest of the day.[36]

During the evening, Jackson improved his position and Longstreet made final preparations for an assault against the Union left. Pope mistakenly interpreted these movements as a general retreat, ordering his army to pursue the Southerners the next day. A series of Federal assaults stalled in front of Jackson's troops on August 30: Pegram and his cannoneers could hear a great uproar of musketry on their right and see the smoke hugging the tree line. Pope made only a few jabs at Hill's division that day, however, and it appears that Pegram's cannon were used sparingly. Walker reported that Hill's artillery was "engaged at intervals on the left and rear of the infantry." Because the battle centered on Longstreet's assault, Pegram and his men had limited opportunity to use their sponge and rammers.[37]

Relegated to the unaccustomed position of spectators, Pegram and his gunners watched as Longstreet's late-afternoon assault crushed Pope's left flank. Pope's entire army gradually came unhinged, flooded the Warrenton Turnpike, and retreated toward Centreville. "On this day was fought the largest battle of the war," Pegram wrote his mother. Though "the enemy had double the number we drove them miles back, completely routing them—capturing six thousand prisoners, and any number of can[n]ons small arms &c." After the Federals had been chased across Bull Run Creek, Pegram walked the field of Second Manassas. "I visited the different battlefields immediately after the fights," he observed, "& think that in all of these fights we killed fifteen or twenty to one—It exceeds anything you ever saw." The passage reflects Pegram's propensity to exaggerate the disparity between Confederate and Union forces. In reality, close to 14,000 Federals fell while Lee suffered nearly 9,000 casualties—not even two to one. What proved more important than the terrific losses, though, was Lee's use of this victory to launch his first raid into the North.[38]

FOUR

YOU WILL PRONOUNCE THIS A PRETTY BATTERY

A GENTLE RAIN BLANKETED THE BATTLEFIELD EARLY IN THE MORNING hours of August 31. According to Albert S. Drewry of Pegram's battery, an air of discontent hovered over the unit because on August 29 Pegram had volunteered the Purcell Artillery for "a very dangerous position" where "a whole gun's crew were cut down with one shell." When Willy learned of these grumblings, he formed his cannoneers into line and announced that he had "heard that I have been blamed for the disaster that occurred to our company at Manassas." He then asked "every man who is not willing to follow me where I choose to take them" to step forward. If a majority did so, he would resign his commission and enter the ranks. But if only a minority signified discontent, he would "give them a transfer to another command, such as they may select." Drewry noted that although Pegram "waited some time," "not one man stirred." The young captain then warned his men: "Let us have no more of this talk. A soldier should always seek the most desperate post that is to be filled."[1]

While Pegram dealt with problems within his battery, Lee sought to destroy Pope's disheartened army. The commanding general instructed Jackson to take his weary troops on yet another flanking movement around the enemy, who lay behind fortifications outside Centreville. Stonewall put his men in motion across Bull Run at Sudley Ford, then onto the Little River Turnpike toward Fairfax Court House. Fatigued and hungry, the men dragged their feet along roads sloppy from recent rains. An artillerist under Lindsay Walker noted that "after traveling until something after dark we encamped within ten miles of Fairfax C.H.—pretty tired and sleepy."[2]

Jackson engaged the Federals near a country mansion named Chantilly the next day. A storm swept the field as the Confederates deployed for an assault. Because of the soggy atmosphere, gun smoke clung to the ground, making it virtually impossible to distinguish friend from foe. The entire scene must have had a surreal appearance, as the dark landscape swarmed with figures that were no more than amorphous shapes and bright sheets of flame sprayed from leveled muskets. In this dense atmosphere, attacks quickly bogged down and regimental organizations disintegrated. Although not involved in the fighting, Hill's guns lay vulnerable to the enemy's fire. After a few rounds exploded amid the Confederate gunners, the batteries quickly dispersed without sustaining serious damage. The fight ended near dark as a stalemate, extinguishing Lee's hopes of crushing Pope's army. Pegram admitted that the Federals "made a pretty stout fight" at Chantilly, but "night and rain" prevented Jackson from wrecking the enemy's force.[3]

Lee embarked on his first raid into the North three days after Chantilly.

Concerned not only about protecting the fall harvests in Virginia but also with gaining recruits in Maryland, he pushed the Army of Northern Virginia across the Potomac River. It was a dramatic moment that remained etched in the memory of every veteran who participated in the crossing. With mountains in the background and the notes of "Dixie" and "Maryland, My Maryland" drifting through the air, Hill's soldiers splashed across the river on September 5. Pegram thought it was a "grand . . . spectacle." "But there was one thing wanted to complete the scene," he added, "that was, a crowd on the opposite bank welcoming them as their deliverers." Western Maryland overflowed with pro-Union sentiment, unlike the eastern part of the state, where the institution of slavery remained an integral part of the economy. Confederate sympathizers in the area consequently hesitated to express their support.[4]

As his battery reached the opposite shore Pegram "could see disappointment written on the face of every man." There were a number of Marylanders in the Purcell Artillery, some of whom muttered that "they had as soon be in Virginia as in Maryland." Pegram complained that "even Virginia opposite to this point is much tainted" and thought it better to have "crossed at some other point." Marylanders failed to flock to the army, which led Pegram to postulate that "the Southern people are restrained, because they don't know how soon they may again be in the enemy's lines, & the union men are spies upon them— It will take a good victory to bring them to our ranks." He wished that his brother John was present because "I know it has always been his wish to be with the army that went into Maryland."[5]

Jackson's column arrived at the outskirts of Frederick by September 6, although the army presented a sorry spectacle when it established camp along the Monocacy River. Filthy, clad in tattered uniforms, and scarecrow-thin from scanty rations, Lee's soldiers neared the limit of their physical endurance. "During our forced marches and hard fights since leaving Orange C.H.," wrote one of Walker's artillerists, "the soldiers have been compelled to throw away their knapsacks and there is scarcely a private in the army who has a change of clothing of any kind. And the consequence is that they are both ragged and dirty." He predicted that the "army will be naked and barefooted" if no victory lay in the near future.[6]

Because of their condition, Jackson allowed his troops to rest for three days, a break that enabled Pegram to summarize the campaign to that point in a letter to his mother. Apart from relating military matters, Willy reported that his brother John's beloved Hetty and her sister Jennie Cary had made it to Baltimore "unmolested." He was sorry to learn that John had been made chief of staff to General Edmund Kirby Smith instead of a brigadier general, "as he had been asked for that position." "I am very anxious to hear how you all are," he added. "I hope things are cheaper & that there is more comfort in Richmond, since the troops have been moved off." Pegram and his men, he wrote, were "lounging about, enjoying the respite allowed us from our truly hard, labours preparatory to, as we suppose, another week of fatigue & danger." If the army continued at its rate of progress, Pegram expected to attend "divine service in Baltimore" by next week. He would "return thanks to the Almighty for His mercies, & pray that through His grace, this Campaign may be as prosperous as it has been so far." With the hope "that God will bless & protect you all," Pegram brought his letter to a close.[7]

While Pegram and his cannoneers relaxed on the banks of the Monocacy, Lee completed the details for a bold campaign. Using South Mountain as a shield, he would send Jackson to capture the Union garrison at Harpers Ferry, thus establishing a clear supply line back into the Shenandoah Valley. Longstreet would block McClellan's forces at the mountain passes until Jackson returned. Once reunited, the army would venture farther north into Pennsylvania. On September 10 Jackson's column filed through the streets of Frederick and marched toward a ford of the Potomac near Williamsport. The men traveled through an intensely pro-Union area, which did little to improve their strained relations with Marylanders. The sight of the Potomac brought a feeling of relief to virtually every soldier in Jackson's command. One of Hill's artillerists wrote that "every Company gave a cheer as it formed on the south bank of the River and I doubt whether there was a man in the army that did not rejoice that he was out of Maryland."[8]

Jackson's troops tramped through Martinsburg and then turned eastward toward Harpers Ferry on September 12. Unfortunately, McClellan had discovered Lee's intentions after an Indiana soldier found a lost copy of Special Orders No. 191 outlining the movements of the Confederate army. As a result, Stonewall needed to invest the town as soon as possible, for otherwise the scattered parts of Lee's command might be destroyed. Despite the need for rapid action, Jackson did not get his troops into position until September 13. He massed his regiments on School House Ridge, a thousand yards west of Bolivar Heights, where Colonel Dixon S. Miles had positioned several thousand Union soldiers. Bolivar Heights extended a mile and a half from the Potomac on the north and to the Shenandoah on the south. Maryland Heights, the most striking topographical feature in the Harpers Ferry area, towered above Bolivar Heights and Loudoun Heights, the two other mountains that dominated the town. Miles had posted 2,000 foot soldiers on the mountain to thwart any Confederate advance from the interior of Maryland, but before Jackson had completely surrounded Harpers Ferry on September 13, the Northerners mysteriously abandoned this position. Harpers Ferry was doomed.[9]

The Confederates unlimbered artillery on Maryland and Loudoun Heights as well as on School House Ridge, which created a triangular converging fire on Miles. But Jackson realized that his cannon alone could not pound the Federals into submission. Late in the afternoon of September 14, he ordered A. P.

Hill to take his division behind School House Ridge and then slide along the bank of the Shenandoah until it had enveloped the Union left on Bolivar Heights. As his men struggled through undergrowth choking the banks of the river, Hill "discovered an eminence crowning the extreme left of the enemy's line, bare of all earthwork." This feature of the terrain became the focal point of his assault.[10]

The Purcell Artillery along with the rest of Lindsay Walker's batteries were ordered to the front after sunset. As cannoneer Albert Drewry recalled: "We had gone into camp about 10 o'clock at night, all tired and worn out. . . . Everybody went to sleep just as quick as possible." Suffering from insomnia, Drewry heard the sentry challenged. In a few minutes a staff officer asked, "Where is the officer in command of this battery?" Drewry told him where Pegram and the other officers in the battery had made their beds for the evening. The man walked over to Pegram, awakened him, and ordered him to limber up two of the company's guns. Willy pulled his groggy cannoneers into line with the Crenshaw, Fredericksburg, Letcher, and Pee Dee Batteries for a night march.[11]

Moving near the rushing waters of the Shenandoah, Walker's artillerists soon discovered that it was virtually impossible to get their guns across the broken terrain. Drewry remembered that "we started out through the woods, pulling the gun[s] over logs and rocks, around boulders, across ravines and gullies until we were absolutely tired out." The commander of the Letcher Artillery reported with disgust: "We were scrambling up hills that we could not have pulled over in daylight if our lives had depended upon it." The men expended a tremendous amount of energy to get the five batteries into position around four o'clock in the morning. The pieces sat atop a prominent hill, a thousand yards to the rear of Miles's line on Bolivar Heights. Hill complimented the "indomitable resolution and energy" of his battery captains and Lindsay Walker.[12]

The staff officer who accompanied the Purcell Artillery informed Pegram's men "that if the worst happens it will be considered no disgrace to run. You are now immediately under the guns of Harpers' Ferry, and the Yankees can open up seventy siege guns on you if they choose." The officer then puffed on his cigar, the burning embers glowing in the gray dawn. As it turned out, he had exaggerated the capabilities of the Federal ordnance because even though Union batteries commanded Hill's artillery and enjoyed the protection of earthworks, the Northerners had not detected Hill's movement. As a result, Miles's men were not properly positioned to contest Hill's cannon.[13]

A blanket of fog receded before the morning sun to reveal Confederate guns pointed at Miles's troops from every direction. Almost as soon as the Southern artillerists had unlimbered their pieces in a field of clover, the order came to commence firing. Projectiles soon whistled across the sky and plowed into the Northern line. Miles's soldiers hugged the ground as dirt flew in all directions

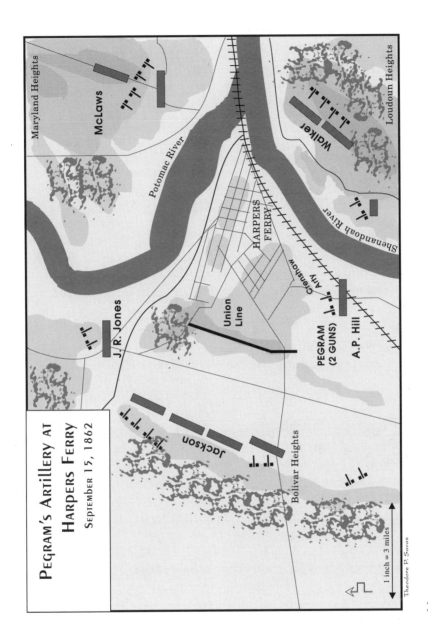

PEGRAM'S ARTILLERY AT
HARPERS FERRY
SEPTEMBER 15, 1862

Maryland Heights

McLaws

Potomac River

Loudoun Heights

Walker

Shenandoah River

HARPERS FERRY

J. R. Jones

Union Line

Crenshaw

Arty

PEGRAM
(2 GUNS)

A.P. Hill

Jackson

Bolivar Heights

1 inch = 3 miles

Theodore P. Savas

Map 4.

and tree limbs crashed to the earth. Even though Walker's batteries occupied a relatively unprotected area, his artillerists, according to the commander of the Letcher Artillery, were not "daunted" and "pounded it into them as fast as we could load and fire." Union batteries responded ineffectually; most of their rounds sailed wildly over their targets. Henry Kyd Douglas of Jackson's staff remembered that the artillery duel "filled the air with a din of war that echoed along the Potomac and reverberated in multiplied repetitions against the rocks of Maryland Heights." [14]

After an hour of constant shelling, quiet settled over the field, but it was not long before the Union artillery erupted again. Hill's infantry assault was already under way with General William Dorsey Pender's brigade in the advance. To ease pressure on Pender, Hill rushed Pegram's two guns and the four pieces of the Crenshaw Artillery four hundred yards closer to the Federal works. Both companies dashed across the field, their caissons bouncing while the cannon rocked from side to side. In the words of Lindsay Walker, the Virginia cannon-eers "opened furiously" against the enemy. Through patches of drifting smoke, Pegram's artillerists saw white flags above the Federal earthworks within ten minutes. Jackson's men received the surrender of the garrison with childlike enthusiasm. One of Walker's artillerists noted that "you never in your life heard such cheering as greeted the hoisting of the white flag." In the natural amphi-theater of Harpers Ferry, their exultations echoed for miles. [15]

The Confederates had good reason to celebrate. Seventy-three pieces of ar-tillery, thirteen thousand small arms, two hundred wagons, and more than twelve thousand prisoners had fallen into their hands. Yet the Army of North-ern Virginia still faced a difficult situation. Lee's forces were decisively outnum-bered and badly dispersed. Yet, because of Jackson's success, Lee imprudently decided to fight it out in Maryland, ordering his troops to concentrate at Sharpsburg. The next day Jackson's men, excluding Hill's division and its artil-lery, marched north from Harpers Ferry. The climactic battle of the campaign commenced at dawn on September 17. McClellan began his assaults against the Confederate left, shifting his attacks toward the center. Lee's battle line buckled but managed to hold. Union troops under General Ambrose E. Burnside stormed a bridge across Antietam Creek and threatened Lee's right flank late in the day. With Federals advancing toward Sharpsburg and jeopardizing the Confederate avenue of retreat to the Potomac, Lee called for reinforcements.

In one of the most dramatic moments of the war, A. P. Hill's division rescued the Army of Northern Virginia. Starting the day at Harpers Ferry, seventeen miles from the battlefield, Hill set a grueling pace for his men. A dusty haze quickly settled over the rapidly moving column. Hill's troops crossed the Poto-mac River at Boteler's Ford near Shepherdstown and, without even pausing to allow their animals to drink water, hastened toward Sharpsburg. Lee had been growing increasingly anxious as Burnside neared the outskirts of town, but suddenly, on the Union left, there arose a high-pitched yell, followed by lines of Southern infantry that delivered volleys into Burnside's exposed flank. Hill's well-directed counterattack forced the Federals to retire.[16]

Pegram carried only a single piece into the fight because his ammunition chests had not been refilled after the bombardment at Harpers Ferry. He planted his cannon on a prominent hill to the right of the Pee Dee Artillery, from where, in Hill's estimation, the gun commanded a "wide field of fire." Although drooping with fatigue from their seventeen-mile march, Pegram's cannoneers fired several shots at Burnside's retreating infantry. Walker reported, though, that "Captain Pegram's gun was withdrawn after a few rounds, the men being exhausted by the march from Harper's Ferry and the labor at the guns." Before his cannoneers moved to the rear, a shell exploded directly over the company and a fragment grazed Pegram's head. Witness John Chamberlayne later wrote, "Willy Pegram was hit at Sharpsburg, a moment after I had moved from him, on the head, not serious." The battery's captain was the company's only casualty at Sharpsburg. Hill noted in his official report, "My gallant Captain Pegram, of the artillery, was also wounded for the first time."[17]

Hill's determined march and attack stabilized Lee's lines, something the Confederate force desperately needed. One more major Union assault probably would have pushed the jaded Southerners over the edge. "The night after the battle of Sharpsburg was a fearful one," wrote Henry Kyd Douglas. "Not a soldier, I venture to say, slept half an hour." The next day the battered units of both armies held their positions. The Army of the Potomac had lost more than 12,000 men; the best estimate of the losses for Lee's army is approximately 10,000. Although the battle was a tactical draw, Lee's soldiers, including Pegram's battery, withdrew across the Potomac during the evening of September 18. Once back on the shores of the Old Dominion, many of the men professed a wish never to hear again the tune "Maryland, My Maryland."[18]

By the end of September Jackson's troops had made their way up the Shenandoah Valley to Bunker Hill, a hamlet located halfway between Winchester and Martinsburg. The soldiers welcomed a respite at Bunker Hill that Kyd Douglas believed gave them "a new lease of life." By October 7, though, Pegram had tired of the sedentary existence. Whenever he saw white tents, he started to crave the smell of burning powder. "Since my last letter home, we have been lying quiet in camp," Willy told his sister Jennie. "After an active campaign this seems very stupid and dull to a soldier." Quite apart from his sheer enjoyment of combat, Pegram hungered for action because he believed the war would end sooner if the South maintained constant pressure on the North: in his view, a passive Confederate strategy would only prolong the struggle. But, sounding a more upbeat note, Pegram also assured his sister that "we have not been idle." "General Lee is getting rid of all incompetent officers & cowards, by a simple order relieving them from duty, without any Court." Pegram was referring to the reorganization of the army's artillery, which resulted in the consolidation of a number of batteries and intentionally left many officers considered unfit without a command. This purge pleased Pegram because it sharpened the army's discipline. "Should we have any more fighting shortly," he thought, "there will not be the same amount of straggling & cowardice, that usually attends a large army." [19]

Pegram also manifested an anxiety "to hear from home, since the school has commenced." From the inception of the war it appears that enrollment declined at his mother's academy, forcing her to accept the distasteful expedient of receiving families as borders instead of female students. Pegram's brother Jimmy had mentioned in a letter "that the prospects were pretty fair, and that in all probability it would not be necessary for Mother to take any Families." Willy hoped this was the case, "as I know how much Sister & Mother dislike that." "When you write to me," he asked Jennie, "let me know all about the school, & also about the other schools" in the city. Pegram particularly inquired about "our gallant neighbour, who made such a brilliant retreat towards the mountains, when Richmond was threatened." This, the earliest surviving example of Pegram's hostility toward civilians who did not remain steadfast to the Confederacy, marks the beginning of a gulf between him and many people on the home front that by 1864 would become a chasm. As did soldiers on both sides, he increasingly denounced civilians who showed the slightest signs of disloyalty or whose courage waned in times of crisis. [20]

Pegram happily reported that Colonel Stephen D. Lee had given him good news on October 6. During the brief siege of Munfordville, Kentucky, from September 14 to 17, Lee reported that John Pegram had retrieved his sword from the Union officer who took it at Rich Mountain the previous year. Willy was "very glad to hear" of this because it would "have a good effect with the public." As usual, Pegram asked about Hetty Cary and her sister Jennie. He had heard that they made it to Baltimore, but "I fear they have been arrested before this." "Write often," he added, signing with "love to all" after apologizing for his messy "scroll." [21]

While the army regained its strength during the first weeks of October, R. E. Lee established clear and rigid regulations for the use and care of horses in the artillery. The recent campaign had virtually exhausted the army's mounts, creating a problem that plagued the Army of Northern Virginia throughout the war. To preserve this vital resource, Lee impressed "upon all officers in charge of horses . . . the urgent necessity of energetic and unwearied care of their animals." Stiff penalties awaited anyone who violated the guidelines. Concerned as well about the condition of his artillery, Lee instructed General William Nelson Pendleton to examine thoroughly the army's field batteries to identify those lacking sufficient men, officers, or horses to work their guns efficiently. He suggested that a test based on services rendered, the leadership abilities of officers, and the existing condition of a battery should determine which companies would be disbanded. A subsequent restructuring of the long arm of the Army of Northern Virginia followed Pendleton's blueprint, resulting in the elimination of eighteen batteries. Reduced in men, horses, and cannon, the Purcell Artillery faced possible consolidation with another depleted unit, but A. P. Hill interceded on behalf of his favorite artillerist, making certain that Pegram would not lose his command.[22]

Pegram eventually reaped the benefits of the artillery's consolidation: two cannon and ninety-six men from the Dixie Artillery and John R. Johnson's Battery joined the Purcell Artillery. It is difficult to say whether any major problems attended this merger of three disparate companies. Johnson's Battery and the Dixie Artillery came from rural Bedford and Page counties, respectively, while most of the men originally in the Purcell Artillery had lived in Richmond before the war. Nevertheless, Pegram boasted in a letter to his sister on October 24 that "my battery is in as good, if not better order, than ever. I have two Parrots & two Napoleons, with plenty of men, & the probability of getting out all six pieces." "If you know anything about guns," he added, "you will pronounce this a pretty battery."[23]

Pegram's refurbished company found itself among the rest of Hill's batteries at Bunker Hill. John H. Munford, a friend and fellow artillerist in Hill's division, wrote on October 24: "We are now in a Battalion composed of all the artillery in our Division, commanded by Lt. Col. R. L. Walker." He found this arrangement "very agreeable" because "we are all encamped together & have a good opportunity of becoming well acquainted." "Wm. Pegram is over to see us every day & I to see him," Munford noted. "He is one of my special favorites, [and] he is my gran[d] ideal of a man."[24] Munford's high opinion of Pegram largely rested, in all likelihood, upon the latter's zealous behavior in battle. Soldiering offered Southern men an opportunity to uphold antebellum notions of male honor and carry out their military assignments according to a code of duty and chivalry, while at the same time fulfilling paternalistic obligations to the people they left behind, whom they were now protecting. Although soldiers like Pegram often felt helpless when their families suffered from food shortages and enemy depredations, they maintained their social identities and paternalistic obligations to their communities through military service.

Even as Pegram's men grew accustomed to the new faces in camp, internal troubles arose when a number of soldiers from Hill's division, including some of the artillerists, carried off fence rails from some nearby farms. Hill exploded when he discovered this destruction of civilian property, charging his battery commanders with neglect of duty and placing them all under arrest. Their honor offended, Pegram and the other officers submitted a petition protesting that they had not allowed "the men under our command to burn the rails near our encampments." "On the contrary," they argued, "we declare that we have used every means in our power to put a stop to it." "Because rails are constantly burned by almost every company in the Division," insisted the petition, "it is wholly impossible to enforce the order in one command, unless it is enforced throughout the Division." Although refusing to admit their men had committed such an offense, the officers expressed a willingness "to repair the damage done, by paying a fair price for the amount of fencing destroyed." This gesture apparently placated Hill, who dropped the charges.[25]

Pegram believed that Hill had not reached an equitable settlement, however, and did not wish to accept "a release" from arrest. He and William Graves Crenshaw, commander of the battery that bore his name, presented their case to General Maxcy Gregg, the fire-eating politician from South Carolina. Gregg reviewed the pertinent documents and told Pegram and Crenshaw that "both parties had misunderstood each other, & upon going to see Genl. Hill, we found that he was correct." Even though "Genl. Hill expressed his regret that the affair had occurred," Pegram wrote to his sister, "it seems a very hard case, that we should be charged with neglect of duty & placed under arrest, and then not even allowed the privilege of a Court." (Ironically, a few weeks earlier he had approved of Lee's decision to dismiss a number of officers from the army without a court of inquiry.) All in all, Pegram regretted "that the affair ever occurred," noting that when he saw Hill shortly after the controversy, the general "was very cordial in his greeting."[26]

During the third week of October the Purcell Artillery and most of Hill's division moved toward Shepherdstown, where Pegram's artillerists exchanged their rammers and sponges for picks and axes. In the brisk fall air, they destroyed nearly twenty miles of the Baltimore & Ohio Railroad. Pegram wrote on October 24 that destroying the railroad track signaled "the breaking up of the fall campaign, and [we] are looking out daily for the order to fall back to some convenient point, for the establishment of our lines." He predicted the army would hold a position "probably to Manassas on the Rappahannock" but admitted that "all this is mere surmise." "We all content ourselves," Willy assured his sister, "with the reflection that Genl. Lee knows what he is about & consequently regard all things as for the best."[27]

But late in October Pegram's thoughts traveled away from military matters back toward home. The war had discouraged most families from sending their daughters to Richmond, creating a number of vacancies at his mother's boarding house. Pegram expressed the hope that these would soon be filled but nonetheless thought the family certainly had "a great deal to thank God for." Inquiring as usual about his brother John, Pegram also asked after Francis W. Dawson, the old friend who had served in his battery at Mechanicsville. "Tell him also that if he gets tired of Richmond, he must come up & pay me a visit," Pegram wrote. "I am always glad to see him . . . because his presence always predicts a fight."[28]

The Purcell Artillery left camp at Bunker Hill with the rest of Walker's battalion on October 29. Three days later the cannoneers established a new bivouac near Snicker's Gap, overlooking the Shenandoah River at Castleman's Ford. During the first part of November Pegram's men endured a miserable tour of picket duty along the river. Winds howled across the frozen landscape and pierced their thin clothing. On November 3, though, a brisk fight with the Federals interrupted this numbing duty. Unlimbered behind Archer's and General Edward L. Thomas's brigades, Pegram's gunners helped prevent the Federals from crossing the river at Castleman's Ford. Hill approved of how his men "handsomely repulsed the enemy." [29]

Relieved from picket duty on November 12, Pegram's company joined the rest of Walker's batteries in a move toward Winchester. Unfortunately, the area that Walker selected for the battalion's winter quarters offered little protection against the cutting winds and icy snow that swept across the Valley. An artillerist in Crenshaw's Battery complained in his diary that "Col. Walker could not have picked a meaner camp if he had tried." Pegram's men spent the days constructing their stables, attending to their personal cabins during free moments. By the time the cannoneers had completed their animals' housing, however, they received orders on November 21 to cook two days' worth of rations and be prepared to march at daylight. Captain Greenlee Davidson captured the frustration of the artillerists, who had been eagerly anticipating the comfort and warmth their half-constructed cabins would shortly provide: "How provoking. Just when we have made ourselves comfortable we are ordered away." [30]

The Army of the Potomac had opened a new campaign from its base at Warrenton with Ambrose E. Burnside as McClellan's replacement in command. Abandoning his predecessor's plan to push directly below Warrenton and strike James Longstreet's corps before Jackson could cross the Blue Ridge Mountains, Burnside decided to slide around the Confederates and march southeast toward Fredericksburg. He wanted to cross the Rappahannock rapidly, pass through the town, and then race toward Richmond. Speed was essential for Burnside to reach the capital of the Confederacy before the Army of Northern Virginia blocked his path. Unlike McClellan, Burnside drove his army in a march that would have fatigued Jackson's foot cavalry, and by November 19 the Army of the Potomac occupied the hills opposite Fredericksburg. Only a token Confederate force held the town. Although Lee was clearly taken by surprise, Burnside lost the advantage because his army's pontoon bridges had lagged behind, a fatal delay that gave Lee time to shift troops from the west. Longstreet's men reached the commanding heights above Fredericksburg first, blunting Burnside's drive for Richmond.

On November 22 Jackson started for Fredericksburg. He marched through Winchester, passing the Kernstown battlefield, before resting for the evening.

His column continued south the next day through Middletown and Strasburg and encamped near Woodstock. That night some of Pegram's men and others from the Letcher Artillery snuck into town and acquired some whisky. According to a member of the Crenshaw Artillery, the soldiers quickly became drunk and "kicked up the devil of a row." A guard detail rushed to the scene to round up the offenders. The next day, as the division's batteries rolled through Woodstock, Lindsay Walker grabbed "two barrels of Apple Brandy" and poured the precious contents onto the frozen ground.[31]

By November 29 Jackson had his troops across the Blue Ridge Mountains and passing through Orange Court House, where Pegram dashed a letter off to his sister Jennie. He acknowledged receipt of "the spectacles you kindly sent me, by Capt. Brockenbrough this afternoon." "It is needless for me to express my thanks for your thoughtfulness," added Willy, but unfortunately his new eyewear did not allow him to focus on objects at long distances—obviously a serious problem for an artillery commander. "Those glasses you sent me are too weak, and I send them back by Mr. James Chamberlayne, with a glass [of] the desired strength." Sorry to put his sister "to so much trouble," he asked her to exchange the lenses and send the new pair up with John Munford. Turning to a brief summary of the military situation, Pegram wrote that his command "marched to this point this afternoon, & resume the march in the morning. I don't know exactly for what point." Perhaps he feared giving away army secrets if he told his sister the exact movements of Jackson's column, because it had become apparent to every man in the ranks that Fredericksburg was Stonewall's destination.[32]

On December 3 Walker's battalion reached Fredericksburg. Moving behind Longstreet's troops, they encamped near Guinea Station. Ewell's division, commanded by Jubal Early, moved farther east, near the vicinity of Skinker's Neck, to support D. H. Hill's division at Port Royal. Lee feared a Union strike in that area, never imagining that Burnside would charge the heights above Fredericksburg. But given the present scheme, Lee reasoned, no matter which way Burnside aimed the point of his attack, Jackson would be able to rush troops in either direction. While the Army of the Potomac prepared to cross the river, Lee's men suffered terribly. "It rained, snowed, and hailed all day," Jedediah Hotchkiss, Jackson's mapmaker, noted in his journal on December 5, making it "a very hard [day] for the soldiers."[33]

A foggy morass imprisoned the woodlots and fields surrounding Fredericksburg on December 11. Shielded by the white curtain, Union engineers constructed pontoon bridges at three locations along the Rappahannock. When the fog lifted it revealed Federal intentions to storm the heights above Fredericksburg; however, Confederate marksmen in the town prevented Northern engineers from completing their assignment. Burnside retaliated with a massive artillery bombardment that ignited fires in the town but failed to dislodge Lee's sharpshooters. Undaunted, the Federals resorted to ferrying infantrymen across the river to establish a bridgehead, after which the bulk of the army crossed the river. Most of Burnside's 130,000 soldiers stood on the western side of the Rappahannock by the next day. This impressive display of force convinced Lee that Burnside wanted to punch through the Southern lines, manned by roughly 75,000 soldiers whose fighting spirit had been aroused by Federal depredations in the town. The Confederate commander deployed his army along a seven-mile front, ordering Jackson's corps to occupy the right wing from Deep Run to Hamilton's Crossing. Longstreet's troops held the other wing, which stretched from Deep Run to Taylor's Hill.[34]

A. P. Hill arrived first on Jackson's front and posted his brigades along a wooded crest that ran parallel to the Richmond, Fredericksburg & Potomac Railroad. Three clusters of artillery supported the infantry, including Lindsay Walker's fourteen cannon on Prospect Hill, an open eminence that anchored the southern tip of Jackson's line. Pegram unlimbered his four pieces on this admirable site, which, in the words of Stapleton Crutchfield, Jackson's chief of artillery, afforded a number of advantages "against a direct assault from infantry." Moreover, Crutchfield determined that the guns at Prospect Hill "so controlled the ground in front" that the enemy had no choice but to "open a heavy cannonade upon" Walker's batteries "before they could move any considerable mass of their infantry down the plain." But the batteries on the hill did face two potential problems. For one thing, the artillerists maintained a fixed position that invited concentrated fire from Burnside's artillery. Crutchfield also noticed that the "formation of the ground at the top of the hill" did not "afford much protection to men and hardly any to horses." All in all, however, Crutchfield considered it "a position of great importance."[35] Perched on a commanding knob eight hundred yards west of Walker's batteries and just below Deep Run was another group of nine guns unlimbered next to some abandoned slave cabins of the Bernard farm. Below these nine pieces rested twelve cannon just in front of the railroad tracks. Jackson's ordnance thus covered virtually every possible Federal approach to the Confederate right.

Behind the clusters of artillery and Hill's infantrymen, Jackson stacked his brigades as if they were dominoes. The strength of this line prompted Stonewall's stern remark to the Prussian observer Heros von Borcke: "Major, my men have sometimes failed to take a position, but to defend one, never!" It was an unusual situation for Jackson and Lee, who were used to maintaining paper-thin lines with few reserves. But there was a defect in Jackson's position. Near the center of Hill's division, between Archer's and General James H. Lane's brigades, yawned a dangerous gap in the line. A bog, full of trees and annoying saplings, created a six-hundred-yard space between the two units that the Con-

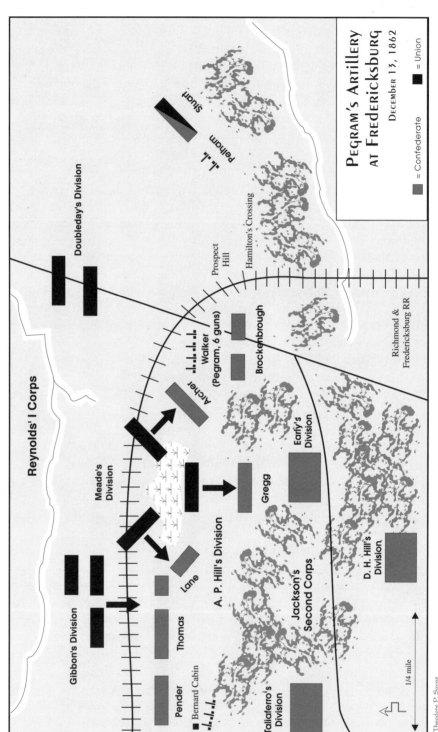

Reynolds' I Corps

Gibbon's Division

Pender

Thomas

Bernard Cabin

Lane

Meade's Division

A. P. Hill's Division

Taliaferro's Division

Jackson's Second Corps

D. H. Hill's Division

Gregg

Early's Division

Brockenbrough

Archer

Walker
(Pegram, 6 guns)

Prospect Hill

Hamilton's Crossing

Richmond &
Fredericksburg RR

Doubleday's Division

Stuart

Pelham

Pegram's Artillery at Fredericksburg

December 13, 1862

■ = Confederate   ■ = Union

1/4 mile

Theodore P. Savas

Map 5.

federate artillery at Bernard's Cabins and Prospect Hill could not cover. Hill nevertheless remained confident that the Federals would not be able to manage an assault across such treacherous ground.[36]

A dripping fog that rose from the Rappahannock River on December 13 limited visibility to a few yards. The Federal divisions of General George Gordon Meade and General John Gibbon maneuvered into position near the Old Richmond Stage Road, three-quarters of a mile east of the Confederate ordnance on Prospect Hill. The creak and rumble of Northern artillery and the shuffle of marching feet warned Pegram and his men of an impending attack. It was mid-morning as Federal officers dashed back and forth making final preparations and giving last minute instructions. Burnside's infantry stared across a plain that was virtually level until it ran into the Southern line along the railway. Recent thawing left the ground soft and muddy in places. Before the advance commenced, the sun gradually "rose red and firey and soon drove away the fog."[37]

With a clear, cloudless sky in the background, the Federals edged their way past the Old Richmond Stage Road. Suddenly, Confederate missiles slammed into their exposed flank from the left and rear. Major John Pelham of Stuart's horse artillery had raced two cannon to the intersection of the stage road and the road that led from Hamilton's Crossing. The Union assault was forced to a halt as Meade shifted troops to this vulnerable area. Pelham stifled the Northern attack with a series of well-executed maneuvers—launching a few shots, then running his guns to a new position before the enemy's artillery could determine his range. Those who witnessed Pelham's performance expressed admiration, including Pegram, who heaped words of praise on Stuart's youthful artillerist. Many of the men standing near Pegram on Prospect Hill could see "the light of battle kindling in his eyes," and they knew he "was burning to 'go in.'"[38]

Pelham withdrew with the loss of one gun after about thirty minutes. Meade then turned his attention to the Confederate cannon at Prospect Hill. It was close to ten o'clock when the artillery of the Army of the Potomac poured an avalanche of shot and shell on the Southern guns crowning the bare knoll. Crutchfield counted twenty-five to thirty enemy fieldpieces aimed at Walker's batteries. Most of the Union missiles crashed into the timber behind the Confederate guns, splintering trees, knocking limbs to the ground, or hitting horses whose shrieks of terror unnerved the cannoneers hugging the cold earth. In fact, the animals at Prospect Hill probably sustained more casualties than the artillerists: according to a member of the Crenshaw Artillery, "nearly every horse was killed or wounded" in one section of the battery. After the fight, Walker's artillerists bestowed the titled "Dead Horse Hill" on the area.[39]

But Southern gunners made no reply to their Northern counterparts, for Crutchfield had ordered Walker "to keep his guns concealed as well as he could, and not to allow himself to be drawn into an artillery duel." Ammunition must be reserved for Burnside's infantry "when it should come within effective range." The commanders of the other two clusters of Confederate artillery had received similar instructions. After thirty minutes of constant shelling, during which a Confederate caisson exploded on Prospect Hill, the Federals mistakenly believed they had silenced Jackson's artillery. The assault resumed as two Northern divisions moved snugly abreast with their banners snapping in the winter breeze. This array of force impressed a cannoneer in the battery adjacent to Pegram's: "I could see fully half the whole Yankee army, reserves and all. It was a grand sight seeing them come in position this morning; but it seemed that the host would eat us up anyhow." [40]

When the Federals came within eight hundred yards of Walker's batteries, though, the signal to fire echoed along the line. Pegram commanded his own four cannon as well as a section of guns from the Crenshaw Artillery. At his order they sent shells screeching toward Meade's three brigades, staggering the Union infantry. Walker complimented Pegram, as did David Gregg McIntosh, for breaking up the charging Union lines with a "murderous fire." In the meantime, Crutchfield had rushed fifteen guns to the right of Prospect Hill, producing a converging fire that pinned Meade's men to the ground. The Union troops withdrew behind a slight rise in a cultivated field as Meade called his batteries back into action. Protected by their ordnance, the Federal brigades again went forward. The assault gained momentum as the attackers drifted toward the gap in the Confederate line. Pegram's men worked their guns at a feverish pace, sending their rounds into the left flank of Meade's division. Yet the Federals swept toward the swampy ground, according to Walker, "in defiance of our guns, which were served rapidly and with great havoc upon their dense ranks." [41]

Two of Meade's three brigades plunged into the hole in Jackson's line; the third engaged Confederate infantry directly below Prospect Hill, along the railway. Many of these Federals looked at Walker's cannoneers over the sights of their rifles. One casualty in Pegram's battery was Peter G. Foster, who instantly "knew he had received his death wound" from an enemy bullet. Before he closed his eyes for the final time, he muttered: "Poor Foster's killed." The Northerners launched volley after volley; at one point their fire drove Pegram's men from their posts. In a letter published in a South Carolina paper, a private in McIntosh's Battery saw Pegram take his battery's battle flag and drape it around his body. Wrapped in the banner as if it were a shawl, he tried to rally his men by walking "up and down among his deserted guns." As at Malvern Hill and Cedar Mountain, Pegram hoped that his reckless behavior would inspire his men. [42]

But before Pegram's cannoneers regained their nerve and return to their guns, the cheers of Jackson's reserve brigades could be heard. Having been unable to expand their foothold in the Confederate line, Meade's troops found themselves virtually surrounded by a swarm of Southern soldiers. Jackson had launched a savage counterattack that sent Meade's Pennsylvania Reserves scurrying out of the woods and across the soggy plain in disorderly fashion—a perfect target for artillery. Pegram's cannoneers punished the Federals one last time.[43]

The failed assault against Jackson's position resulted in some twenty-five hundred Union casualties. On the Confederate left, repeated Federal charges against Marye's Heights had proved disastrous. In all, the Army of the Potomac suffered more than 12,000 killed, wounded, and missing at Fredericksburg, whereas Southern losses amounted to only about 5,000. During the night of December 15, the battered Army of the Potomac evacuated the town, crossed the Rappahannock, and took up its pontoons. Lee had achieved an overwhelming defensive victory.[44]

Though the battle had not been particularly costly to the Army of Northern Virginia, Pegram's battery sustained high losses. Fourteen men were wounded, three died instantly in battle, and one man succumbed to his wounds a few days after the fight. The battery's horses were depleted as well. But, regardless of casualties and the fact that his men had temporarily abandoned their guns, Pegram's ordnance had done much to seal the fate of Meade's division. Nor did the services rendered by the Purcell Artillery, as well as the other batteries on Prospect Hill, pass without notice. Lindsay Walker complimented all of his gunners. He wrote in his official report that "the artillery of the Light Division did theirs in this engagement," adding that "comparison would be invidious." Applauding the efforts of his artillerists, A. P. Hill specifically mentioned Willy's role in the fight: "Pegram, as usual, with McIntosh to help him, managed to find the hottest place." The Richmond press also heralded the performance of Pegram and his men. While visiting Walker's artillery camp shortly after the battle, a correspondent for the *Examiner* was introduced to Willy. "I was much pleased with meeting Captain PEGRAM commanding [the] Purcell Battery," he reported. "He is a small man, wears spectacles, is quiet and modest . . . yet he gets his battery always into the hottest place, and always is conspicuous."[45]

FIVE

FORTUNATELY WITH US,

THE SOLDIERS MAKE THE OFFICERS

PEGRAM'S BATTERY FINALLY SETTLED INTO WINTER QUARTERS AT THE end of December. In camp one mile south of Bowling Green, not far from Mulberry Place, the home of Jourdan Woolfolk, the men and animals endured a winter of skimpy rations and scarce fodder. Uniforms and equipment were also in short supply. To make matters worse, the men rarely received leaves of absence. "There seems to be no probability of my getting a furlough," Pegram informed Jennie on January 8, 1863, because "active operations may be resumed at any time." "This is a great disappointment to me, dear Jennie, for I had hoped to see you all, whom I long so to see." Yet Pegram "cheerfully submitted" to this inconvenience because he knew "that General Lee has the interest of the service at heart, & will do whatever is right." If he was lucky, "special business connected with the artillery" might take him to Richmond, and he assured his sister that "I will endeavor to get down in this way during the winter."[1]

Beginning in 1863 Southern civilians experienced serious hardships. Pegram's mother and sisters found it increasingly difficult to feed their boarders. In February Willy's mother paid the outrageous sum of $45.00 for twenty pounds of butter, $1.75 for a dozen eggs, and anywhere from $18.00 to $29.00 for turkeys. "Mrs. Pegram talks about starving us very often," reported one student, adding that "the Pegrams don't live so extravagantly in the front parlor this year as they did last." In fact, the strain of feeding boarders forced Pegram's mother to request that the students pay for the dormitory's housekeeper. By March 1863 fourteen boarding houses had closed in Richmond because of the scarcity of foodstuffs and other necessities. One resident of the Pegram household remarked that she "wouldn't be at all surprised if Mrs. Pegram closed before June."[2]

While Pegram's mother struggled to maintain her boarding house, his cannoneers routinely saw picket duty near Port Royal. "Once a week," wryly recalled an artillerist in Crenshaw's Battery, "a detachment might be seen leaving camp, marching through the village of Bowling Green and on to the Rappahannock, where we would report to the officer in command, go to the position assigned us, and remain there six days watching the sluggish river, to see that it did not overflow its banks." Unhappy with such cheerless tasks, Pegram wrote on January 8 that "everything is quiet and dull in this region, and there is nothing of special interest to give you." Because the Army of Northern Virginia lay dormant, he turned his attention to matters outside the state. The recent Confederate defeat at Murfreesboro, Tennessee, in a battle fought between December 31, 1862, and January 2, 1863, prompted the sarcastic gibe that "Bragg's victory, like all our western victories, turned out to be scarcely any victory at all." Like many of his comrades, Pegram considered the Southern armies in the West no match for Lee's force in Virginia.[3]

Pessimism about the Western Theater turned to anger when Pegram read an article in the *Richmond Enquirer* suggesting "that France is going to recognize us!" "What a pity!" he exclaimed, "I have always been of [the] opinion that we would be better off in the end to fight the battles out ourselves." "Convinced of the correctness of this opinion now," he expressed the hope that "they will let us alone." Why bring Europe into the war, he reasoned, if "the result of our victories has just begun to be shown at the North the past month." Pegram distrusted Louis Napoleon because intervention would "benefit the French people more than any other." "If they would not help us when we seemed to need their assistance, twelve months ago," Pegram concluded, "we do not want them to come in now, and get the credit and benefit of our hard struggles." Pegram desired a Confederate nation that forged its own independence: the birth of his country must not involve a European midwife. This hostile attitude toward foreign recognition was far from unique in the Confederate ranks. "For one I desire to see no foreign intervention," wrote Charles Jones, Jr., in 1862, "and fully concur with you in the conviction that if we are only true to ourselves we will be able, with the blessing of Heaven, to whip our own battles and secure our own freedom."[4]

Reorganization of the army's artillery, rather than European recognition, dominated conversation around the campfires of Walker's battalion in the winter of 1862–63. After consulting with Stapleton Crutchfield and Colonel Edward Porter Alexander, General Pendleton devised a plan in early January to arrange batteries into independent battalions, a system that had been partially implemented in the fall of 1862. Pendleton believed that brigade commanders already had too many responsibilities with respect to the infantry, which prevented their meeting the special needs of the artillery. He also criticized the old system because it gave battery commanders little control over the placement of their guns on the battlefield. Obliged to answer to brigadiers, who generally saw the removal of an attached battery as a violation of a "vested right," artillery officers had not been free to detach and reassign their companies "without producing some difficulty." All in all, the old organization made it impossible for the artillery of the Army of Northern Virginia to level its full weight on the enemy. Pendleton proposed assigning batteries to battalions of about sixteen guns, each commanded by lieutenant colonels and seconded by majors. Instead of answering to a brigadier general of infantry, the officer in charge of the battalion would follow the instructions of his corps's chief of artillery. Batteries could be detached in a more systematic manner, allowing Lee's army to concentrate its artillery fire without brigade and division commanders working at cross-purposes with artillery officers.[5]

Pendleton's plan included promotion for a number of officers. The artillery chief suggested that Lieutenant Colonel Lindsay Walker receive the rank of full colonel and take control of Battalion L, which included the Letcher, Crenshaw, Fredericksburg, and Purcell Batteries, all from Virginia, as well the South Carolinian Pee Dee Artillery. He offered Pegram's name for the position of major in the battalion, noting that Willy has "fully earned" his recommendation for promotion "by efficient service, and would no doubt be highly approved by Lieut.-Col. Walker and by Gen. Hill." Lee and Pendleton implemented the new system during the first days of March, and Pegram received his promotion on the second of that month. Pegram almost certainly savored his boost in rank and the additional responsibilities it entailed, but contemporary evidence of his reaction has not survived.[6]

Army inspectors pronounced Walker's battalion in "good order & effectiveness" during the winter of 1862–63—and this despite a shortage of fodder because supplies had to trickle "some 60 miles" across dreadful roads into Bowling Green. Pegram grappled with the problems typical of an artillery battalion. Harnesses and other equipment must be repaired, inferior ordnance culled, and the stock of horses replenished. Most of all, Pegram sought to protect his animals from disease. Religious worship was also one of his chief priorities. According to William Gordon McCabe, one of Pegram's heartfelt personal cares on going into winter quarters "was to assemble the men and say a few words to them concerning the importance of building a chapel and holding regular prayer-meetings." "It was a common sight," noted McCabe, "to see him sitting among his men in the rude log-chapel, bowing his young head reverently in prayer, or singing from the same hymn-book with some weather-beaten private."[7]

Pegram retained his sense of humor through it all. On a trip to Richmond at the end of February he saw Sallie Munford, who had recently broken off her engagement to Lieutenant Edward A. Marye of the Fredericksburg Artillery. Returning on the train to Bowling Green, the jilted Marye told Pegram he left the city "without many regrets, and would be contented to remain in Camp for the future." Back at quarters, Pegram proceeded to go around asking his comrades if any young woman had given Marye "his walking papers."[8]

The winter of 1862–63 also offered a variety of diversions from work, worry, and material shortages. Relying on various means of chicanery to slip past the guards at the depot, the men in Walker's battalion frequently "ran the blockade" for Richmond. The boredom of winter quarters took an especially heavy toll on the men in the Crenshaw Artillery, who held a bogus election and then told W. G. Walker that he had been chosen for the position of lieutenant. A member of the battery informed his diary that "we played off on him for two or three days," and that Walker even went so far as to have "bars put on his collar and put on airs generally." Conferring a dubious distinction upon Walker, the diarist pronounced him "the greatest fool I ever saw." Less creative men in the battalion engaged in snowball fights with neighboring batteries. Others sat around the campfire and listened to Martin DeLaney, an Irishman in the Letcher Artillery, who relished the opportunity to sing "The Moon Behind the Hill." But these pastimes could not erase all feelings of homesickness. "Camp is as dull as possible," John Munford informed his cousin Sallie in Richmond on April 24, "although we have enough to keep us employed."[9]

Joseph Hooker, who had succeeded Burnside in army command, ordered his Union troops to abandon their winter quarters on April 27 and took a third of his 134,000 troops on a flanking march northwest of Fredericksburg. The rest of his men maintained their position in front of the town. They threw pontoon bridges across the Rappahannock the next day, convincing Stonewall Jackson that the enemy would strike near Fredericksburg.[10]

In response to the Federal crossing, "Ole Jack" consolidated his corps around Hamilton's Crossing. On April 29 Walker's battalion "received very suddenly an order to the front," but because of "inevitable entanglements & delays," Walker and Pegram did not get their column started until eleven o'clock in the morning. Twenty-five miles of water-soaked roads lay ahead. "The march was through mud, mud, mud," Captain John H. Chamberlayne of the Crenshaw Artillery wrote, "& cold northeast rain, no sleep, no food." Pegram's men almost fell "asleep as they stumbled through the dark clinging mist." At one point the road virtually swallowed one of Pegram's guns. The cannoneers fell in "at the word into knee-deep slush & mud to play at horses and push the guns up on the fagged out brutes." Curses filled the air, but Chamberlayne noticed that there still was "a will *to do it*." The column halted with annoying regularity during the march, a disturbing pattern as "every pause in front makes a stop in the whole line & every carriage makes the road worse." Pegram's horses grew restive and uncertain during these lulls, often refusing to move once the column restarted.[11]

The last of Walker's cannoneers dragged into camp about three o'clock in the morning, Prospect Hill rising behind them. Pegram and his men would not have another opportunity to fire their guns from this commanding position, however, because according to Stuart's reports of April 28 and 29 large numbers of Federals had approached Germanna and Ely's Fords on the Rapidan River. If the enemy continued on that course, Hooker's forces would converge at Chancellorsville, about twelve miles west of Fredericksburg. Although caught in a vice and outnumbered two to one, Lee contemplated attacking Hooker at Fredericksburg, but Jackson objected on the grounds that the Union artillery on Stafford Heights would wreck any such assault. Lee then devised an audacious scheme, ordering Jubal Early to hold Fredericksburg with approximately 10,000 men while General Lafayette McLaws's troops and Jackson's three divisions moved west to reinforce General Richard H. Anderson's division, which blocked Hooker's advance eastward from Chancellorsville. Jackson's and McLaws's veterans marched to the west during the early morning hours of May 1. Hooker kept his army bottled in the Wilderness, an area covered with scrub oaks and pines, which effectively nullified his superiority in numbers and artillery.[12]

Anderson's men waited in a set of entrenchments near the confluence of the Orange Turnpike and Orange Plank Road. Jackson's and McLaws's soldiers reached Anderson's position by eight o'clock, whereupon Jackson quickly ordered an advance down the Turnpike and Plank Road, the latter route taken by Jackson's men, with Walker's battalion in reserve. As soon as Stonewall's troops collided with the Federals at Zoan Church, Hooker ordered a general retreat toward Chancellorsville, where his men were preparing a line of breastworks. Jackson pursued, but the Union rear guard firmly held its ground. Although dense forests retarded the artillery on both sides during the day, Pegram managed to bring the Purcell Artillery into the fight late in the afternoon, driving the enemy back to their fortifications.[13]

Jackson and Lee had not only snatched the initiative from Hooker, but they had also trapped the Union army in the Wilderness by the end of the day. As the moon illuminated the gloomy forests around Chancellorsville, Lindsay Walker positioned his battalion on the Confederate left, not far from the intersection of the Plank and Catharine Furnace Roads. Only a few hundred yards separated the antagonists. Brief artillery duels erupted throughout the night, denying the men badly needed hours of rest. "After dark we went into position," wrote John O. Farrell, one of Pegram's men, "and shelled some Yankees out of the woods in front of us."[14]

Not far from where Farrell recorded his thoughts, Lee and Jackson evaluated events of the day and deciphered intelligence reports. Sitting on a fallen log beyond the range of the enemy sharpshooters, the two generals concluded that an attack against Hooker's center or left flank would be costly and futile. Jackson predicted that the Army of the Potomac would be on the other side of the Rappahannock by sunrise; Lee disagreed that Hooker would give up so easily and thought the prospects of driving the Army of the Potomac into the river dim. But had anyone discovered the location of Hooker's right flank? Jackson had not ventured beyond Catharine Furnace that day, so his knowledge of the area was murky at best.

Jeb Stuart cleared up the situation. His subordinate, General Fitzhugh Lee, had discovered Hooker's right flank "in the air." Lee then decided to strike Hooker's vulnerable right flank, and the next morning he and Jackson completed the final plans. Stonewall suggested he take his entire corps, some 28,000 men, around the enemy's flank. Lee would face five Union corps around Chancellorsville with the 14,000 muskets in Anderson's and McLaws's divisions. The commander of the Army of Northern Virginia approved his subordinate's suggestions, thus embarking on one of the most daring maneuvers in American military history.[15]

As the morning light of May 2 peeked through the trees, Pegram "was directed to advance as many rifled guns" as possible up the Plank Road toward Chancellorsville. Federal pickets who could observe Confederate movements along the Catharine Furnace Road threatened to foil Jackson's and Lee's plans. Pegram ordered the Pee Dee and Purcell Artillery to the front, prompting a reply from Northern guns near the stately Chancellor House. One of Pegram's men wrote that "a stream of fire was seen to shoot from the crest in front." An enemy round sailed high above Pegram's cannon, knocking four horses to the ground and killing two men. Pegram called for support, and two pieces from the Crenshaw Artillery rumbled to the scene. Pegram saw the limited effect of his rounds and reported this to Henry Heth, who ordered Willy to withdraw. A shell slammed into a retiring caisson of the Pee Dee Artillery, filling the air with burning wood and flames. The earth shook from the explosion and one South Carolinian artillerist crumpled to the ground, his leg torn to shreds. This poor man managed to jot a few lines to his wife before a surgeon amputated his limb. He would die a few weeks later in a Richmond hospital.[16]

Pegram's artillery fire, though not destructive in its results, partially shielded the beginning of Jackson's march around Hooker's flank. The column started between seven and eight o'clock in the morning. Rodes's division led, followed by Raleigh E. Colston's and A. P. Hill's veterans. Around ten o'clock, Walker's battalion took its place near the end of the column. It was a pleasant day for the men in the ranks. Light rainshowers had left the roads soft and virtually dust free, and Jackson added to the comfort of his soldiers by not setting a blistering pace for his last and most famous march.[17]

When the column reached Catharine Furnace, Jackson turned the men to the south. Hooker mistakenly interpreted this movement as a general Confederate retreat, but Jackson soon directed his men westward on narrow roads. Close to two o'clock, Fitzhugh Lee galloped up the former Virginia Military Institute professor and convinced him to ride to a small eminence above the Plank Road. There the two officers saw General Oliver O. Howard's Eleventh Corps arrayed along the Orange Turnpike. Unionists sat around their campfires, puffing on their pipes, relaxing under trees, reading papers, or napping. Jackson saw a golden opportunity to roll up the right flank of the Army of the Potomac, but knew he must swing his troops down the turnpike instead of the Plank Road, as he had earlier proposed. He managed to get his troops into position with a few precious hours of daylight left. Savage yells announced a ferocious Confederate assault that rolled past Howard's right flank near Wilderness Church and sent Federals stampeding toward Chancellorsville. Abandoned accoutrements, muskets, caissons, and fieldpieces spoke of the hasty Union retreat.[18]

The sounds of fighting swelled to a fearsome crescendo and then rolled across the treetops like an approaching storm, while Pegram and the rest of his cannoneers remained in reserve just below the turnpike. Gunfire brought the battalion into motion. The Confederate batteries followed the victorious infantrymen, but darkness halted the Southern advance before Pegram could put his guns into action. Jackson hoped that a final assault would drive Hooker's army into the Rappahannock. But before such an attack could begin, Stonewall was accidentally shot by his own men. Hill briefly assumed control of the Second Corps until shell fragments bruised both his legs, at which point Brigadier General Robert E. Rodes took command. Rodes then relinquished authority to Jeb Stuart around midnight.[19]

Any hope of making a night assault evaporated with Stonewall's wounding. Stuart would continue the attack at dawn but lacked familiarity with the tactical dispositions of either army. He instructed Colonel Edward Porter Alexander to open his guns "at day break everywhere along the line," a vague order that revealed the cavalry officer's limited understanding of the terrain. Alexander knew that suitable ground had to be located for the artillery before dawn. A bright moon cast eerie shadows in the forest as Alexander reconnoitered close to the perimeter of the Southern battle lines. The Federals were constructing entrenchments that stretched north from Hazel Grove across the turnpike and anchored on the Rappahannock. Alexander found only five suitable locations to unlimber the Second Corps's cannon. One vista, about a hundred feet wide and two hundred yards long, ran through a second growth of pine and afforded a partial view of the enemy's batteries and infantry at Hazel Grove.[20]

With this information, Alexander headed behind the lines to find Walker's battalion. "Drunk with sleep," his bleary eyes faintly made out Jackson's men "lying on the ground in line of battle with their guns in their hands." "In the pale moonlight," Alexander believed they "looked like an army of dead men." He finally located Walker's battalion, parked near the Wilderness Church with "the horses still in harness & the men lying scattered around the guns." Finding Walker asleep under a haw bush, Alexander asked him to move his guns to the edge of the vista that led to Hazel Grove. Walker replied that "it would not take five minutes to get the batteries in the road, as all were ready hitched, & only the men had to be roused." Pegram had posted two guns of the Crenshaw Artillery on the turnpike behind Pender's brigade, stationing two other cannon south of the road in support of General Samuel McGowan's brigade near the vista. On a number of occasions, when phantom Union attacks were supposedly surging toward their line, Pegram's gunners arched their shells over the

infantrymen. Willy thought he inflicted "heavy damage on the enemy's infantry," but his missiles probably did no more than disturb the enemy's sleep.[21]

Because Stapleton Crutchfield had also been wounded, Walker replaced him
at the helm of the Second Corps artillery and turned command of the battalion
over to Pegram. Close to five o'clock on the morning of May 3, Willy received
instructions from Alexander to relieve the two cannon of the Crenshaw Artillery on the turnpike with the Fredericksburg and Pee Dee Artillery. After he
posted the former's four cannon behind Pender's brigade, Pegram positioned
the Pee Dee Artillery three hundred yards to the rear of the Virginia battery.
While the Fredericksburg gunners trained their sights on Hooker's batteries
down the turnpike, the Pee Dee artillerists faced the option of either shelling
the enemy's infantry in the woods on either side of the road or dueling with
the Northern batteries. If they chose the second target, they would have to
arch their rounds over the heads of the Fredericksburg cannoneers. It was
an awkward situation, but, as Alexander explained, "in no other way could
sufficient fire be thrown down" the road.[22]

Pegram collected his other two companies, the Purcell and Letcher Batteries, and moved toward the vista where two pieces of the Crenshaw Artillery
had been unlimbered and lay masked by pine trees. Alexander wanted more
guns in the area and directed Pegram to place a battery on a small knoll about
four hundred yards to rear of the vista. Uncertainty regarding Hooker's exact
position was evident in Alexander's final words of advice to Pegram: when the
Confederate attack rolled through the woods, Willy was to "fire over the pines
at the enemy's smoke."[23]

Pegram's men stood silently by their cannon in the early morning darkness.
Suddenly, James J. Archer's brigade lurched forward and drove the Federal rear
guard away from Hazel Grove, as Hill's division, now commanded by General
Henry Heth, advanced on both sides of the turnpike. Hooker's men retired to a
set of well-prepared entrenchments, where they repulsed Confederate attacks.
Stuart ordered his other two divisions to the front and his artillery to occupy
Hazel Grove. It was close to 6:30 and through patchy smoke Pegram could see
that the enemy had abandoned Hazel Grove. Riding up to Archer, Pegram said:
"General, if you will hold this ground [Hazel Grove] until my guns are in position you may then retire your men under the hill to a safer position." He then
raced the Crenshaw and Purcell Batteries down a narrow lane, wheeling his
companies into position on an open plateau that afforded a panoramic view of
the Chancellorsville plain some two thousand yards away. Because his batteries
faced east, he could enfilade the enemy artillery on the turnpike or fire
obliquely into the Northern guns at Fairview. Working behind a curtain of vegetation that stretched along the crest of Hazel Grove, Pegram's men fired their
guns from a position slightly higher than Fairview. A noted historian of Lee's

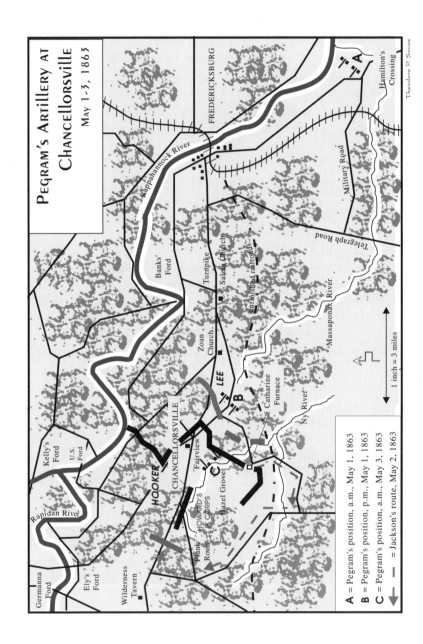

PEGRAM'S ARTILLERY AT
CHANCELLORSVILLE
MAY 1-3, 1863

FREDERICKSBURG

Hamilton's Crossing

A

Military Road

Rappahannock River

Telegraph Road

Banks' Ford

Turnpike

Salem Church

unfinished railroad

Massaponax River

Zoan Church

Ny River

Catharine Furnace

LEE

B

CHANCELLORSVILLE

Fairview

C

Hazel Grove

HOWARD'S XI CORPS

Plank Road

HOOKER

Kelly's Ford

U.S. Ford

Rapidan River

Germanna Ford

Ely's Ford

Wilderness Tavern

1 inch = 3 miles

A = Pegram's position, a.m., May 1, 1863
B = Pegram's position, p.m., May 1, 1863
C = Pegram's position, a.m., May 3, 1863
— — — = Jackson's route, May 2, 1863

Theodore P. Savas

Map 6.

artillery considered the sight below Pegram's cannon "one to fill the soul of an artilleryman with joy."[24]

His artillery reinforced by additional units, Pegram instructed four batteries to shell Hooker's guns on the turnpike. Rounds plunged down among the Union guns with a "telling effect." Ammunition chests exploded, sending bursts of yellow and orange flames into the sky, as Pegram watched the enemy's cannoneers scamper from their posts. Just when it appeared the Southerners were on the verge of driving Hooker from the field, a Union counterattack forced the Confederate infantrymen to a position they had held earlier in the morning. A "heavy line of skirmishers" suddenly appeared in the woods in front of Pegram's cannon. They laid down a brisk fire that killed or wounded a number of artillerists. With his infantry assault at an impasse, Stuart recognized the importance of Hazel Grove and instructed Alexander to "immediately crown the hill with 30 guns." Willy welcomed the additional support, and Alexander's own battalion unlimbered on the plateau. Hooker's men had advanced dangerously close to Pegram's fieldpieces, and Willy instructed his gunners to ignore Hooker's batteries and concentrate on the enemy's footsoldiers. Twenty-five cannon immediately raked the woods, sending the Northerners scattering for cover.[25]

As soon as Stuart's infantrymen regained their poise, they launched a counterattack that allowed Pegram to renew his duel with Hooker's ordnance at Fairview. Even though many of the Confederate shells were defective and failed to explode over their target, the Southerners still delivered an effective fire that crippled the enemy's batteries. Pegram's men worked their pieces at a feverish pace, firing their cannon three times a minute. While Pegram shuffled units that had expended their rounds to the rear, Alexander funneled more batteries into Hazel Grove. This mechanical process allowed Pegram to maintain at least forty guns against the enemy at all times. The efficiency of Alexander's operation and Pegram's execution of the plan resembled a well-oiled assembly line.[26]

By nine o'clock the converging fire from the Confederate guns at Hazel Grove and the Orange Turnpike had silenced Hooker's batteries at Fairview. The Northern artillerists limbered up their cannon and retired toward the Chancellor House; Lee's artillery had crushed the backbone of Hooker's defense. Pegram subsequently reported that "at the moment of victory" Greenlee Davidson, one of his most reliable battery commanders, received a mortal wound from a bullet fired eight hundred yards away. Nonetheless, Pegram rejoiced when Hooker's batteries withdrew, exclaiming to Alexander, above the din of battle, "a glorious day, Colonel, a glorious day!"[27]

Linked with Richard H. Anderson's troops on the right, Stuart's men clawed their way to the top of the Chancellorsville plateau. If the reunited wings of the army were to drive Hooker into the river, they needed support. Alexander quickly ordered the batteries at Hazel Grove to occupy the enemy's gun pits at

Fairview. Three other batteries also galloped down the turnpike. Deploying his cannon at Fairview, Willy beheld an artillerist's dream: a sea of stragglers, wagons, horses, and guns stretched from the Chancellor House toward the river. Alexander considered it "the part of artillery service that may be denominated 'pie'—to fire into swarming fugitives, who can't answer back." Shells exploded in the confused mob while a few rounds struck the house, sparking a fire that soon engulfed the building in flames. "After a heavy cannonading of an hour," Pegram noted, "we inflicted a heavy loss on the enemy, [and] suffering but slightly ourselves, we succeeded in driving them entirely off the field." [28]

Although Hooker's defense had crumbled, the Army of the Potomac held a secure avenue of escape. The Federals retired to a set of trenches that followed the Ely's Ford and United States Ford Roads. When the fighting had subsided, Pegram's men rummaged through the personal effects of the Union dead. One of his soldiers picked up a grisly trophy: "We got a great many things from the Yankees. I had a tooth that I got out of one of their heads. I will send it to you in the next letter. . . . It is a Yankee tooth, that I know, for I got it myself." Pegram's cannoneers were able to scour the battlefield for souvenirs until about ten o'clock, when Pegram placed his guns along the turnpike and behind some hastily built earthworks. His men sensed that the army was on the verge of a spectacular victory. "We completely routed the Yankees from their positions, which were as strong as any I have ever seen," one of Pegram's artillerists wrote in his diary that night. "So far we have gained a splendid victory, and were it not for the miserable country through here, we would have demolished their whole army before this." [29]

While Pegram's cannon and the rest of Stuart's command held Hooker against the river, Lee shifted McLaws's and Anderson's divisions toward Fredericksburg and a new Federal threat. Jubal Early's line at Marye's Heights had been broken by John Sedgwick on the morning of May 3. That afternoon and the next day, Lee blunted Sedgwick's drive around Salem Church, three miles west of Fredericksburg. During the evening of May 4 Sedgwick pulled his troops back across the river at Scott's Ford. Convinced that his army had been whipped, though his subordinates argued otherwise, Hooker ordered a general withdrawal north of the Rappahannock. The Army of the Potomac was safely across the river by May 6. [30]

Lee had achieved a remarkable victory in the face of overwhelming odds, but his audacity cost him close to 13,000 soldiers, nearly one of every four engaged. Pegram's friend and subordinate, Ham Chamberlayne, wrote his mother that "our loss in Officers was unparalleled, in men not so great—I regard it as by far our greatest victory. . . . Our army was in fighting trim at the end of the engagement, no disorganization, no panic any where." Walker's battalion suffered moderate casualties. In five days of fighting, the battalion had lost some thirty-three men, including Captain Greenlee Davidson of the

Letcher Artillery, whom Pegram considered "one of the most gallant, meritorious, and efficient officers in the service."[31]

Willy and his comrades in the long arm of the Army of Northern Virginia could feel especially proud about the recent victory. On May 3 the well-coordinated fire from Hazel Grove and the turnpike forced Hooker to abandon Fairview. As predicted by Alexander, the battalion system had maximized the firepower of Lee's artillery. "The most noteworthy feature of the Battle was the efficiency of our Artillery," Chamberlayne observed. "Owing to the issue of good guns replacing bad & the organization into Battalions we massed it & produced effects unknown [and] unhoped before." Another one of Pegram's friends in the battalion, John Munford, seconded Chamberlayne's positive evaluation of the artillery's performance. "Some of their Arty. Officers who were captured," he wrote, "said we took them completely by surprise this time with our artillery & that nothing on earth could stand against the shower of missles [sic] we gave them." "Think of 20 or 30 guns opening at once," he added, "& each gun firing twice a minute." Pegram also marveled at the artillery's performance at Chancellorsville. "Throughout this series of engagements both officers and men have acted with great gallantry," he stated in his official report. "The firing was the best I have ever seen."[32]

Chancellorsville solidified Pegram's standing as one of the most talented and promising artillerists in the army. His alert seizure of Hazel Grove and his ability to maintain a well-directed counterbattery fire earned him accolades from his superiors. Rodes and Alexander specifically mentioned Pegram in their official reports, Alexander crediting Pegram and Chamberlayne for "the first footing" at Hazel Grove. Colonel J. Thompson Brown, commander of the Second Corps artillery reserve, urged Pegram's promotion after Chancellorsville, calling him "a good officer in camp and a splendid one in the field; he has done invaluable service in this war and can do more with higher rank." Pegram also impressed the enlisted men of his new command. "This was the first battle Maj. Pegram commanded us in," John Munford told his cousin Sallie in Richmond. "He was everywhere on the field, encouraging and cheering the men to do their duty, he is the bravest and noblest fellow I ever saw, [and] has won the confidence & esteem of the whole command." Munford urged his cousin to tell Pegram's mother that "her Willie is the admiration of the Batt. & of all who know him, & if he had his deserts he would have three stars on his collar, instead of one." Munford's praise and Pegram's actions in battle suggest that notions of courage had not changed since the beginning of the war. Officers and men still admired soldiers who showed contempt for the enemy's bullets in battle.[33]

These plaudits must have pleased Pegram, but he probably drew more satisfaction from the army's latest triumph. Writing from Hamilton's Crossing on May 11, he enthusiastically reported to his oldest sister: "The more we think of

our recent victory, the grander it seems. Every one, high & low, considers it
the greatest victory of the war." "Our troops fought better," he averred, "and
the enemy's worse than ever before." Unless the Federals transferred soldiers
from the West, Willy believed that "we have very little to fear from the troops
opposite." He admitted that "this was undoubtedly the best planned movement
on the part of the enemy of the war, but Hooker *executed* [it] so badly on the
field, that we can scarcely give him the credit for it." [34]

Pegram also offered a number of explanations for Lee's failure to deliver a
crushing blow to the Army of the Potomac. "If we had been on equal ground,"
he speculated, "or Longstreet had been present with the other two divisions,
or Genl. Hill or Jackson on the field on Sunday, or it had not rained, or Early
had managed better below, at Fredericksburg, in either event, we would have
had a much more effectual victory." Pegram predicted that Hooker would
withdraw toward Washington and expressed his ardent hope for a rapid pursuit. After five days of rest from active campaigning, camp already seemed "in-
sufferably dull." [35]

Shortly after the battle, Pegram's family learned that he had not been injured, which was a great relief to him because "all that annoyed me was your
anxiety about me." He also wondered what his mother and sisters thought
of George Stoneman's cavalry raid on Richmond. Reflecting the growing gap
between the civilian and military experience, Pegram poked fun at the people
back home, imagining that the residents of Richmond reacted to this small
affair as if it were a full-scale invasion. "The excitement in Richmond must have
been amusing, on the occasion of the approach of the Yankee Cavalry." It "was
certainly a bold affair," Pegram acknowledged, "& puts Stuart up to his
trumps." Still, raids that ended without decisive results irritated Willy. He desired "that we will make a permanent raid on a larger scale." Willy had also
recently learned of unruly behavior in John's cavalry brigade in the Western
Theater and hoped his brother would transfer to the Army of Northern Virginia. With the openings in Lee's command structure after Chancellorsville,
Pegram thought "there is a fine chance for Brother to get here now, if he wishes
an infantry brigade." "You had better write to him immediately," he commented, "& let him known of the vacancies in this army." [36]

The euphoria in Lee's army after Chancellorsville dissipated, however, with
the news of Jackson's death on May 10. Accidentally shot by his own men on
May 2, Stonewall had been taken to Guinea Station to recover from his wounds
but had succumbed to pneumonia. "There is quite a gloom over the army
today, at the news of Jackson's death," Pegram informed his oldest sister on
May 11. "We never knew how much we all loved him until he died." But because
Pegram saw the tragedy as part of God's plan, he did not interpret the general's
loss as a critical blow to the Confederacy. "His death will not have the effect of
making our troops fight any worse," he asserted. "Besides being the bravest

troops in the world they have the most unbounded confidence in their *great leader*, Genl. Lee." As for Jackson, Pegram thought that "some of our troops made too much of an Idol of him, and lost sight of God's mercies." [37] In Willy's mind, faith in God, not human action alone, would decide the outcome of the war, leading him to insist that all would be well if the army and the Southern people remained true to God's word and performed their Christian duty. Similar attitudes prevented many Southerners like Pegram from ever feeling downcast about the war. Failures and hardships were part of God's plan and their purpose would be revealed to Southerners with independence.

In addition, Pegram took note of fears in some quarters that "the Yankee troops will fight better, since they will not hear any more that Jackson is in their rear." He looked to A. P. Hill "as the man to fill his place, & after he once gets a shew, the enemy will fear him as much as they ever feared Jackson." Although Willy thought it "a great pity that we should have lost Jackson," he was sure that the "troops will fight well under anybody." "Fortunately with us," he reasoned, "the soldiers make the officers, & not the officers the soldiers." [38]

Walker's battalion left Hamilton's Crossing for the pastures of Caroline County during the second week of May. The cannoneers bivouacked near Bethel Church, approximately six miles north of Milford and in view of the Mattaponi River valley. While the men relaxed along the banks of the river and their horses grazed in lush fields, their officers worked to refit the companies for the approaching campaign. Emaciated horses, unserviceable guns, and worn accoutrements had left Lee's artillery in need of immediate attention after Chancellorsville. Ham Chamberlayne complained on May 31: "I have had all the labour over again of fitting out the Battery with caissons, horses, harness &c and besides have had drills and reviews to attend. So my time has been filled quite completely." [39]

Lee reorganized the Army of Northern Virginia into three corps at the end of May, a long-contemplated change triggered by the death of Jackson. The First Corps remained with Longstreet, Ewell assumed the helm of the Second, and a newly created Third Corps went to A. P. Hill. Lindsay Walker became Hill's chief of artillery, and his old battalion, with Pegram in command, also joined the Third Corps. Refitted and reorganized, Pegram's battalion anticipated the start of a new campaign. [40]

Rumors and speculation concerning the army's destination dominated conversations in camp. Pegram thought Lee would take the war to Northern soil, a sentiment commonly expressed in the ranks. Chamberlayne informed a friend in Richmond on June 4 that "we are on the eve of things yet untried in prose or verse—The army is in motion up stream" and that time "will soon see us victorious pressing to leave the sacred soil behind." Many Southern papers also called for Lee to launch a second raid across the Potomac to relieve Virginia from the ravages of war. By the spring of 1863 the land could no longer provide for Lee's soldiers. A raid would allow his army to draw from the bountiful farmlands of Pennsylvania, while also protecting Virginia's crops for the fall harvest. Taking the war above the Mason-Dixon Line could bring other advantages as well. The presence of a Southern army might boost the growing strength of the Northern peace movement or precipitate European recognition.[41]

Prompted by such compelling reasons, Lee moved Ewell's and Longstreet's corps toward the Shenandoah Valley on June 3. Hill's troops stayed near Fredericksburg as a decoy. Two days later Pegram's artillerists broke camp near Bethel Church and marched to Hamilton's Crossing, where they deployed their guns in line of battle. Although Hooker's soldiers made their presence known to Hill's troops, one of Willy's men doubted there was "the slightest chance of a fight here." Then, on June 11, Pegram was attacked by a severe fever. He tried to remain in camp, but his temperature burned with more intensity as the hours passed. The next morning his comrades brought him to a Mr. Marye's house, located near Hamilton's Crossing. "I am in hopes," John Munford told his cousin Sallie in Richmond, "he will be well enough to take command again in a few days." Willy's condition did not improve, however, and he returned to Richmond. Captain Ervin Brown Brunson assumed command of the battalion, joining Lee's column as it pushed toward the Shenandoah Valley.[42]

When Pegram learned that Hill's corps had joined the rest of the Army of Northern Virginia on its march north, he pulled himself out of bed, gathered his things, and bid farewell to his family. Pale and drained by lingering fever, he rested in an ambulance for the bumpy journey to his battalion. Shortly after Hill's soldiers crossed the Potomac on June 25, Ham Chamberlayne asked his mother: "Let me know always how Willy P. is, and let him know when you hear from me, and where we are—He must be anxious to hear." "Tell him we need him," Chamberlayne added, "but he must be careful not to come before he is well." On June 30, Pegram reached Hill's soldiers while they rested at Cashtown. Among the first individuals to encounter Pegram was General Lee, who said to A. P. Hill a few moments later: "General Hill, I have good news for you; Major Pegram is up." "Yes," responded Hill, "that is good news." A staff officer repeated this exchange to Willy, who said "he valued those few words from the General of the army and the General of his corps more than another star upon his collar."[43]

Pegram must have noticed the wretched condition of his horses when he resumed command of his battalion. The limestone pikes in Pennsylvania had lacerated the beasts's hooves and left them bloody. By the time the battalion had reach Fayetteville on June 27, twenty-seven animals lay dead along the roadsides. The next day, Ham Chamberlayne organized a foraging party to impress local horses. Riding into Millerstown, a cozy hamlet west of Gettysburg and not far from Fairfield, Chamberlayne's band acquired a number of

Figure 10. Ambrose Powell Hill (1825–1865), who considered Pegram his finest artillerist. After the death of Stonewall Jackson, Pegram wrote that "everyone looks to A. P. Hill as the man to fill his place, & after he once gets a shew, the enemy will fear him as much as they ever feared Jackson." (Photograph courtesy of the Library of Congress)

animals outside a church. Unfortunately, though, a sizeable force of Union cavalry surprised the detail and captured the commander of the Crenshaw Artillery and four men, as well as the confiscated horses.[44]

Another of the battalion's expeditions for fresh mounts also produced few rewards. A sergeant in the Fredericksburg Artillery complained that this was "very distasteful service" because every animal he seized happened to be "the special favorite of the women and children of the family, who with 'wailing and crying,' begged that their 'pets' might be spared." Worst of all, according to the cannoneer, the horses commandeered in Pennsylvania "were big, fat, and clumsy, totally unfit for the quick movements and long, forced marches." The Confederates abandoned most of the beasts before the army returned to Virginia.[45]

Many foraging missions during the Gettysburg campaign did, however, secure abundant riches. In a letter published in the *Richmond Daily Enquirer* on July 15, an unidentified soldier in Pegram's battalion confided that "I have not lived exactly up to what my conscience tells me is right, for I have been living on the 'fat of the land.'" Rejecting government rations since "we *left the Confed-*

Figure 11. John Hampden Chamberlayne (1838–1882), long one of Willy's closest friends. During the war, Pegram wrote of his dear friend: "I am sorry to say that I see very little of him now, as we are so far apart. I miss him exceedingly as he is one of the most agreeable and amusing friends I have." (Photograph from *Ham Chamberlayne—Virginian*, ed. C. G. Chamberlayne, Dietz Printing Co., 1932)

eracy," Pegram's men loaded down their tables with "eggs, butter, milk, roe herrings, cheese, apple-butter, pickles, strawberries, cherries, molasses, syrup, veal, green peas, [and] early cabbage." It seemed cruel to have "feasted myself on the good things of life at the expense of other people," the cannoneer admitted. Still, fresh provisions and the sight of land untouched by vandalous armies rejuvenated Lee's veterans. "We have not a single man in the ambulance, and have been marching continually for *twelve days,*" the artillerist boasted. "You can see the boys are determined to urge their every faculty in this campaign." [46]

While many of his soldiers feasted, Lee faced a difficult situation. His corps lay widely scattered, and Jeb Stuart, separated from the army on a fruitless raid, provided no information about the enemy's movements. By June 30, Lee had learned of Federal positions and hastened to concentrate his army. Hill's corps rested at Cashtown, about eight miles from Gettysburg; Ewell, who had marched nearly to Harrisburg, was en route toward the Third Corps; and Longstreet had also moved within supporting distance of Hill, halting his column about seven miles east of Chambersburg. Lee thus had four of his nine infantry divisions east of South Mountain and within less than a day's march from one another. Gettysburg was the obvious point of concentration for the Army of Northern Virginia. [47]

Under dreary skies and a spitting rain, Heth's division left its camp at five o'clock in the morning on July 1 for Gettysburg. Confederates had stumbled into the Federals in town a day earlier in an effort to secure shoes. After pleading for permission from his superiors, Pegram brought his battalion from reserve to the van of the column. Pegram's astonished men, believing that their commander was still absent, looked "to see our 'Fighting Major,' galloping up to our camp, crying out 'harness and march.'" Parked behind Pender's division, Pegram's men proceeded down the Cashtown Road and brought their guns behind Heth's four brigades. A cannoneer in the Crenshaw Battery saw this as clear evidence that "our boys (the battalion) are never sought for in vain, and can always be depended upon."[48]

Another man offered a different perspective, though, maintaining that only Pegram's zealousness could account for the battalion's spot near the head of the column. A month after Gettysburg he wrote that Pegram was "a perfect gentleman and is moreover a fine officer, though *rather* too fond of fighting. In fact he has been known to beg to be allowed to take his batt'n into a fight." This man thought it peculiar that "in going to Penna. we marched behind our whole corps and were considered as in reserve but when the time came for fighting we opened it." He heard Pegram say that "'we happened to be in front that day' [1 July]." Willy's explanation puzzled his subordinate because "such chances as a batt'n *happening* to be in front after marching some two or three hundred miles in extreme rear is rather extraordinary are they not."[49]

This soldier correctly observed that Pegram possessed more zeal for battle than most of his officers. His complaint reveals the beginning of a gulf between men like Willy, who still embraced courage in its 1861 form, and soldiers who realized they could not fight the war the way they had set out to. Still, while many Southerners began to question the purpose of eagerly seeking battle or exposing themselves to Northern bullets, they still admired men who fought with reckless abandon. As for Pegram, he remained convinced that God wanted "his people" to make every exertion to defeat the enemy. Not only did he demonstrate his devotion to the Confederacy and God by his actions on the battlefield, but he also expected the same behavior from his men.[50]

Pegram's caissons followed Heth's soldiers as they plodded toward Gettysburg. The sun penetrated gray skies and a morning breeze drifted through the ranks, transporting the men's careless chatter and laughter across wheat fields bracketing the road. Shoes were the purpose of the expedition. The previous day General James J. Pettigrew's brigade had ventured into Gettysburg for this scarce commodity but had found Federal cavalry instead. Hill disagreed with Pettigrew's findings, insisting that only the Pennsylvania home guard occupied the town. The Third Corps commander approved Heth's plan to send his entire division to secure the footwear. But as his men neared Gettysburg, Heth became more concerned about what lurked in his front. "I was ignorant [as to]

Figure 12. Henry Heth (1825–1875). Heth considered Willy one of the few men who was "supremely happy" in battle. (Photograph courtesy of the Library of Congress)

what force was at or near Gettysburg," he complained in his after-action report. About three miles west of town, Heth spotted movement near the crossing at Marsh Run and called for Pegram and a section of rifled pieces from the Fredericksburg Artillery.[51]

The distance, as well as the briars and trees along the banks of the creek, concealed the identity of the soldiers. Pegram and his subordinates debated the allegiance of these men and had concluded that they were Confederates of the First Corps before a sergeant in the battalion announced "that he had passed Longstreet's corps and that it was two days' march in our rear." With the debate settled, Pegram swung both rifled guns onto the road. "Load with shrapnell shell," he ordered. As his cannoneers executed their instructions, a man from a nearby house yelled from his porch: "My God, you are not going to fire here, are you?" He then "threw up his hands and disappeared at top speed." At the command to fire from Pegram, Confederate cannon shattered the morning calm with eight or ten rounds that flushed Federal cavalry from the timber along Marsh Run. Heth then continued the advance down the Cashtown Pike. The irregular firing of skirmishers increased with every step toward Gettysburg.[52]

Heth's skirmishers ran into stiff resistance at Willoughby Run, about a mile from town. Heth spotted Union battle lines across the face of McPherson's Ridge. A seventeen-acre woodlot marked the crest of this prominent landmark. McPherson's barn and farmhouse stood just north of the grove, and a railroad

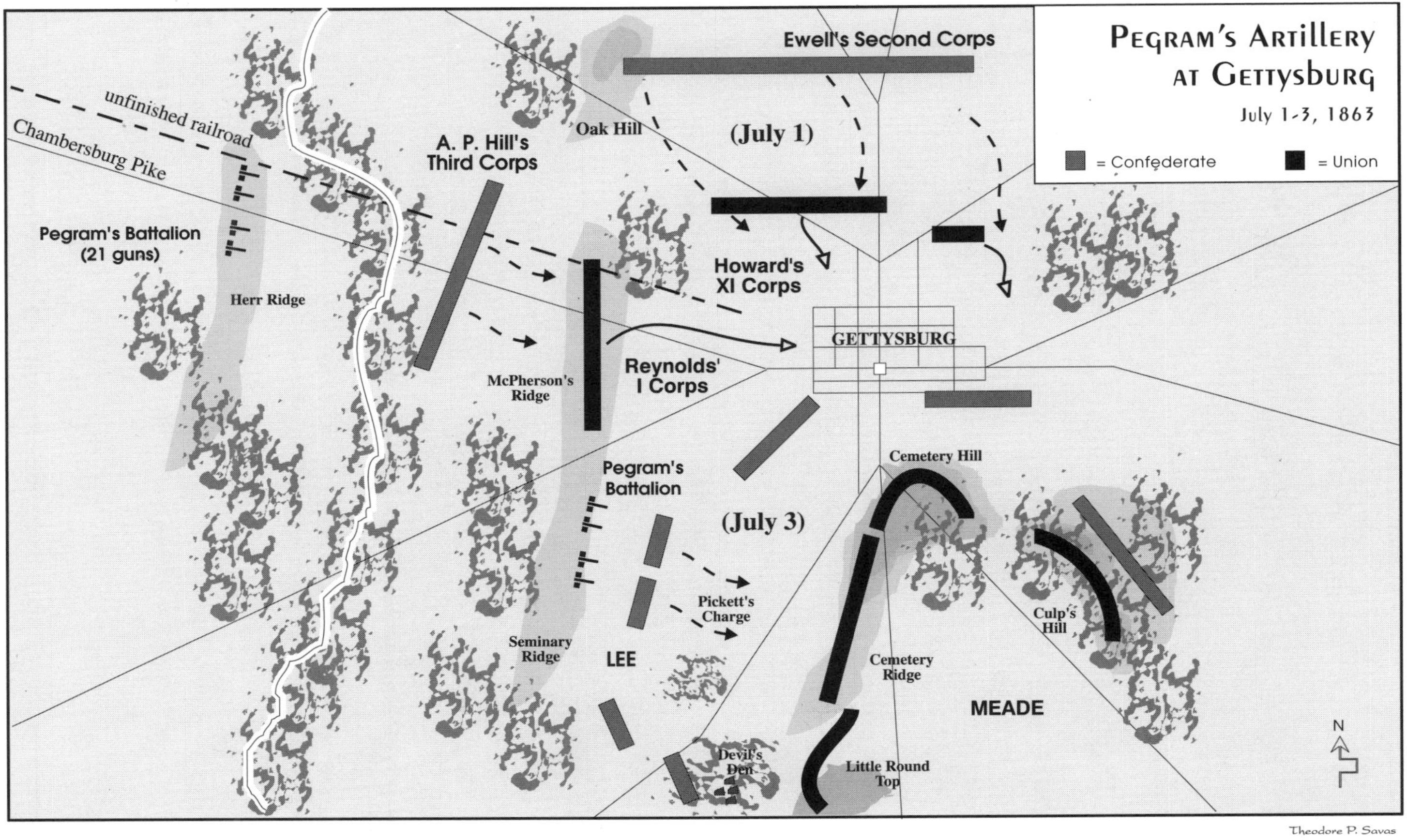

PEGRAM'S ARTILLERY AT GETTYSBURG

July 1-3, 1863

■ = Confederate

■ = Union

N

Ewell's Second Corps

(July 1)

Oak Hill

A. P. Hill's Third Corps

Howard's XI Corps

Reynolds' I Corps

unfinished railroad

Chambersburg Pike

Pegram's Battalion (21 guns)

Herr Ridge

McPherson's Ridge

Pegram's Battalion

(July 3)

Seminary Ridge

LEE

Pickett's Charge

Devil's Den

GETTYSBURG

Cemetery Hill

Culp's Hill

Cemetery Ridge

Little Round Top

MEADE

Theodore P. Savas

Map 7.

cut paralleled the pike four hundred feet to the north. Uncertain of the enemy's strength, Heth instructed Generals Joseph R. Davis and James Archer to make a forced reconnaissance, with the former to the left of the turnpike and the latter to the right. The Confederates met General John Buford's dismounted cavalrymen, who easily repulsed the attackers with their rapid-firing carbines. Pegram's batteries raced to the support of the retreating infantry. Unlimbering his units on both sides of the turnpike, Willy trained most of his twenty-one cannon on Calef's Battery, a thousand yards away.[53]

The opposing guns banged away at each other for more than an hour. Pegram tried to take advantage of the higher elevation of Herr Ridge but could not overwhelm the enemy's lone battery. The Unionists, in fact, managed to reply with an occasional well-directed shot. Then, against orders, Willy's trusted ordnance officer and acquaintance from the University of Virginia, John Morris, left the ammunition train. Roaming among the battalion's guns, he had just congratulated one of the officers on his performance when a stray shell "struck him upon the knee-joint, carrying it away entirely." The shock to his system was too great, and Morris died two hours later at a field hospital.[54]

By this time Heth had reformed his brigades and renewed the assault. Buford's line started to waver under the mounting pressure. It was close to ten o'clock when General John F. Reynolds and his Union First Corps deployed opposite Heth. Reynolds immediately sent Calef's guns to the rear and placed Daniel Hall's Battery between the turnpike and the railroad cut. Reynolds wanted Hall to draw Pegram's shells while his infantry made its final dispositions. The scheme worked. Essentially ignoring the Union infantry advancing from Seminary Ridge, Pegram directed all of his batteries to fire against the enemy's cannon. Although Hall's cannoneers managed to escape the Confederate barrage by pulling their cannon into a depression behind McPherson's barn, Reynolds had left Hall in an isolated and vulnerable position. Davis's Mississippi brigade threatened the battery's flank from the north, but General Lysander Cutler's Union brigade stabilized Hall's position by advancing past the brim of the cut.[55]

Pegram noticed the arrival of Cutler's infantry and alertly sent the Letcher Artillery to Davis's aid. Five hundred yards from Hall's fieldpieces and just behind the Southern skirmish line, the Virginia artillerists poured their missiles into the cut. This barrage sent Federals scampering to the rear in a "'rough-roll, and tumble' fashion." At the same time, the Mississippians slammed into Cutler from the north and west, forcing the Northerners to retire for a quarter of a mile until they were able to regroup behind a ditch along the turnpike. The situation did not entirely favor Heth because the other Federal brigade on the field, the Midwest's famed Iron Brigade, had sent Archer's men fleeing toward Herr Ridge, minus its commander and a good number of prisoners.[56]

One regiment from the Iron Brigade, the Sixth Wisconsin, hurried from

Reynolds's left and bolstered Cutler's sagging line. A countercharge pushed Davis's men into the cut, while some Federals managed to get astride the railroad embankment. From there, they sent volleys crashing into the Confederate's flank. Many of the men were unable to escape because of the cut's precipitous banks. About three hundred surrendered, while the rest of Davis's brigade and the Letcher Artillery scurried down McPherson's Ridge. The Federal right flank had been saved.[57]

A silence settled over the field between twelve and two o'clock, disturbed occasionally by Pegram's guns firing at the enemy's exposed batteries. Reinforcements from the Union First Corps extended the Union line along McPherson's Ridge and Seminary Ridge from the Fairfield Road to the Mummasburg Road. The Federal Eleventh Corps assumed a position that slanted north of town. Heth also reorganized his command during the lull. He brought Colonel John Mercer Brockenbrough's and Pettigrew's brigades to the center of his line, while Archer and Davis protected the right and left flanks, respectively. Pegram received reinforcements from his friend Major David Gregg McIntosh, who arrayed his battalion's sixteen cannon along Willy's firing line on Herr Ridge. Hill arrived on the field next and quickly spotted his ailing artillerist. Spurring his horse toward Pegram, he shook hands with the major under the battalion's flag. With Pender's division within supporting distance, Heth resumed his advance toward McPherson's Ridge while Pegram and McIntosh maintained a brisk but deliberate fire over the heads of the infantry. The opposing battle lines swayed back and forth, neither side able to hold a decisive edge over the other.[58]

Gunfire erupted from the north about 2:30 in the afternoon, as Robert Rodes's division poured out of the woods covering Oak Hill. Although his assaults initially failed, his batteries raked the troops who faced Heth. When portions of the First Corps turned to meet Rodes's attack, Pegram and McIntosh hurled their shells into the flanks of the Northerners. They paid special attention to exposed Union batteries, which impressed William Nelson Pendleton, who stated in his official report that the Federals "were handsomely enfiladed by the batteries of McIntosh and Pegram." Heth also complimented Pegram for skillfully directing his battalion during the first day of fighting, stating in his report that "my thanks are particularly due to Major Pegram for his ready cooperation. He displayed his usual coolness, good judgment, and gallantry."[59]

Rodes's presence on Oak Hill significantly weakened the Northern grip on McPherson's Ridge. When Jubal Early's division struck General Oliver O. Howard's exposed flank north of town, the men of the Eleventh Corps tumbled through the streets of Gettysburg before rallying on Cemetery Hill. Their flight forced the exhausted men of the First Corps to retire as well. Pender's fresh troops, intermixed with Heth's soldiers, pursued the retreating Northerners, who made a final stand on Seminary Ridge. A few of Pegram and McIntosh's batteries followed the Confederate infantrymen. Eighteen Federal guns blasted huge gaps in the Southern lines as they marched in parade-ground fashion from McPherson's Ridge. Although Pegram and McIntosh's cannoneers focused on the enemy's batteries, they inflicted little damage.[60]

When Dodson Ramseur's and Junius Daniel's brigades gained a foothold on the northern tip of Seminary Ridge, the First Corps fell back to the heights above Gettysburg with the remnants of Howard's command. The Confederates, however, did not pursue them up Cemetery Hill. While the Southerners caught their breath, the Federals assumed a defensive posture on a series of ridges that resembled a fishhook. Throughout the night of July 1, General George G. Meade, the new commander of the Army of the Potomac, positioned his troops from Power's Hill and Culp's Hill southeast of town to Cemetery Hill. From this point, his line extended south along Cemetery Ridge. Not only did the high ground allow Meade's artillery to cover every possible Confederate approach, but if the Southerners threatened a segment of his line, Meade could exploit his interior lines to summon reinforcements.

While the Army of the Potomac braced itself for the next day's combat, Pegram's weary cannoneers rested on the field near Seminary Ridge. A few of the artillerists broke into an abandoned house and rummaged through its cabinets and drawers. Wine and food quickly surfaced, and someone struck up a rendition of the "stag dance" on a piano in the parlor. The foraging expedition turned into a bacchanal. Laughter mixed with the music of the piano floated across the battlefield, forming an eerie counterpoint to the moans and cries of the wounded. While most of his cannoneers either slept or caroused, Pegram probably enjoyed little rest. Readiness for the next day's action required that horses be watered and fed, crippled animals destroyed, and harnesses removed from the dead beasts. The men also needed rations. Limbers and caissons must link up with ordnance wagons so that empty boxes could be refilled with cartridges, shell, fuses, and primers.[61]

In the dim morning light of July 2, Pegram's cannoneers harnessed and hitched their teams and moved a mile south of the Cashtown Turnpike. Pegram unlimbered his batteries behind a stone wall that looked toward the Union center, only fourteen hundred yards away. One of Pegram's artillerists considered the battalion's position "rather weak": exposed to the Northern guns crowning Cemetery Ridge, the level ground offered men, horses, and caissons little shelter. Fortunately, this portion of the line remained relatively quiet on the second day of fighting, although an artillery duel occasionally flared between the opposing batteries. Pegram's companies suffered few human casualties, though they lost twenty-five precious horses.[62]

The hottest action centered on the flanks of the armies. Two divisions of James Longstreet's corps crashed into Meade's troops near the Peach Orchard and almost captured Little Round Top, a prominent hill that dominated the area. On the other side of the field, Ewell struck the Union right at Culp's Hill and East Cemetery Hill but could not dislodge the Federals. Although his lines had wavered, Meade's army remained intact and prepared to resist further assaults.

The air was heavy, almost suffocating, on July 3. One of Pegram's artillerists wrote that the atmosphere "produced a feeling of nervous expectancy, which sometimes is felt when an electrical storm is pending." Small arms fire rattled in front of Pegram's guns around eleven o'clock. Only a few hundred yards away, Union sharpshooters had infested the barn on the Bliss farm. Portions of the Third Corps's artillery, including Pegram's battalion, tried to blast the pesky marksmen from the wooden structure, with Meade's guns on Cemetery Ridge joining the chorus. For thirty minutes a hundred cannon dueled for possession of the barn. E. P. Alexander could not believe that Hill had squandered powder on such a meaningless target and wrote after the war that "I would not [have] let one of my guns fire a shot." Eventually, Confederate skirmishers flushed the Northerners from the structure, then burned it.[63]

Silence fell on the field. Lee massed more than 13,000 men behind Seminary Ridge for an assault against the center of Meade's line. Shortly after one o'clock in the afternoon, the ground trembled with the thunder of 150 Confederate guns. "It was the most terrific and deafening artillery fight of the war," commented one of Pegram's cannoneers. "Such cannonading as was on that day, was never heard before on the American continent." Their jackets tossed on the ground and sweat streaming down their faces, Pegram's gunners rammed round after round into their pieces. Standing behind his guns, not far from General William Mahone's brigade, Pegram tried to gauge the effect of his batteries, which was difficult to do through the thick smoke. Suddenly he waved his hat in the air and yelled to the footsoldiers that "he had exploded one of the enemy's caissons." His celebration was short-lived, though, as a Federal round plowed into one of his ammunition chests, sending burning splinters in the air.[64]

Even though Lee's artillerists smothered Cemetery Ridge with a blanket of missiles, most of their shells flew harmlessly over Meade's batteries. The astute Northern artillerist Charles S. Wainwright noted that "the enemy fired full three shots to our one. I have never known them to be so lavish of ammunition. . . . But it was by no means as effective as it should have been, nine-tenths of their shot passing over our men." Damaged, but hardly crippled, the Northern batteries responded with a vengeance. "Shell, grape and solid shot were hurled as thick as hail over our battalion," a member of the Crenshaw Artillery reported. Again Pegram's horses fell victim to enemy rounds. "Ripped open and disemboweled" by the jagged pieces of metal, the beasts let out all-too-human screams as they collapsed to the ground. One of Pegram's men thought the scene "was enough to try the stoutest heart."[65]

After twenty minutes of firing, E. P. Alexander realized that ammunition was running low and urged General George E. Pickett to begin the assault. With Pettigrew on the left and Pickett on the right, perfectly dressed Confederate battle lines emerged from Seminary Ridge near two o'clock, prompting cannoneers on both sides to put down their sponges and rammers as if to pay homage to this grand spectacle. Because their fuses were unreliable, Lee's artillerists could not support the Southern infantrymen when they rushed Cemetery Ridge. Alexander recalled that "we were always liable to premature explosions of shell & shrapnel, & our infantry knew it by sad experience." He remembered times when Confederates threatened "to fire back at our guns if we opened over their heads." [66]

Pegram watched Lee's infantry advance toward immortal fame and death. To his surprise, the supposedly disabled Federal batteries punished the charging Southerners with shotgun blasts of canister. A handful of men broke Meade's line near the clump of trees. Deprived of additional support, the Confederates streamed back across the field toward the protective apron of their ordnance. Some of Pegram's men spotted Pickett crying as he rode up to Lee. Willy ordered his cannoneers to return to their posts to resist a possible counterattack, but like the rest of Lee's batteries, his battalion was in no condition to resume fighting. Pegram's position "presented a sad spectacle of war's destructive work," recalled one of Mahone's men, "the shot and shell of the enemy having killed and wounded several men and the horses and considerably damaged the pieces of artillery." [67]

Pegram's men had sustained terrible losses. Ten lay dead and thirty-seven wounded; thirty-eight horses had been killed; three guns and one caisson had been disabled and two caissons exploded on July 3. Over three days of fighting Pegram's cannon had expended 3,800 rounds, 2,000 more shots than any other battalion in the Third Corps. In fact, Pegram's companies only had sixty-nine rounds left for each fieldpiece, the lowest rate in Lee's force. Sadly, Pegram's command reflected in microcosm the condition of the entire army. The Confederates had lost more than 25,000 men, dropping the army to two-thirds of its former strength. Gettysburg had effectively destroyed the offensive capabilities of the Army of Northern Virginia. Fortunately for Lee and Pegram, however, Meade did not pursue the broken Confederate legions. A member of the Crenshaw Artillery captured the impact of Gettysburg in one simple sentence: "I think it was the hardest battle of the war." [68]

The following morning, Independence Day, Pegram and his cannoneers waited on Seminary Hill to resume the battle. With little ammunition, Pegram must have been anxious about the prospect of more fighting. "We lay in line of battle all day," a member of the Crenshaw Artillery scribbled in his diary. "We have very little ammunition, scarcely 30 rounds to the gun." In the gathering darkness, Pegram's cannoneers limbered up their pieces and headed toward Virginia. A driving rain pelted the men as they hobbled along the muddy roads.

The cries of the wounded echoed in their ears. Many injured Confederates, recalled one of Pegram's veterans, begged their "comrades to leave them on the wayside or else to shoot them." [69]

On July 6 the battalion entered Hagerstown, not far from the Potomac River. "Our boys have stood this march like veterans," observed a gunner in the Crenshaw Artillery, adding that "I hear of few cases of sickness in our battalion." After supporting Heth's division for three days at Saint Mary's College, Pegram's batteries rattled across pontoon bridges that spanned the Potomac. His cannoneers then moved toward the familiar camping grounds of Bunker Hill—the spot where the Army of Northern Virginia had recovered from the rigors of the 1862 Maryland campaign. Pegram had returned to his native state for good. [70]

SIX

THE MUSIC OF A SHELL WOULD BE DELIGHTFUL

PEGRAM'S CANNONEERS HAD SETTLED INTO CAMP NEAR ORANGE COURT House by the first week of August, where their health and spirits recovered from the trials of the Gettysburg campaign. "We have bacon and fresh beef issued to us alternately," a member of the Crenshaw Artillery wrote. "We are living very well." Yet one of Pegram's soldiers complained about Lee's order that only granted leave for two men out of every hundred in a regiment. "I endeavored to obtain a furlough under this order," he groaned, "but had to give way to two fellows who had wives." [1]

A number of soldiers circumvented bureaucratic channels and simply ran away from camp, never to return. "A good many men," observed one of Pegram's cannoneers, "are deserting from the N.C. & Ala. regts." Desertion also afflicted Pegram's battalion; between July and September 1863 his four Virginia batteries lost a shocking thirty-five men. One member of the Fredericksburg Artillery believed, however, that Pegram's batteries "are all good fighting companies," even the Letcher Artillery, which had received its recruits from the Castle Thunder prison. Even though he criticized Pegram for bringing the battalion to the front of the corps at Gettysburg, this man considered the major's leadership invaluable because he made sure that his "men are provided for and at the same time (what I admire in him) is particular about seeing that his officers and men do their duty." "As brave as a lion" in the face of the enemy, Pegram "deserves all the reputation he has and more." Evoking the name of a dead hero, the cannoneer pronounced Pegram "a second Pelham." [2]

The assessment offered by Pegram's subordinate partially explains how officers, who were usually members of the slaveholding class, managed to gain the allegiance of nonslaveholders who served in Confederate armies. The relationship between officer and private reinforced paternalistic ties that had been established between rich and poor well before the war. By providing for the material comforts of his soldiers and exhibiting the most extreme form of male honor in battle, Pegram legitimated his authority in the eyes of his men. Indeed, it was such antebellum attitudes toward male identity and paternalism that enabled most Southerners to endure the hardships of war and support the Confederacy.

But Pegram was still not feeling well after Gettysburg: the fever he had contracted before the campaign refused to leave his body. When the army reentered Virginia, Pegram went home to Richmond to regain his strength. Returning to camp at the beginning of September, he found the country air therapeutic, informing his sister on the tenth of the month that "my week's sojourn in camp improved me a great deal." According to Pegram, his comrades agreed that he appeared to be "in much better health." Separation from his family, however, dampened his spirits. Because of the war, Pegram could now imagine how much he would miss his oldest sister "if you were away for any length of time on one of your European trips." That said, he relieved the seriousness of his missive by teasing Mary about her kissing a gentleman while on a recent vacation. This impropriety, Pegram thought, demonstrated that "your trip has turned your head, and that you are becoming fast!" He closed the letter with a final jab: "I expect you will get notions in your head & will not be contented to remain in this quiet place."[3]

In the meantime, the army's uncertain future had generated heated discussion in the battalion's camp, a debate intensified by the departure of Longstreet's corps on September 9. A day later, while detailed on a mission to Richmond, Pegram spotted Longstreet's troops passing through the city and felt certain they were moving to Tennessee on "a temporary arrangement." He had also heard that Lee might try his hand in the Western Theater. These developments caused Pegram to speculate that the focus of the war might shift from "Virginia to Kentucky and Tennessee," a change he would welcome. The movements of the army in Virginia, Pegram noted, were shrouded in "a great deal of mystery." With the loss of "so many troops," Pegram feared that "the army will have to fall back upon Richmond to winter." While he hoped that "it may not be necessary," there was still no need to worry because "Genl. Lee seems to be at the bottom of it all."[4]

In fact, Lee had no intention of drawing his lines around Richmond. The Army of the Potomac also had been reduced in size that fall, and Lee hoped to strike Meade before he could receive reinforcements at his camp north of Culpeper. In light of this goal, Lee's army started north on October 9. Hill's corps, including Pegram's battalion, halted outside Culpeper two days later. The Federals had made a hasty retreat toward Warrenton, leaving abandoned camps and a few stragglers to greet the Confederates. The arrival at this point of his brother John, who had transferred from his cavalry brigade in the West to command "Extra Billy" Smith's brigade, must have brightened Pegram's day. Willy had always desired to serve in the ranks with his oldest brother.[5]

Fearing the Army of the Potomac would have time to retire to its impregnable Washington defenses, Lee hoped to sever Meade's line of retreat. On October 14 Hill caught the Union column at Bristoe Station and pushed Heth's men forward without making a proper reconnaissance. This proved a fatal error, since three undetected Northern divisions waited behind a railroad bank. In less than forty-five minutes, more than a thousand Confederate casualties littered the ground. Pegram hurried the Crenshaw Artillery to the scene, but his cannoneers never received an order to fire. Hill's battered forces subsequently retired across the Rappahannock, and Pegram's battalion encamped near Brandy Station.[6]

Pegram moved his batteries toward Culpeper on November 8 before embarking on a night march toward Orange Court House that continued until noon the next day. Eagerly anticipating the army's hibernation from active campaigning, Pegram's cannoneers began constructing winter quarters. These plans went awry on November 26, when Meade threatened Lee's line along the Rapidan. Ewell's corps, under the command of Jubal Early, confronted the Federals near Locust Grove at the western edge of the Wilderness. Meade hoped to turn the Southern right flank, but Lee adroitly parried each of his jabs. By November 28 the Confederate commander had massed his army behind the waters of Mine Run, Hill's corps occupying the right while Early guarded the left. Pegram's battalion rolled into line just below the Orange Plank Road in support of Heth's division.[7]

A dull rain soaked Lee's veterans that day, as they constructed a magnificent line of earthworks on the west bank of Mine Run. Meade paraded his long battle lines within view of the Southerners while Pegram prepared for a Federal assault. Because Willy feared a sudden attack, wrote one of his soldiers, "everything was kept in readiness." Pegram ordered charges of canister placed near the muzzles of the cannon and instructed picket detachments to rotate throughout the night. Should the Federals drive their sharpshooters two hundred yards toward the cannon, Pegram had instructed his gunners to "let fly with our grape and canister."[8]

Meade's troops refused to budge from their entrenchments, staring instead across the slippery landscape at the Confederate works. Occasionally they peppered Pegram's trenches, encouraging a few seasoned members of the Crenshaw Artillery to hide in a ready-made bomb shelter formed by an unfinished railroad that rested on top of a rock culvert. A recent conscript to the battery— still brimful of bravado—informed his veteran comrades that "he don't mean to go into the culvert because it might stigmatize him as a coward," which prompted the men to chuckle "at his scruples." They expected "to see a wonderful change wrought in him by the force of example the first time a Yankee shell comes in dangerous proximity."[9]

The Army of the Potomac's timorous behavior gnawed at the patience of Lee's soldiers during the last three days of November. On November 29 and 30 Pegram's guns and the Federal batteries dueled with each other, but without effect. On the final night in November, howling winds and plunging mercury attacked the shivering soldiers. "We had a very cold night last night, the soldiers who had to lay in their trenches no doubt suffered much," wrote James Hart, a member of the Crenshaw Artillery. The next day, though, increased activity warned of an impending assault. Despite the hard conditions, Hart expressed confidence "of success in case they attack us."[10] But once again no Northern assault materialized. His patience exhausted, Lee decided to attack Meade's left the next day. Before he could storm the enemy's position, the Federals slipped across the Rapidan River under the cover of darkness.

Disappointed Confederates put aside dreams about the "knapsacks, over-coats, canteens, oilcloths, blankets, &c that we expected to find when the contest was over," as Hart put it. The harsh elements of December prompted Pegram's cannoneer to tell his mother shortly after Mine Run that "I hope it won't be long before we go into winter quarters." Hart doubtless was happy when Pegram's battalion established its permanent camp on December 16 at Lindsay's Turnout, five miles southwest of Gordonsville, near the Orange & Alexandria Railroad. Shortly after their arrival, Pegram informed his sister Mary that "we have gotten, I think, into a very nice neighborhood." Construction of stables became his top priority, a chore that Pegram estimated would occupy the men's attention for the "next ten days." Hart, who clearly desired the comfort of winter quarters after Mine Run, complained to his mother that "we have to work on the stable every day beginning at 9 o'clock. We work on our own house at night and whenever not otherwise engaged." Because of the demanding work schedule, Hart grumbled that "we have barely time to cook and eat the simplest fare." [11]

While his men finished their stables, Pegram took the opportunity to dine with his cousin Edward Pegram and Dr. Churchill Gordon, both of whom resided on farms located nearby. Willy looked forward to spending more time with his relatives and other friends who lived in the area once matters had been settled in camp. He also sought to rekindle his love for books and learning. During the last year, he had felt "keenly" aware of his "ignorance" but hoped to "make up for lost time." Realizing that he could not "entirely do this" in one winter, Pegram believed "it will take several years after the war is over" to catch up on his studies. "If I can only keep my mind in training," he told Mary, "so that when the war is over, I will not have a distaste for books, I shall think I am doing well." [12]

Pegram's concerns that fall extended far beyond his future education. The fourth session of the First Confederate Congress had opened. Sardonically wondering whether "Richmond is crowded now with illustrious legislators," Willy expressed the hope to his sister "that they will do very much better than they have ever done before." If they were not up to the task, he stated bluntly, "they had better go home." The protests of Congressman Henry Stuart Foote, known as the "Vallandigham of the South," against the Davis administration outraged Pegram, who could not understand why the "citizens of Richmond" had not silenced "Old Foote's mouth" in Congress. Although "his jabbering does not do much harm in Virginia, or amongst sensible people," Pegram argued, among western Confederates, especially in Tennessee, the damage could be irreparable. [13]

Willy's harsh remarks about the Confederate Congress revealed his growing hostility toward men outside military service. While the soldiers bore the cross of the Confederacy, he thought, the nation suffered at the hands of disloyal politicians who managed only to handicap the army with their traitorous language and bureaucratic red tape. Some of the most vocal critics of the Confederacy in fact came from the slaveholding class. Criticism of government policies and politicians, however, should not be interpreted as a rejection of the Confederacy or a weakening of the Southern will to fight. Men like Pegram questioned the commitment and judgment of Confederate authorities primarily out of a fear that the congress might fail to enact measures necessary to prosecute the war. While Willy censured certain politicians and their policies, he never doubted that the Confederacy represented and protected the ideas and values that he had respected before the war.

Pegram did admit that the Confederate Senate's Bill No. 158, debated at the beginning of December, offered a glimmer of hope because it called into service all men between the ages of sixteen and sixty. Armies in the field would only receive soldiers between eighteen and forty-five; the remainder would see duty in the reserve corps or local defense units. Although this legislation enlarged the power of the executive branch while violating the rights of states, Pegram championed the principles behind the measure because it addressed an urgent shortage of manpower in the Army of Northern Virginia. "We must get a large number of men in the field by Spring," he wrote to his sister Mary, "and have a successful campaign in the Summer & Fall." Pegram understood that the war was entering a critical phase, one that could decide the fate of the two nations. With the Northern presidential election looming ahead, he realized that "Lincoln's term of office and the power of the war party depend upon the campaign of 1864." [14]

Jefferson Davis's appeal to the Confederate Congress to expand the draft and employ free blacks and slaves in noncombatant duties also met with Pegram's approval, who consistently supported measures that enlarged the powers of the Confederate government at the expense of states' rights in order to strengthen the South's military capacity. But his rejection of local prerogative under such circumstances did not mean that Pegram had discarded antebellum notions regarding the relationship between citizen and state. Rather, he considered government intervention in the lives of its citizens a temporary measure required by the need to prosecute the war. Once the Northern invaders had been repulsed, the South's antebellum way of life could be restored. Although concerned for the welfare of Virginia, Pegram realized that preservation of his community and his way of life were bound up with the fate of the Confederacy. He would have enthusiastically agreed with the sentiment of one South Carolinian that "failure would be to us universal death." [15]

Politics notwithstanding, Pegram yearned for his family as the holidays approached. His decision to apply for a furlough was a difficult one. Not only did his mother seem "anxious" for him to return home for Christmas but the prospect of the company of Hetty Cary also provided further inducement to leave the army. Slightly smitten by his brother's girlfriend, he had always enjoyed the company of the South's most celebrated belle. Pegram considered her "the greatest [attraction] to me in the world." After careful deliberation, though, he thought it imprudent "to apply for leave of absence just at this time, whilst I have so much to do." He would go to Richmond in February or March, he resolved, "for then all will be quiet in camp and I will have no work to do." [16]

Pegram thus spent Christmas day at cousin Edward Pegram's house, and he could not have passed "forty-eight hours away from home anywhere more pleasantly." "For once I was very glad that Cousin Edward did not allow dancing, but not from religious scruples, which was his reason," Pegram wrote his sister Mary on December 28, although he did not "think there is any more harmless recreation than dancing." But Pegram never disclosed his presumably secular reasons for supporting his cousin's decision. Returning to camp, he heard a rumor that Joseph Johnston had been assigned command of the Army of Tennessee, replacing General Braxton Bragg, who "volunteered to be his chief of staff," something that Pegram believed spoke well for Bragg's "patriotism." [17]

The stay at his cousin's house afforded Pegram a brief but much needed respite from the demands of his battalion. A longer vacation from the army was still in order, though, and the end of February did look promising. John had applied for leave at the same time. How joyful it would be to have all three sons at home on Franklin Street. "I look forward with great pleasure to this visit," Pegram informed his sister Mary on February 11, "and intend to give myself up entirely to pleasure whilst at home." His last trip home after Gettysburg had provided little enjoyment "because I was sick, & constantly anxious about my Battalion." But now, he hastened to add, "I never felt more in the mood for recreation, for I don't think I have ever worked as hard in my life as during the past five months." In addition, the ennui of camp racked Pegram's nerves. "I am exceedingly tired of winter quarters," he confessed in the same letter, "and shall be delighted when the Spring campaign opens." To hear "the music of a shell," he commented, "would be delightful." When active operations commenced, he hoped that "they could continue until the war is brought to an end." Willy believed the soldiers might share his attitude toward the sedentary life of winter quarters, hoping that "this idleness may have a good affect in disgusting all of our soldiers with camp life, and make them more zealous to conquer peace." [18]

While Pegram believed the war had strengthened the moral fiber of the soldiers, he maintained it had produced the opposite effect on most civilians, commenting that he had learned "from all accounts," that "Richmond must be getting fearfully corrupt." Whenever anyone discussed the decadent state of the city, Pegram impressed "upon them the fact that the gayety & corruption exists among the *parvenus* and newcomers." Pegram's misgivings about the future did not stem from ideological contradictions over slavery or other Confederate institutions that had emerged during the war. Rather, his concern centered on newly arrived Southerners who now challenged the traditional class structure of Southern society. In Willy's eyes, these *"parvenus* and newcomers" also jeopardized the South's special relationship with God because they had succumbed to greed and profiteerism. Pegram knew that even "His People" were not immune to Providence's wrath—in fact, he worried that "God will not favor us" if Richmond continued to decay morally.[19]

Pegram's fear that "a great many formerly good people are being contaminated" manifested itself when he encountered "three fair specimens" who "were about as much demoralized as any I have seen anywhere." It disgusted him that "one half of a community" reveled in "dance & festivals, when the other half are mourning for their dead friends." By 1863 Southern soldiers increasingly held to the conviction that large elements of the civilian population disparaged the army's sacrifices, were concerned above all with prospering from the war, and encouraged the faithful to abandon the Confederate cause. Their traitorous behavior, Pegram and many other soldiers maintained, undermined the moral fabric of the Confederate nation and its ability to prosecute the war. Sharing Willy's disgust with the people back home, Dodson Ramseur complained that "the army, I think, I know is *sound* and will do honor to the state—if the people at home do not condemn us in dying in this cause."[20]

Lack of rations plagued the Army of Northern Virginia during the winter of 1863–64, to the point where they were reduced to a quarter pound of meat per man in January. The situation reached a critical low the next month when Lee's commissary announced that only two days' worth of bread and a few days' worth of meat remained in the army's stores. An overburdened transportation network and greedy profiteers prevented supplies from reaching the front. One of Pegram's men asked his mother to "send me a box for I am getting right hungry now for something to eat that is got some strength in it for I am almost played out on dry bread this time sure." He further claimed that "we haven't had any meat this year and I don't know when we will get any. We did not have but a very small piece of beef for Christmas." On January 22 Lee warned Secretary of War James A. Seddon that "short rations are having a bad effect upon the men, both morally and physically." Without immediate changes, Lee feared, "the army cannot be kept together."[21]

Desertion soared throughout the army, and even many veterans began to question whether they should stay in the ranks. When Pegram proposed reenlistment to four of his companies at the beginning of February, the Purcell Artillery "would not do so, with a few exceptions." "My old battery is composed of three different companies," Pegram noted, "and I think this accounts for the dissatisfaction." But the intransigence of his cannoneers also led Pegram to conclude that "men in the ranks are like children, and when they take up whims, it is hard to get them out of them." Revealing his disdain for conscripts and men brought into the army by lucrative bounties, Pegram stated that "the old men that are left are . . . in favor of reenlisting": these veterans assured him that "they will fight as hard for the cause as ever." Pegram promised to "give them the first opportunity for proving this" and remained staunchly optimistic that all the men "will come around in a day or two." Willy was correct. On February 15 Lee informed Samuel Cooper that Pegram's battalion had reenlisted for the war.[22]

Clearly, though the shortage of food, fodder, and equipment exacerbated administrative problems for Pegram during the winter of 1863–64. As he told his sister Mary, he could not imagine "that any command in the army causes as much anxiety & trouble as a Battalion of Artillery." The difficulties of maintaining a large number of horses fueled his chief complaint about his administrative burdens. If the animals "are kept in good condition," Pegram claimed, he did not "mind the trouble," but his horses had fallen "in low order" by the second week of February. An epidemic had infested the battalion stables, and many animals succumbed to the disease. "This is exceedingly discouraging," Pegram wrote, "particularly as I believe that Gen. Lee regards the horses above everything else."[23]

Apart from worries associated with the maintenance of horseflesh, Pegram was forced to watch his battalion roster dwindle. "Some of the Companies of this Battalion have a great many disabled men, who will never be of service in the field," Pegram stated on February 1. If recruits did not come into units soon, he warned, "they will probably never have another opportunity" to receive replacements. A recent order from the adjutant general troubled Pegram because it forbade "companies which have over *sixty-four* privates on their rolls, to receive recruits." Worried that this cap might eventually be applied to artillery units, he "respectfully" requested through channels that the rule "may be extended to *one hundred & twenty privates*," when applied to the long arm. "In order to be effective," he argued, "an artillery Company should always have at least eighty privates present for duty." Such administrative details consumed most of his time, but Willy did manage to relax by making short visits to Edward Pegram's home. Court-martial service in the middle of February, followed by a furlough home, offered Pegram further relief from the tedium of managing a battalion.[24]

Pegram discovered a lieutenant colonel's commission waiting in camp when he returned to the army in March. Dated February 27, it brought a well-deserved promotion. But despite this accolade, Pegram still faced a number of obstacles in preparing his battalion for the spring campaign, mainly a dreadfully meager supply of horses. According to an inspection report on April 9, only 128 animals serve the battalion's sixteen cannon. Although some of the missing horses were probably grazing on pastures away from Lindsay's Turnout, Pegram's stock remained at a level that threatened to paralyze his command. On a brighter note, recruits and veterans returned to camp in February and March from furloughs and sick leave. Pegram counted 445 men in his battalion at the beginning of April. Eighty soldiers were present for duty in each company, enough in Pegram's estimation to keep a battery in effective operating condition.[25]

"I have received orders, and will move to the neighborhood of Orange Court House this morning," Pegram informed his cousins Edward and Lucy Pegram on May 2. He wished that he "could come up and take leave of you this morning, but as this is impossible, I write to say good-bye." Whenever Willy recalled "the many pleasant hours I have passed at your house during the past winter, and of the great kindness I have received from you, I know not how to thank you," but as a token of his appreciation, he presented them with a copy of the "History of the Prayer Book," a selection that Pegram "enjoyed reading very much." He also hoped that "we may all be spared to meet, well and happily, at the end of the war."[26]

Confederate signalmen perched on Clark's Mountain had spotted Federals moving toward the Rapidan River on May 4. While Ulysses S. Grant, the recently appointed general-in-chief of the Union armies, orchestrated the new campaign, Meade remained in command of the Army of the Potomac. Grant hoped to pass through the Wilderness, turn Lee's right flank, and wedge his force between Richmond and the enemy, instructing his subordinates that "I shall not give my attention so much to Richmond as to Lee's army, and I want all commanders to feel that hostile armies, and not cities, are to be their objective points." A more brutal form of warfare loomed on the horizon for Pegram and his comrades in the Army of Northern Virginia.[27]

As Grant's troops crossed the Rapidan at Ely's and Germanna Fords on May 4, Lee ordered A. P. Hill's Third Corps to leave its camps near Orange Court House and march east on the Orange Plank Road. Ewell's Second Corps also moved eastward, taking the Orange Turnpike from its bivouac near Locust Grove. Longstreet's First Corps would follow Hill on the Plank Road from his camp near Gordonsville. Lee wanted to trap Grant in the Wilderness, where the enemy's superior numbers and artillery would be neutralized. By May 5 the Army of the Potomac had marched to the fringe of this area, only to halt so that it would not outdistance its wagon train. An early start the next day and a brisk pace would find Grant's soldiers liberated from the entangling forests where the armies had clashed the previous year.[28]

Longstreet was too far away to support the other two corps, and Lee warned Hill and Ewell not to attempt a general engagement on May 5. As the Federals snaked down the Brock and Germanna Ford Roads early that morning, Ewell's troops stumbled into their column. Grant's soldiers turned, faced southwest, and pitched into the Second Corps on the turnpike, after which they struck Hill's veterans along the Plank Road. The woods quickly became choked with smoke from battle lines engaged in a savage contest. Pegram's battalion moved up the Plank Road late in the afternoon, its cannoneers itching for a fight. Pulling his cannon off the road near Parker's Store, Willy rode "about in a restless and eager manner," dispatching one courier after another to see "if he could not get in a battery, or at least a section" into the fight. But he never received a call to the front. One Confederate recalled that Pegram was "highly disquieted that his pieces should be silent at such a time"—and he had good reason to feel uneasy. Hill's infantrymen were falling back, pressed hard by General Winfield S. Hancock's Union Second Corps. Dusk rescued Hill's corps from disaster and brought relief to men on both sides. Lee had called on virtually every available unit, and Longstreet had still not arrived. When the First Corps made its appearance the next day, Lee would reopen the battle.[29]

While Pegram missed the fighting on May 5, his brother John had been in the thick of it, receiving a serious wound to the leg while repulsing an assault near the turnpike. It is impossible to say exactly when Willy learned of his brother's injury, but it must have weighed heavily on his mind for the next few days. On May 6 a scorching sun awakened Pegram and his cannoneers. In the hazy dawn, fighting flared along the entire line. Hancock's Second Corps plowed into Hill's jaded veterans around the Plank Road; General Gouverneur K. Warren's Fifth Corps and General John Sedgwick's Sixth Corps advanced down the turnpike toward Ewell's men. Grant had ordered Ambrose E. Burnside's Ninth Corps to fill the middle of the Union line, exploit the gap in the center of Lee's position, and then pounce on Hill's left flank. Hancock drove the Confederates down the Plank Road in confusion, anxiously waiting for Burnside's men to deliver the final blow; however, the Ninth Corps commander had failed to get his men into line at the set time. The tide turned when James Longstreet's soldiers arrived and sent Hancock's troops scrambling for their earthworks along the Brock Road.[30]

Burnside finally located the battlefield about 6:30. Finding the gap that stretched between Ewell and Hill, the Ninth Corps moved across the fields of the Jones farm and started to ascend the Chewning plateau, a stretch of high, open ground that overlooked the battlefield. Possession of this hill would split the Army of Northern Virginia in two. Rodes hurried Stephen D. Ramseur's brigade of North Carolinians to the scene. Although they were able to blunt the leading elements of the Federal advance, a sizeable breach in the line still existed and the full weight of Burnside's corps had not yet reached Ramseur's troops. Lee's center hung in the balance. More troops were needed.[31]

Not long after Pegram's cannoneers had shaken themselves awake, they received their summons to the front. Harnessing horses, they hauled their pieces

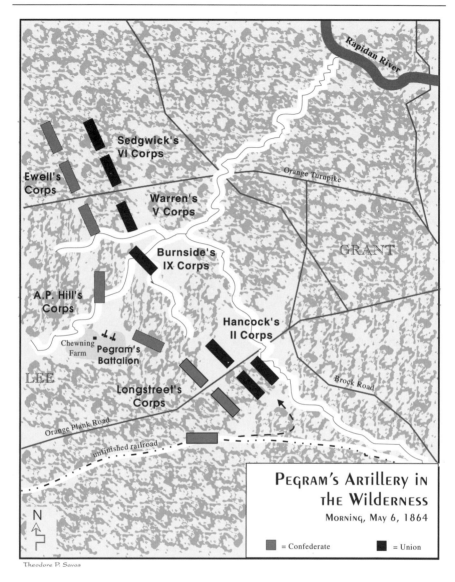

PegRam's ARTillERy iN
THE WildERNESS
MorniNG, May 6, 1864

■ = Confederate   ■ = Union

Theodore P. Savas

Map 8.

northward past the Chewning farm, unlimbering their guns on some high ground behind the right flank of Ramseur's brigade, just south of Wilderness Run. The prospect of facing an entire corps of Federal infantry with only a brigade and a battalion of artillery must have been slightly unnerving for Ramseur and Pegram. Burnside's attack never got off the ground, however, and the threat passed by 8:30 in the morning. The infantry brigades of Generals James H. Lane, Samuel McGowan, and Abner M. Perrin surrounded Pegram's gunners, plugging the hole between Ewell's right and Hill's left. As it turned out, Willy's men had little opportunity to use their ordnance on May 6. One of his cannoneers recalled that "we did very little fighting there, for we could not get a position for our guns, we only shelled the woods some to dislodge some sharpshooters."[32]

As the fighting ended near the center, Lee tried to turn the Union left flank and then the right. Both assaults enjoyed limited success before darkness brought an end to the fighting. The paper wadding that spewed from the soldiers' muskets smoldered on the dry forest floor, igniting small brushfires that dotted the Wilderness. The pathetic cries of wounded men caught in the burning timber echoed eerily throughout the night. As was the case for nearly every Confederate artillery unit, Pegram's batteries had sustained minimal losses in two days of fighting. Infantrymen accounted for most of the estimated 10,000 Southern casualties. Worst of all for the Army of Northern Virginia, James Longstreet had fallen, accidentally shot by his own men under circumstances similar to those that accompanied the wounding of Stonewall Jackson a year before. Grant, however, had lost nearly 18,000 soldiers and seen both of his flanks turned. Would the Federals retire across the Rapidan on May 7, or continue the struggle where the battle had raged on the previous two days?[33]

Both sides caught their collective breath on the seventh, even though occasional bursts of musketry flashed along the lines. By the end of the day Lee realized that his adversary intended to shift his troops to the southeast. He asked Jeb Stuart to "thoroughly inform yourself about the roads on our right, which it would be advisable or necessary for us to follow should the enemy continue his movement toward Spotsylvania Court House." Lee pulled the First Corps out of line at eleven that night. Longstreet's replacement, Richard H. Anderson, led his troops onto a very narrow military road that had been cut by army engineers the previous day. Stumps covered this exceedingly narrow road, making a swift march difficult. But the Confederates had to overcome these obstacles and reach Spotsylvania Court House before the Army of the Potomac. Should they fail, the Federals would own the most direct route to Richmond.[34]

A race quickly developed between the two armies. Grant held the advantage because he controlled the Brock Road—the straightest path to the courthouse. Ewell's and then Hill's corps, under the command of Jubal Early, followed Anderson's troops on May 8. Lee's veterans marched out of the Wilderness sickened by the nauseating stench of corpses and gagged by clouds of dust and smoke. Many soldiers, suffering from sunstroke, collapsed on the sides of the road. Fortunately for Lee, Jeb Stuart's cavalry performed excellent service along the Brock Road. Confederate troopers harassed the Federal column all day, allowing Anderson to reach Spotsylvania Court House and block the Union advance at Laurel Hill.[35]

Pegram's battalion entered the village the next day. Aiming his sixteen guns to the north, Pegram placed his batteries around the courthouse building and the Fredericksburg Road. General Cadmus M. Wilcox's division supported Pegram, with Lieutenant Colonel William T. Poague's battalion on the left and Allen S. Cutts's on the right. The Federals appeared just as the Confederates were throwing up a line of entrenchments. Pegram quickly ran a section of the Crenshaw Artillery down the Fredericksburg Road, supported by Stuart's troopers, which enabled the Confederates to complete the breastworks. His cannoneers then assumed a position on the right flank of Lee's line. The army thus held a compact position that stretched from the Massaponax Church Road to the Shady Grove Road. From flank to flank, the line covered little more than three miles and protected the courthouse and three main roads that led southward from the village. A vulnerable bulge jutted from the center of the line. Called a "mule shoe" by the soldiers, this irregularity invited a Union assault, but Lee thought the position could withstand an attack if protected by artillery. As a precaution, Lee began construction of a secondary line across the base of the salient.[36]

Grant tested the western side of the mule shoe on May 10. Colonel Emory Upton's 3,000 men surprised a Georgian brigade and briefly secured a portion of its trenches before Confederate reinforcements drove the Federals back to their original position. If Upton's small force could penetrate the Confederate lines, Grant reasoned, why not send an entire corps against the salient? The results should be more fruitful and lasting. Two days later, on May 12, 20,000 Federals overran the mule shoe, bagging most of General Edward A. Johnson's division. If the Federals drove to the south, Lee's army would be divided. To stem the tide, Lee ordered a series of countercharges to the north and west that resulted in vicious hand-to-hand fighting across a section of works later dubbed the "Bloody Angle."[37]

During the morning of the twelfth, Pegram heard the roar of musketry to the north as he walked among his guns near Heth's salient, looking "eagerly" at every courier who passed. One of his men recognized a familiar "burning" expression on his face that revealed his desire to "get in" the fight. Close to four in the afternoon, one of Lee's staff officers galloped up to the artillerist with a simple message: Pegram "must hold the heights" but could not expect additional infantry support because of the crisis at the center of the line. "Colonel," responded Willy, "you can say to General Lee that I will hold the place while I have a man to sponge a gun." Riding down the line, Willy instructed his battery commanders to "run up" a dozen rounds of canister to each piece and have their "guns already shotted, primers fixed and lanyard taut." "Captain," he added, "shoot the first man who pulls a lanyard until I raise my sabre as a signal."[38] Moments later Burnside's Ninth Corps advanced within six to eight hundred yards of Pegram's cannon. Willy lifted "his sabre and shouted

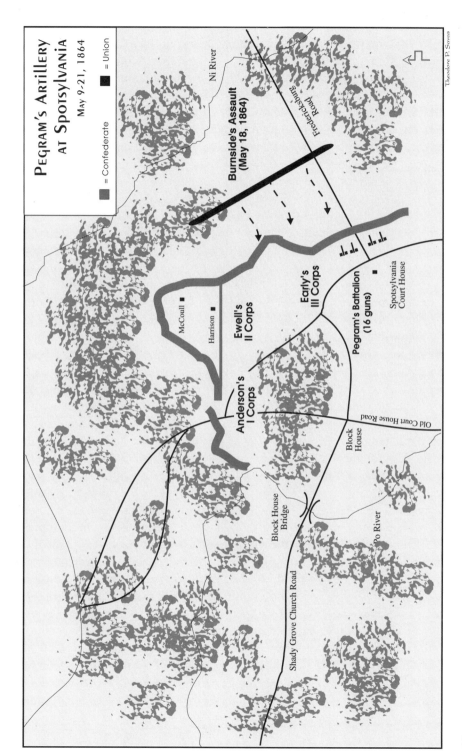

PEGRAM'S ARTILLERY AT SPOTSYLVANIA
MAY 9–21, 1864

■ = Confederate   ■ = Union

Ni River

Burnside's Assault
(May 18, 1864)

Fredericksburg Road

McCoull

Harrison

Ewell's
II Corps

Early's
III Corps

Anderson's
I Corps

Pegram's Battalion
(16 guns)

Spotsylvania
Court House

Old Court House Road

Block
House

Block House
Bridge

Po River

Shady Grove Church Road

Theodore P. Savas

Map 9.

'Fire!'"—then watched as his fieldpieces showered Burnside's regiments with missiles, forcing the Federals to return to their entrenchments. Some of Pegram's cannoneers "sprang upon" their parapets and taunted the Northerners to renew the battle by yelling "come on." The Federals, however, were content to stay safely behind their earthworks. Later that day, while Pegram conversed with Lee behind the lines, a courier handed the commanding general a message announcing that Jeb Stuart had been mortally wounded. As Lee folded up the dispatch he looked away from Pegram, sadly remarking that Stuart *"never brought me a piece of false information."* [39]

During the early morning hours of May 13, the Confederates evacuated their trenches and staggered toward Lee's last line. The Army of Northern Virginia was no longer in immediate danger, and the next few days saw relative quiet along the battalion's front. Ham Chamberlayne, who had returned from imprisonment on Johnson's Island and was now serving on Pegram's staff, informed his mother on May 17: "For myself—I have seen but little danger—the Artillery generally taking little part & ours (3d Corps) less than the rest." His situation was "more comfortable" than his mother could have imagined. Not only had he obtained "a horse & all the trappings," but he also had the services of one of Pegram's slaves because John Pegram no longer needed his servant since his wounding. Chamberlayne closed his missive by assuring his mother that he did not anticipate being "in much danger this campaign." Another one of Pegram's men, though, endured a more trying experience at the courthouse when he "saw my Father's house when it was burned." Only two miles away from his family, he lamented that he "could not get there, as the Yankeys [sic] was between me and home." [40]

Still, on May 18 Grant began to apply renewed pressure against Lee's center. Starting near dawn, twenty-six Northern guns peppered the Confederate works around the courthouse. A Union artillery officer thought the duel "was very sharp," rating the marksmanship as "being excellent on both sides." Some of the Federal artillerists enjoyed an oblique fire on Pegram's guns near the village and dropped their shells with alarming accuracy. A large metal fragment tore Major Joseph McGraw's hand off and shattered the rest of his arm. Chamberlayne quickly "tied a bandage around the upper part of his arm" and sent him to the rear where the major's arm "was cut off 2 inches above the elbow." Shortly after McGraw fell, enemy rounds struck the captain and a lieutenant of the Purcell Artillery as well as a lieutenant of the Letcher Artillery. While the muzzles of Pegram's cannon cooled after an hour of constant shelling, Grant's infantry attacks against the Confederate center evaporated. [41]

Unable to find a weak spot in Lee's lines, Grant resumed his flanking maneuvers around the Confederate right flank during the night of May 20. He aimed his column toward Bowling Green and Milford in another effort to impose his force between Lee and Richmond. Wooded terrain and conflicting intelligence reports made it difficult for Lee to determine either the location or the destination of the enemy. Not until daylight the next day did Confederate cavalry discover Grant's movement. Lee moved to intercept the Union advance at the North Anna River, just above Hanover Junction, twenty-two miles north of Richmond. Ewell's corps led, followed by Anderson's and Hill's. Two weeks of fighting had considerably thinned the ranks of both armies: since May 5 at the Wilderness, Grant had sustained more than 35,000 casualties, while Lee had lost at least 21,000 men.[42]

Pegram's battalion evacuated its position near Spotsylvania Court House close to nine at night on May 21. Ewell's and Anderson's men shuffled down the Telegraph Road; Hill's veterans took roads west of the other two corps. Groping forward in the blackness, many soldiers collapsed from exhaustion. It was hot again the next day, and the men quickly kicked up a cloud of dust before crossing the river late in the afternoon. Early the following morning, May 23, Hill formed the left flank of the army near Anderson's Station. Ewell's troops occupied the right flank of the line near Hanover Junction, and Anderson's corps held the center at Ox Ford. The race to North Anna had been decided, with Less successfully blunting Grant's most recent drive to the south.[43]

But the weary Confederates enjoyed little rest. Not long after Hill's men had broken ranks from their morning march on the twenty-third, Warren's Fifth Corps crossed the river at Jericho Mill. If the Federals maintained that beachhead on the south side of the ford, they could sweep around the Southern flank and prevent Lee from holding the river farther east. General Cadmus Wilcox's division arrived on the scene later that afternoon. Believing he faced only three enemy brigades on the Federal flank, Wilcox ordered his men forward. He also sent Pegram's battalion to cover the ford from high open ground near the Fontaine house. As his cannoneers galloped into action, they passed Heth's infantrymen, who roared: *"Make way, men, make way right and left, here comes the fighting Battalion!"*[44]

Pegram pulled his cannon behind the right flank of Wilcox's division under cover of rising ground. As soon as the Confederate foot soldiers leapt forward, he rushed his batteries to the brow of the hill, followed by Poague's battalion. Wilcox's 6,000 men ran squarely into the front instead of the rear of Warren's troops—but, instead of the expected three brigades he engaged five, numbering close to 15,000 soldiers. Although his intelligence reports had proved erroneous, Wilcox still possessed the element of surprise. The Federals were cooking, chatting, or sleeping when they were shaken from their lethargy by Pegram's shells. The Confederate projectiles initiated a stampede for the river, which included the usually stalwart Iron Brigade. One Union soldier noted in his diary that the Confederates "opened artillery on us which was the hottest I have ever been under." The area around the pontoon bridge resembled a clogged funnel full of panic-stricken soldiers, an ideal target for Pegram's ordnance. In the astute opinion of one Union officer, it was "a very ticklish moment" because "our whole right was open, and unless the enemy could be stopped they would seize our bridge." But twenty Union fieldpieces checked the impending Confederate onslaught, allowing Warren's soldiers to regain their composure and meet the Southern advance. The counterbattery fire across the river gradually quieted Pegram's guns, as the Confederate brigades hit the Federal line without coordination.[45]

His assaults repulsed, Wilcox pulled his men back to Noel's Station. Throughout the night, the Northerners strengthened their entrenchments in an effort to preserve their foothold on the south bank of the North Anna. Because the river no longer served as a barrier to Grant's advance, Lee slid Hill's corps back to Ox Ford: Hill's left rested on the Little River; his right connected with Anderson's troops at the ford, with Ewell's corps anchoring the right. The Confederate line followed the shape of an "inverted V." The Little River secured the left while the swampy ground south of Hanover Junction ensured the safety of the right. Grant tested Lee's center at Ox Ford on May 24, but failing to scale the heights above the crossing, Grant returned to his flanking maneuvers. Three days later the Army of the Potomac vanished from the south bank of the North Anna altogether. The Federals soon crossed the Pamunkey River, only fifteen miles from Richmond. Lee shadowed their movements in an attempt to place his army between the enemy and the capital.[46]

By June 1 the Army of Northern Virginia blocked the most direct route to Richmond. Lee's soldiers threw up a strong set of entrenchments stretching all the way from the Chickahominy River on the south to Totopotomoy Creek on the north. The position was simply impregnable, possibly the strongest the Army of Northern Virginia ever occupied. Pegram posted his battalion on the army's extreme right flank on Turkey Ridge, just north of the Chickahominy. Most of his cannon apparently held the ground between Thomas's and McGowan's brigades. He also stationed some pieces along Wilcox's entire front, including guns from the First and Fourth Maryland Batteries temporarily assigned to him. Because of the river to the south, a flanking maneuver was out of the question for Grant. He decided instead to try to blast straight through the Confederate lines near Cold Harbor.[47]

Intermittent showers throughout the night on the second and third of June brought some relief from the suffocating heat of the previous days. Before the sun peeked through the overcast morning skies, Pegram and his cannoneers saw waves of Federals charging across the fields. Close to 60,000 men made a general attack along three miles of the Confederate front, many with their names scribbled on pieces of paper so that their dead bodies could be identified. Pegram's missiles sailed toward the Northerners as soon as they stepped forward, followed by sheets of musketry from the Confederate infantry. The enemy's ranks disintegrated under this fire. General Francis C. Barlow's division hit the Southern works near Pegram's cannon. "Exposed to a severe fire of artillery on their left flank" the Federals could not locate suitable ground from which to bring artillery to bear on Pegram's batteries. Willy's cannoneers, as a result, worked their pieces virtually unmolested.[48]

Barlow nonetheless managed to penetrate the line just to the left of Pegram's guns and bag two hundred prisoners and one stand of colors. Pegram ordered his batteries to switch to canister, and blasts of round balls smashed into Barlow's flank. Thundering down the hill, General Joseph Finegan's Floridian brigade drove the Federals out of the trenches. The Unionists fell back fifty yards and desperately dug in. At this point, only a narrow stretch of ground "ploughed by cannon-shot and clotted with dead bodies" separated the two armies. The battle was over in a few hours; Grant had lost more than 7,000 men. "We gained nothing save a knowledge of their position," one of Meade's staff officers wrote that night, "and the proof of the unflinching bravery of our soldiers."[49] For the next week and a half Pegram's battalion remained on Turkey Ridge, intermittent firing erupting between the opposing lines.

While Pegram's artillerists took potshots at the enemy's batteries, an unidentified member of the battalion found time to write a letter to the *Richmond Whig*. Signing his editorial with the initials "M.S.," he objected that "not for one moment" had Pegram's cannoneers been accorded "the respite which is the need of good service." "We have never been in reserve," he bluntly put it: even though there were five battalions in the Third Corps. "The day of our relief has not yet come." He offered Pegram's insatiable hunger for combat as a possible explanation for the battalion's unique record. His grievance demonstrates how the attitudes of some soldiers toward duty had changed over the course of the war. Whereas Pegram still upheld the idea that a soldier should always seek action in battle, a notion popular at the beginning of the conflict, many veterans had disassociated themselves from this belief by 1863. The burden of fighting should be equally distributed throughout the army, they thought. After all, the men who eagerly engaged the enemy were usually the first to die, while the skulkers survived even though they had behaved dishonorably. This evident dichotomy between those constantly called upon to fight and those who managed to escape their duty on the battlefield drained many men's enthusiasm for battle, even as Pegram continued to seek the most dangerous posts for his men. This cannoneer also criticized the people of Richmond for not giving the men in the battalion the recognition they amply deserved. "The private has not the accessaries of name and place and notice," he stated, "but he has that prouder prerogative of doing all and daring all for the consciousness of rectitude and duty."[50]

Duty called Pegram's men again on June 13. Lee had lost touch with the Army of the Potomac, and he hoped to discover the enemy's whereabouts by sending Wilcox's division and Pegram's Purcell Artillery down the Long Bridge

Road toward Riddell's Shop. The Confederates ran into elements of Warren's Fifth Corps near Riddell's Shop. In a brief encounter, Wilcox's infantry and Pegram's cannoneers held the Federals in check. The exchange of gunfire at Riddell's told Lee that Warren's corps would lead a general Union advance down the Long Bridge Road toward Richmond. In reality, however, the Fifth Corps merely served as a screen for the rest of the Army of the Potomac, which was marching on roads further to the east, heading south for the James River. Beyond the observation of the Confederates, the Federals crossed the James on a special pontoon bridge during the night of the fourteenth and over the next two days. In a perfectly executed flanking maneuver, Grant brought his troops to the Petersburg trenches.[51]

On June 14 communiqués began to trickle into Lee's headquarters, reporting that a large Federal force was approaching Petersburg, but the general refused to believe that Grant had slipped below the James. Beginning on June 15 and continuing for the next three days, Grant hurled his legions against P. G. T. Beauregard's 6,000 Confederates who manned the outer works of Petersburg. In the meantime, the Army of Northern Virginia, in the words of Edward P. Alexander, "was sucking its thumbs by the roadside." Lee reacted slowly to Beauregard's perilous situation, telling the Louisianian on June 17 that until "I can get more definite information of Grant's movements I do not think it prudent to draw more troops to this side of the river." Forced to resort to more "radical measures," Beauregard sent three staff officers to Lee within two hours. The last messenger finally persuaded Lee that the Army of the Potomac indeed stood outside Petersburg, whereupon the general hurried reinforcements to the scene of the crisis.[52]

Close to 3:00 A.M. on the eighteenth, the Third Corps received orders to break camp south of the James and move for Petersburg. Under a boiling sun, Hill's men marched toward the sounds of booming guns. Lacking adequate supplies of water, many of Hill's men fell by the side of the road from heat exhaustion as regiments dwindled "to the dimensions of companies." Straggling became so severe, recalled one soldier, that "a brigade would stretch for miles." Covered with dust and bent over from fatigue, the Confederates staggered into Petersburg late that evening after completing a twenty-mile march—only to discover that their assistance was no longer needed, as portions of the First Corps had reinforced Beauregard earlier in the day. They could take heart, though, from the news that Federal charges had failed under the increased Southern firepower. Pegram's battalion and the rest of Hill's troops moved to the extreme right of the Confederate line, between the Jerusalem Plank Road and the Weldon Railroad.[53]

Siege operations settled over both armies, as Confederate and Union engineers constructed intricate sets of entrenchments. "Everything is quiet" along his portion of the line, Pegram told his sister Jennie on June 28. Rumors said

Early's corps would soon return to the army after its raid into Maryland. If this were true, he believed, "we will most certainly . . . attack the enemy," going on to boast that "every confidence is felt of our ability to whip them off." News that General Robert F. Hoke had failed to carry out instructions from Lee had also reached Willy's ears. Although he failed to mention the date or place of the proposed assault, Pegram reported that Hoke "was to make the attack, with his entire division, supported by another on the river." Because the success of the attack had hinged on Hoke's movement, Lee was apparently "very severe on him." Willy feared that Lee "must feel that he can put very little dependence on most of" his generals. Pegram also mentioned that he considered Cadmus Wilcox one of Lee's less capable lieutenants and thought he "is fast ruining" his division—although this piece of information should be regarded as *"entre nous,"* Pegram informed his sister. He went on to say that he wished that Lee would give John command of Wilcox's men.[54]

Pegram's sister Jennie hoped to visit her brother in camp. Although Willy would "be delighted to see" her, enemy missiles sailed over the battalion's trenches on a regular basis. "Whilst I think there is very little danger," he observed, "there is certainly some." Prudence thus dictated that she should wait before visiting. Writing on the day before his birthday, he asked Jennie to tell his mother to send some collars and a "couple of pairs of the *unmentionables* that she had made for me." He then scribbled some final thoughts on the side of his letter: "Just to think! That I will enter my *24th* year tomorrow, & am not even engaged to be married to any one!! Ask Sister if she does not think this is horrible, & that I ought to be hurrying up?"[55]

But Willy's marital fate was hardly the concern of General Grant. The Weldon Railroad, the main transportation artery that fed Petersburg from the south, became the focus of the Union general's new design. To sever this important link with the Carolinas, Grant sent the Second and Sixth Corps to turn the Confederate right and occupy a position on the tracks. In conjunction with the infantry, General James Wilson and 6,000 cavalrymen moved farther south to cut the line. Even though the Federal infantry received a thrashing near the Jerusalem Plank Road on June 22, Wilson's cavalry successfully severed the line near Reams Station. His troops continued west toward the Southside Railroad and the Richmond & Danville Railroad, where they destroyed the track at Blacks and Whites depot the next day before returning to Reams Station. Chased by the horsemen under Generals Wade Hampton and Fitzhugh Lee, Wilson still believed that his destination remained in Union hands. R. E. Lee had ordered two brigades of Mahone's division and Pegram's Purcell and Letcher Artillery to the scene, however, turning Wilson's haven from the hard-riding Confederates into a trap.[56]

On June 29 Wilson's cavalrymen ran into Confederate infantry near the station. The Northern officer wanted to punch a hole through the Southern line but abandoned the idea when gunfire erupted near his left flank and rear. Fitz-hugh Lee's horsemen had used an old country lane to slash at Wilson's rear, while Mahone's infantry, supported by Pegram's two batteries, hit the Federals in front. Surrounded and fearing capture, Wilson ordered his men to grab what ammunition they could, set torches to abandoned wagons, and save them-selves. Mahone's soldiers pursued the Northerners, as Pegram fired his guns rapidly for a few minutes, limbered his pieces, and then advanced with the infantry. The burning wagons ignited portions of the surrounding woods, send-ing black smoke across the field. Through the haze, Confederates spotted pis-tols, carbines, ordnance wagons, and caissons "scattered over the ground in wildest profusion." In all, nine hundred of Wilson's men were killed, wounded, or declared missing, in addition to which he was forced to abandon twelve artillery pieces, four mountain howitzers, and thirty wagons and ambulances. The Confederates had preserved the Weldon Railroad.[57]

Many of the Union prisoners captured at Reams Station had plundered from civilians during Wilson's raid. Revealing their fondness for women's clothing, a number of captured Yankees tossed "dresses" and items that "make-up a lady's wardrobe" along the roadside. Pegram's men chuckled at the sight, enjoying a rare smile during the summer campaigning of 1864. The grinding monotony of siege life tested the resolve of the most hardened veteran. The locations of Pegram's batteries along the southern portion of the Dimmock defensive line cannot be determined. Every morning mortar rounds hissed toward his can-noneers, who responded with warnings: "'Here she comes'; 'Lie down'; 'Grab a root.'" Many of Pegram's soldiers were hit "while lying in their tents." It was a "villainous mode of warfare," said one of Willy's cannoneers, who never wanted "to see such instruments of death at work again."[58]

Pegram echoed his subordinate's disdain for trench fighting. Writing to Jen-nie on July 14, he declared that he "would like to have this kind of warfare broken up, and get to field fighting once more." "Every thinking man in the army," Pegram speculated, desired such a change. He also preferred to fight in the field because his notions of courage meant little in trench warfare, where enemy sharpshooters made acts of heroism impossible. A few days before Pe-gram wrote his sister, Lee had visited Hill's headquarters while Willy was pres-ent. Hill read a paragraph out loud from "a Yankee paper" stating that Grant "could never catch us [Confederates] from behind our works; that if they could they would fight us." Lee "looked up & remarked that 'he hoped that Gen. Grant was of the same way of thinking.'" Lee wanted nothing more "than a 'fair field fight.'" "If Grant would meet him on equal ground," he grimly prom-ised to "give him *two to one.*" Pegram regarded Lee's words as "very strong for the Old General."[59]

An ice-cream social at the beginning of July with his friend David McIntosh and "eight gentlemen" offered a brief respite from the pestilent conditions in the trenches. Because he was not far from Richmond, Pegram could see his family on a more regular basis. Although this must have alleviated his homesickness, it created a host of new problems as his sisters and mother demanded that he visit more often. They frequently told Willy, "'Now do come,' as if the matter rested with" him. "You had almost as well say 'now do fly over to Richmond,'" Pegram sarcastically told Jennie, "for one is about as impossible as the other." He could "run the blockade" but imagined that his family would "rather see me brought over in my coffin, than come in this way." In no way did Pegram want "to convey the idea that I am dissatisfied with restraint of being in the army." "I voluntarily sought it," he stated, "and am willing to suffer it all my life, for the cause in which we are engaged." Pegram rejected anyone who disagreed with these words as "a moral coward, and no time patriot."[60]

During 1864 the gap between the military experience and life on the home front widened in Pegram's mind. He possessed little patience for his family's inability to grasp the restrictions of army life and condemned conscripts or men who failed to give their complete devotion to the cause. Unlike that of many soldiers by the later stages of the war, Pegram's sense of duty and commitment to the Confederacy had not softened. Rather than leave his battalion without permission, Willy preferred a coffin as transportation home—a powerful testament to his dedication to the army and his nation.

Pegram could not even slip away from camp to celebrate his youngest sister's twenty-first birthday on July 15, an occasion on which Jennie had hoped they could eat ice cream together. But although he could not be there, Pegram wanted her to "know how much I am thinking of, and would like to be with you." Now that she had obtained her "majority," Jennie could enjoy "freedom from all restraint." "So many young ladies," he wrote, "cut themselves off before they attain it, by getting married," adding that, because she had avoided the altar, "I think you are particularly to be congratulated."[61]

Pegram also supposed that news from Jubal Early's raid on Washington had elated the family. Early had crossed the Potomac, defeated a Federal force at the Monocacy River on July 9, and reached the outskirts of the Northern capital before returning to Virginia. "'We haven't taken Washington,'" Early quipped, "'but we've scared Abe Lincoln like h—!'" In his letter of July 14, Pegram rated Early's maneuvering in Maryland as a "very brilliant & successful 'raid' so far." But not only was he afraid that the Confederates might meet "disaster in getting back" to Virginia, he also worried that Early would not be able to draw Grant's army away from Richmond and Petersburg. Although he knew that his brother John anxiously wanted to join his command in Maryland, he was also aware that John "was not mending as rapidly as at first." Even if he was well, Pegram did not think his brother could locate his brigade because "all communication with Early is for the time cut off." In the event John made a sudden recovery, Pegram would return his brother's slave, Henry. Willy closed his birthday greetings to his sister by "praying that you may have a long & happy life." [62]

At the end of July Pegram's other brother Jimmy was appointed paymaster on a man-of-war scheduled to leave shortly for Europe. Willy wrote to his sister Mary on July 21 that he "would regret the separation from him, and feel all the time anxious about his safety." "As far as his safety is concerned," Pegram reasoned, "life is so uncertain, that I believe he will be equally as safe there as here." Although he wished that Mary could travel with Jimmy, Willy asked her to "cheer up! & do not despair" because "our time will come yet." When the opportunity presented itself, Pegram hoped "to go there *with you*." It would only be Mary's "fault if you do not go with me," he added. Pegram had also heard from a visiting cousin that John planned to return to Early's corps in a few days. Conversing with his relative stirred his feelings for home and "made me long to be with you all." After his cousin "gave me a very interesting insight into the family circle," Pegram felt as if he had been back home on Franklin Street. [63]

At the same time, recent Confederate setbacks in the West had a sobering effect on Pegram. Although the "general news" from Atlanta was "very cheering," he doubted the veracity of the stories. Pegram's skepticism of western armies had turned into outright mistrust and derision. In particular, he found Jefferson Davis's removal of Joseph Johnston as commander of the Army of Tennessee very distressing. According to Pegram, the replacement of Johnston by General John B. Hood on July 17 "caused great indignation against the President" in the Army of Northern Virginia. Only if Johnston had refused to hold Atlanta would Pegram agree with the president's action. But if he was relieved because of "the influence of Bragg, and prejudice of the President," Willy's confidence in Davis "will be entirely lost." After all, any man who sacrificed "a General . . . to his prejudice" could not "be a patriot." Because Johnston "gives up too much territory, without fighting," Pegram was nonetheless "inclined to believe" Davis "has acted right in removing Johnston." [64]

Bragg's appointment as chief of military affairs for the Confederacy, a position that gave him rank superior to virtually every other Confederate general, including Lee, further weakened Pegram's faith in Davis. Willy's confidence in Lee soared to new heights with every passing day. He believed more than ever that "our cause" depended upon Lee's leadership, which was under the care of "Providence." Pegram could not understand how the government could deny Lee "entire control of all military operations through out the Confederate States." Ranking the general as "one of the few great men who ever lived, who could be trusted," Pegram "should like to see him King or Dictator." "Are you not gratified at the tribute paid his generalship in the Northern papers?" he asked Mary.[65]

Pegram's unyielding faith in Lee was common throughout the army by 1864. Ham Chamberlayne, then a twenty-four-year-old Virginia officer, had claimed as early as 1862 that Lee would rank "at the side of the Greatest Captains, Hannibal, Caesar, Eugene, Napoleon." In his view, Lee moved "his agencies like a God, secret, complicated, vast, resistless, complete." Feeling betrayed by the politicians in Richmond as well as alienated from the people back home, many soldiers, including Pegram, looked to the army for some reason to continue fighting. It was Lee's success on the battlefield and his Christian bearing that kept the rank and file of the Army of Northern Virginia in the field. In the eyes of the men, he symbolized the Confederacy, exemplifying everything that was virtuous about the old South. Veterans such as Pegram pointed to Lee as irrefutable proof of why God would never turn his back on the South. Whereas noble men like Lee led the Southern cause, Willy maintained, Union generals had duped the Northern people to their own political advantage while waging an immoral war against helpless Confederate civilians.[66]

As the army's morale was thus tested, little rain, extreme temperatures, the constant threat of sharpshooter's bullet, and sheer boredom made life miserable in the front lines during the summer of 1864. To relieve the tedium, some members of the Forty-Eighth Pennsylvania Infantry tunneled more than five hundred feet beneath the Confederate line at Pegram's salient. As a result, two South Carolina regiments and a Virginia battery commanded by Richard Pegram, one of Willy's cousins, unknowingly sat atop of eight thousand pounds of gunpowder. At 4:45 A.M. on July 30 a sudden cataclysm shook the earth. In wake of the explosion, a hole some 170 feet long, 60 to 80 feet wide, and 30 feet deep stood in place of Pegram's salient. The Confederates who survived the blast scurried from the scene. Lee's line had been breached, but for some reason the Crater seemed to beckon the attacking Federals inside its steep walls. Instead of skirting the rim of the chasm and rolling up the exposed Southern flanks, the Federals piled inside the vortex. As the men jammed together, lacking decisive leadership, the possibility for a stunning Union triumph faded away by mid-morning.[67]

Lee immediately rushed units from other portions of the line to the threatened point. Alerted to the crisis by Hill at seven in the morning, Pegram ordered the Purcell and Letcher Artillery through the streets of Petersburg at a "sharp trot," halting his batteries at General Bushrod R. Johnson's headquarters, located directly north of Blandford Cemetery and the Crater. Johnson said little to Pegram about the situation. Gordon McCabe, Pegram's adjutant, later remembered that Johnson "knew nothing of the extent of the disaster" because he had not ventured to the front. Spurring his horse down the Jerusalem Plank

Road, Pegram decided to conduct his own reconnaissance. He returned in but a few minutes to inform McCabe that a "severe fire" swept the road, making it impossible to move the guns in that direction. Pegram then headed back in the direction of the city, where he discovered a ravine leading to the Gee house approximately five hundred yards to the rear of the Crater. A steep hill, however, impeded Pegram's advance. Undaunted, Pegram instructed his men to leave the caissons in the ravine and harness the extra horses on the guns. The ascent up the precipitous banks placed men, beasts, and cannon "almost perpendicular." "It was the steepest pull" that McCabe "saw during the war." [68]

After this exhausting climb, Pegram unlimbered both batteries just behind and to the right of the Gee house, a position commanding the western side of the Jerusalem Road. Pegram instructed his artillerists to hold their fire "unless the enemy attempted to reinforce the troops in the Crater" or rushed Cemetery Hill. In case the Federals launched a quick attack, "piles of canister" had been placed next to each gun. Pegram and McCabe ran into the Gee house, climbed upstairs, and "peeped" through the bullet ridden walls to get a better view of the field. "I never saw such a sight as I saw on that portion of the line," Pegram informed Jennie two days after the battle. "For a good distance in the trenches," he wrote, "the yankees, white & black, principally the latter, were piled two or three or four deep." [69]

Pegram also caught a glimpse of Mahone's soldiers "lying down in the ravine." About 8:00 A.M. the infantrymen suddenly jumped up and raced across the field. Infuriated by the explosion of the mine, the Confederates responded with even greater fury upon realizing they faced black troops. Pegram noticed that his comrades became "exasperated" if they were wounded by the "negroes." After the battle Mahone told Pegram that he saw a black soldier run a bayonet through a Confederate soldier's cheek, infuriating the Southerner, who refused to "throw down his musket & run to the rear, as men usually do when they are wounded." Instead, he managed to kill "the negro." Engaging black troops heightened the fighting spirit of Lee's veterans. Pegram himself always had desired that "the enemy would bring some negroes against this army" because "it has a splendid effect on our men." [70]

Mahone's counterattack pushed the Federals back to the Crater, where hundreds of them surrendered. In a number of cases Mahone's men refused to show quarter to their black opponents. During a lull in the fighting Pegram left the Gee house and witnessed "a fight between a negro & one of our men on the trench." After the black soldier had surrendered, the Confederate "told the negro he was going to kill him." "Desperate," the black man lunged for a musket and "fought quite desperately" with the Confederate until a bystander dropped the "negro" with one shot. In every bomb proof, Pegram counted "one or two dead negroes . . . who had skulked out of the fight, & been found & killed by our men." Fewer than half of the blacks who put down their arms, he estimated, "ever reached the rear." "You could see them lying dead all along the route" that led behind the lines.[71]

Pegram considered it "perfectly" correct to slaughter captured black soldiers "as a matter of policy." Imagining, though, that Jennie might think it was "cruel to murder them in cold blood," he explained that the men who committed these acts "had very good cause for doing so."[72] Seeing blacks carrying weapons confirmed Pegram's view of Republicans and Northerners as people determined to destroy the social order of the South. Blacks occupied a predestined and permanent station in Pegram's opinion. He understood that his way of life rested upon the continuation of slave labor. Although Willy saw blacks assert their right to freedom by serving in Union armies or running away from their owners, he continued to deny the basic humanity of African Americans and to accept the fundamental assumptions of the master-slave relationship. The destruction of slavery and its material foundations during the war did not create an ideological crisis for Pegram in which he questioned the master class's rationale for the institution. Rather, war strengthened his commitment to the ideas of the antebellum world, which had given birth and meaning to his nationalistic beliefs.

By one in the afternoon, Mahone's division had recaptured the main line of works. Although Pegram's batteries received scattered shelling and small arms fire, he never brought his guns into action. An enemy bullet plucked his hat "just over the place [where] I was wounded at Sharpsburg," something that he regarded as "quite a singular coincidence." "Through the merciful kindness of an all & ever merciful God," Pegram considered July 30, "a very brilliant day to us." He correctly estimated the Union loss at "three to our one": Burnside suffered 3,798 casualties, while Confederate losses amounted to 1,500. The "moral effect" of the victory particularly impressed Pegram. As he remarked to Jennie, the Crater proved the enemy "cannot blow us out of our works" and underscored "the supremacy of veterans to new troops—i.e. of Lee's to Beauregard's troops" because Lee relied on Mahone to fill the breach at the Crater.[73]

Shortly after the battle Pegram found his cousin Dick Pegram, whose battery had been obliterated by the explosion. Fortunately for Willy and his family, his relative "had been relieved, & was not in the trenches when the mine was sprung." In matters aside from the army, Pegram remained concerned about his family's welfare. Aware of John's intention to return to the army at the beginning of August, Willy knew how badly his brother's departure would devastate his mother and sisters. He also worried that the congestion and putrid air of the city might damage his family's health. A trip to rural Virginia, Willy thought, might bolster their fortitude and temporarily divert them from the anxiety of having three family members in the army. Retire "to the country somewhere," he suggested to Jennie, "as you will all be benefitted by the change." More than anything else, he wished he could be with everybody at Linden Row, but, as he acknowledged, "this is impossible." Yet he believed that these troubles should not overshadow the fact that "God has been so merciful to us." "We will be reunited again in this earth," Pegram trusted, and "if not, then certainly in a far better home." [74]

TELL MOTHER & BOTH MY SISTERS
THAT I COMMEND THEM TO GOD'S PROTECTION

PEGRAM RETURNED TO THE SOUTH SIDE OF PETERSBURG WITH THE PUR-cell and Letcher Artillery after the battle of the Crater. His batteries stretched east from the Boydton Plank Road to the "Lead Works," located on the Weldon Railroad. Pegram's men sustained themselves on corn meal, a few peas, and Nassau pork, rations that one cannoneer dyspeptically characterized as "not sufficient in quantity or very elegant in quality." The same man judged the pork "the most unpalatable meat" he had ever tasted, complaining that the July sun turned the meal "sour" and the meat would often run "out of the haversack." [1]

In August Grant resumed his flanking maneuvers around Lee's right flank: with the Weldon Railroad as its objective, Warren's Fifth Corps vacated its trenches on August 18. Under "an oppressive, warm rain," the Federals brushed aside some Confederate cavalry at Globe Tavern and took possession of the tracks. To secure his lodgement on the railroad, Warren immediately deployed a strong picket line facing west and north. Southern horsemen alerted Beauregard of the Union advance, and around noon he ordered Heth to take Davis's and Walker's brigades as well as Pegram's Letcher Artillery to the scene. Outmanned and outgunned, Heth stood little chance of driving the Northerners from the Weldon Railroad. [2]

As the Confederates moved down the Halifax Road, the air thickened with humidity and dust "as severe" as any Heth had "ever experienced." But not a murmur of discontent drifted from the ranks. About four miles south of Petersburg, Heth formed Davis's brigade on the right side of the road and Walker's on the left, placing Pegram's four cannon behind the center of the line near the Davis house. Below the Southerners stretched a field of corn and a patch of woods that obscured Warren's view of the Confederate force. Before the Federals could strike, Heth pushed his men forward through the tall corn into the woodlot, surprising Warren's pickets and capturing two hundred prisoners. Heth's men continued the advance in "good order," crossing "several lines of breastworks," as Pegram's artillerists arched their shells over the heads of the infantrymen. His guns engaged Union batteries a mile to the south, near the Blick house. When Warren's gunners saw their infantry support running, they opened a telling fire on Heth's troops and Pegram's cannoneers. The Confederate attack quickly faltered, and Pegram's battery fell silent, forcing Heth to withdraw his infantry to the Davis house. The general bluntly reported that his "two Brigades had done all that could be expected of them." The Confeder-

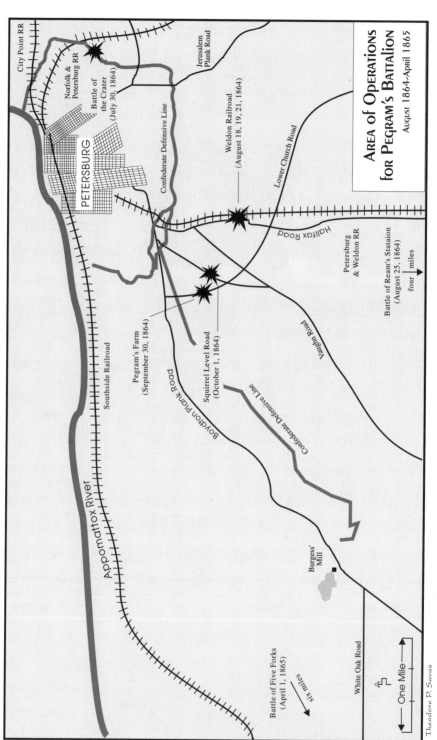

Area of Operations for Pegram's Battalion

August 1864–April 1865

City Point RR

Norfolk & Petersburg RR

Battle of the Crater
(July 30, 1864)

PETERSBURG

Confederate Defensive Line

Jerusalem Plank Road

Weldon Railroad
— (August 18, 19, 21, 1864)

Lower Church Road

Halifax Road

Petersburg & Weldon RR

Battle of Ream's Station
(August 25, 1864)

four miles

Vaughn Road

Pegram's Farm
(September 30, 1864)

Squirrel Level Road
(October 1, 1864)

Boydton Plank Road

Confederate Defensive Line

Southside Railroad

Appomattox River

Burgess' Mill

Battle of Five Forks
(April 1, 1865)

six miles

White Oak Road

One Mile

Theodore P. Savas

Map 10.

ates had lost approximately 350 men, the Federals 900, including those taken prisoner.[3]

The Fifth Corps fortified its position astride the Weldon Railroad that night, while Grant sent reinforcements toward Globe Tavern. Heth's soldiers spent the evening near the Davis house. Heth predicted that he could drive the enemy from the railroad if he received reinforcements, but Beauregard informed Lee that Heth "has already all I can spare," forcing Lee to admit that the Weldon line could not be recaptured. He wanted Grant to pay a heavy human price for its possession, however, so the next day he sent Heth three brigades of Mahone's division, along with Pegram's Purcell, Crenshaw, and Fredericksburg Batteries.[4]

A steady drizzle fell on the morning of August 19, while Pegram unlimbered at least eight guns near the Davis house. Where he positioned the rest of his cannon is impossible to determine. Two Northern divisions awaited the Confederates behind entrenchments that ran perpendicular to the north-south Halifax Road and the Weldon Railroad; a third division rested parallel to the road and the tracks. At dusk Mahone's three brigades slammed into the enemy's exposed right flank. The Federals fell back in confusion, while Heth ordered two brigades forward at the Davis house to act as a diversion. Mahone's attack also brought Pegram's gunners into action, and a furious counterbattery fire developed between them and the Union gunners near the Blick house. "Never before or after," Heth wrote, had he been exposed "to such a terrible fire of artillery." Warren's cannon all too quickly silenced Pegram's guns.[5]

The Northern artillerists then turned their attention to Mahone's men, who were sweeping around the crumbling right flank, firing away until the sudden arrival of a fresh Federal division blunted the Confederate attack. Mahone reluctantly pulled his troops off the field, escorting 2,700 Union prisoners behind the lines—an amazing figure considering that total Northern losses amounted to 3,000. In Heth's and Mahone's troops, six hundred men were killed, wounded, or captured.[6]

Unshaken by two days of failed attacks, Lee decided to strike the Weldon Railroad one more time with a larger force. He accordingly alloted eight brigades to Mahone and three fresh North Carolina brigades to Heth for a final assault on the twenty-first. Warren's troops had constructed a formidable set of entrenchments over the course of the three days. His line now ran north-south, paralleling the Halifax Road and the Weldon Railroad until it reached the Blick house where it turned east so that the Federals could also resist an assault from the Davis house. A nearby signal station scanned the countryside for any Southern movement. In contrast to the fighting on the nineteenth, this time Mahone would find Warren's veterans well prepared for his attack.[7]

Hill's column plodded down the Vaughan Road through a steady drizzle and a light fog on the morning of the twenty-first. Leaving eight guns back at the

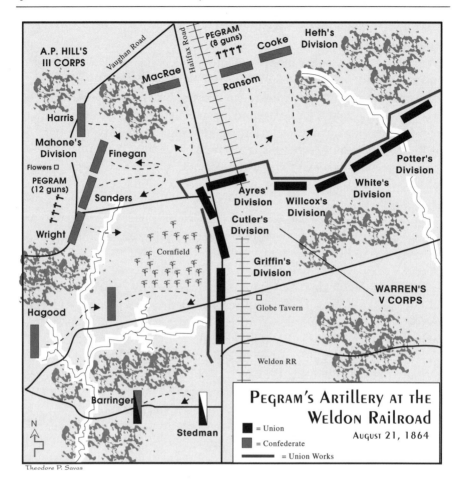

Map 11.

Davis house, Pegram concentrated twelve pieces among Mahone's eight brigades near the Flowers house, which bordered the Vaughan Road. His position
lay opposite the western face of the enemy's works. Once the fog lifted, Hill
and Mahone peered across a cornfield several hundred yards wide between
the opposing lines, at which point they realized that Warren's entrenchments
extended much further to the south than they had expected. Refusing to cancel
the attack, Hill and Mahone decided to send most of the men straight across
the open ground, while one brigade moved further south to outflank the
Northerners.[8]

Somewhere between eight and nine in the morning, Pegram ordered his
gunners near the Flowers house to cut their fuses to one second. They pushed
case shot down the barrels of their guns, stood back, and watched their missiles
soar toward the Federal lines. Hearing the cannon fire to their right, Pegram's

other section, at the Davis house, joined in the bombardment. Because of the disposition of his pieces, his shells converged on Warren. "It was a very ugly fire for us," wrote the chief of the Fifth Corps artillery, "coming from two direction[s]." Another Union soldier recalled that "we had seldom been placed under a hotter artillery fire than this." Many frightened men tried to escape the cannonade by "lying half buried in the mud."[9]

Most of Pegram's fuses failed to detonate, however, causing his rounds to ricochet harmlessly off the enemy's fortifications. After Pegram warmed his cannon, Mahone's men advanced into the corn, their heads bobbing just above the stalks and their red flags hanging overhead. Northern gunners depressed the barrels of their pieces and sent solid shot skimming off the ground and careening into the dense Confederate ranks. Wainwright grimly remarked that the attackers' battle cry "was stopped in their throats before it was well out." Within minutes Mahone's men retired toward Pegram's batteries.[10]

For the rest of the day the Confederates repeatedly tried to carry Warren's position, only to fall back in confusion. After each attempt, though, Pegram's cannoneers stepped up to their posts and reopened fire. The Federals also repulsed Heth's infantry at the Davis house. Toward nightfall, Mahone's and Heth's commands hobbled back to Petersburg, having sustained some thirteen hundred casualties, whereas Warren had lost fewer than five hundred men. Artillery fire on both sides, according to Wainwright, accounted for most of the injured and killed. Still, Pegram had managed a credible performance despite his faulty ammunition, directing a powerful converging fire that pinned the Fifth Corps to its trenches. If Warren had contemplated a counterattack, Pegram's missiles must have extinguished the possibility. A correspondent from the *Richmond Dispatch* learned "from high official testimony that the conduct of Pegram and his men was almost beyond praise." Impressed by the fact that Pegram's cannoneers had placed their guns approximately four hundred yards from the enemy, the writer incorrectly concluded that it was "the shortest distance that artillery has been made available for assault during this war."[11]

The failure of Hill's assaults on August 21 left the Weldon Railroad firmly in the hands of the Army of the Potomac. On top of this severe blow to Lee's already overburdened supply line, both the Southside and the Richmond & Danville Railroads were already operating at partial capacity because of Wilson's raid the previous June. Thus, by the end of August, the army had exhausted its supply of corn and faced an increasing shortage of food. Even civilians in Richmond started to feel the pinch, a troubling development for Pegram and his family. "Some millers here are selling new flour at $27," noted John B. Jones in his diary on August 30, adding that the price of "meat is still too high for families of limited means."[12]

To further weaken Lee's army, Grant instructed Meade to destroy the Weldon Railroad "as far south as possible." By August 24 two divisions of Hancock's

Second Corps had wrecked seven miles of track south of Warren's position at Globe Tavern. Hancock's men completed their work near Reams Station, where roughly 6,000 Federal infantry, 2,000 cavalry, and sixteen guns occupied a poorly engineered set of trenches that formed a salient. This force, which included many green troops, might threaten Dinwiddie Court House, making Petersburg and Richmond virtually untenable. Lee responded by dispatching A. P. Hill with eight infantry brigades, seventeen guns (including Pegram's Purcell and Letcher Artillery), and two divisions of cavalry to attack Hancock. Hill's force vacated the lines south of the city on August 24. Federal signal officers spotted the Confederate column moving southwest on the Vaughan Road and warned Hancock to prepare for the enemy's advance.[13]

Hill's soldiers traversed a series of obscure roads before halting that evening near Armstrong's Mill, two miles from Reams Station. Hill's men did not return to the road until seven o'clock in the morning, locating the Union entrenchments at Reams Station at noon. Hill initially left the tactical arrangements to subordinates, who assaulted the Federal position for several hours without any coordination. As a result, the Confederates had failed to gain any advantage over the enemy when Heth's troops and Pegram's batteries arrived on the field at three o'clock. Hill, Heth, and Wilcox conferred and decided to break the stalemate by resuming the assault.[14]

By five that afternoon they had completed arrangements for a final rush against Hancock. Pegram arrayed his batteries behind the crest of a cornfield, only four hundred yards away from the enemy. As his guns dashed into position, General William MacRae's North Carolina brigade greeted the cannoneers with hearty cheers. One Confederate recalled Willy's "young face aglow with the light of battle, carrying into action a battery of artillery at a full gallop," commenting as well that it would have been an "inspiring . . . scene for a painter." Pegram and Wilcox then reported to Heth, received their orders, and synchronized their watches. Pegram would bombard Hancock's line for thirty minutes, after which the infantry would follow with a frontal assault.[15]

When Pegram gave the signal, his seventeen cannon fired at the astonishing pace of three times per minute, so that nearly every second a round exploded in the vicinity of the Union works. Pegram's shot dropped "just over the breastworks," noted one Confederate sharpshooter, and "not a Federal dared to raise his head above the works." The faulty configuration of the Union entrenchments enabled Pegram's guns to rake a portion of the line with special effect. Although the massive cannonade actually inflicted few casualties, it thoroughly demoralized the untested Northern soldiers. As Hancock's reliable division commander, General John Gibbon, reported, he had never before "witnessed a sight" where "every man seemed to be seeking personal safety in flight."[16]

After twenty minutes Pegram's gunners put their rammers and sponges aside to watch Heth's cheering soldiers move forward. The infantry met little

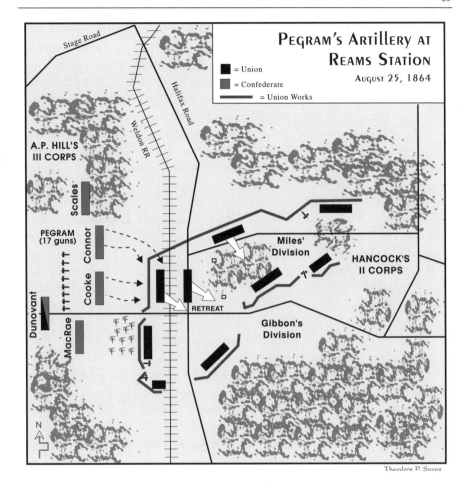

Map 12.

resistance, surging across the Northern breastworks and firing at fleeing Federals. Union officers implored their men to turn and face the charging Confederates, and Hancock was heard saying, "I pray God I may never leave this field!" His troops established a final line of defense only after surrendering nine pieces of artillery, ten caissons, thirty-one hundred arms, twelve flags, and more than two thousand prisoners. Six hundred Federals also lay dead or wounded. All in all, this fiasco was not only a humiliating defeat for the veterans of the Second Corps but it also damaged Lincoln's prospects for a second term. Nevertheless, the Federals still held the Weldon Railroad, forcing Lee to cart his provisions over thirty miles of roads from Stony Creek depot.[17]

On August 27 the Confederates returned to their lines south of Petersburg claiming a decisive victory, in which Pegram's artillery had played a pivotal role. His cannonade had shielded the infantry as it stormed the enemy's position.

Heth stated that he "measurably owed my success at Reams's Station" to Pegram, and William N. Pendleton similarly attributed the victory to "the efficiency of Colonel Pegram and the good conduct of his officers and men." Two days after the battle Ham Chamberlayne informed his mother that "Willy Pegram especially distinguished himself & the arm which he directed" at Reams Station. Wishing he "could get a chance," Chamberlayne nonetheless rejoiced with Pegram, "notwithstanding a natural envy at the luck which gives him all the hot places & chances for helping on the cause & making a name at the same time."[18]

From the trenches below Petersburg, Grant intensified his bombing of the city, leading Pegram to suppose that they were "venting their spleen for their recent losses." It angered him that the Federals claimed a "great victory" at Reams Station, "one of the most complete victories we have ever had." "Meade's lying dispatches" shocked Willy, "as he has always been so truthful." Pegram attributed Meade's distorted account of the battle to the recently convened Democratic convention in Chicago, predicting that the Democrats would select George B. McClellan as their presidential candidate. But, in Pegram's opinion, the Democratic choice could not "affect us much" because Lincoln would sweep the polls in the fall. Speculation that a peace candidate might enter the White House only instilled a false sense of hope in many Southerners. As far as peace was concerned, he was weary of hearing "sensible men expressing the opinion that we will have it in the winter." Pegram accordingly expressed his hope that his sister Mary had not deluded herself into thinking that peace was near, for he did "not believe that the war will end in less than two years—probably much longer." The South, he wrote, should prepare itself for the sacrifices of an extended conflict.[19]

As the end of the summer neared, Pegram earnestly desired to escape siege warfare. Unable to "see how the troops can live in the trenches" much longer, he dreaded the coming winter more than any other the army had passed. Assaults against the Federal trenches "would be madness," and Pegram admitted as well to Grant's "advantage over us, as he has plenty of firewood while we have none." "Something may turn up to take him away," Pegram assured Mary, while confessing that he could not imagine "what it will be."[20]

A visit from his sister Jennie at the end of August brightened Pegram's spirits, even though he "scarcely saw anything of her" because a crowd of admirers usually occupied her attention. Willy could not remember a time that she looked "so beautiful." Her company provided a pleasant interlude from the drudgery of camp, but it made him wish that Mary and his mother could visit him in September, especially because there was not "the slightest chance of my getting home." He also wondered about the "charming little girl" that Mary was "keeping for me." Jennie had "guessed that it was Ellen Anderson." Pegram disagreed as "she was too old."[21]

Men and beasts alike suffered in the stagnant trenches outside Petersburg that fall. At the beginning of September Pegram sent his horses to graze west of the city near Sutherland Station. He also received instructions to move his command north of the James sometime during the month, but Lee subsequently grew concerned about the safety of Petersburg and rescinded the order. Only the Fredericksburg Artillery left for the Richmond defenses, never to rejoin Pegram's battalion. Willy also made a short visit to Richmond during the second-to-last week of September, meeting A. P. Hill on the way. When Pegram told him that "the people of Richmond were expecting Richmond and Petersburg to be evacuated," Hill "laughed very much." From what he could see, Willy remained satisfied that "Gen. Lee has not the most remote idea of evacuating this place." [22]

Pegram pronounced Jubal Early's defeats at Winchester on September 19 and then three days later at Fisher's Hill "most unfortunate." But, he insisted to Mary, the Confederates "should not allow two or three disasters to depress us." "The worst of this struggle" lay ahead, he warned his sister. Certain that his brother John "was in the thickest of it," Willy admitted that he had been "feeling very anxious" about his safety. "As I have seen no mention of his meeting with any mishap," he assumed that John had come out of the recent battles unscathed. Whenever his family learned about John's actions, they must let him know. Finally, Pegram declared, if the Union victories in the Valley signaled the beginning of the final crisis, "we can congratulate ourselves on its coming so soon." The "sooner the crisis," he added, "the sooner comes peace." His faith in the Confederacy remained unshaken. [23]

To meet demands of the war, Pegram admonished Mary that "we must arouse ourselves to exertion, and not stop to despond." While the army did not have "more than half of our strength in the field," he complained that "every city & county is filled with clerks, petty state officers, & details for this or that business." Angered by these bureaucratic exemptions, he insisted that all men should serve in the ranks of the army. He pointed to the North's ability to maximize its manpower when Early threatened Washington as "a very good example in this." Nevertheless, since the Third Battle of Winchester, Pegram conceded that "the whole aspect of affairs has been turned against us in a very short time." Yet he could see no reason "why it cannot be again changed in our favor," especially "if the President will only give everything into Genl. Lee's hands." But regardless of human decisions or who was in charge of the armies, Pegram knew that ultimately God would ensure the independence of the Confederacy: "By the blessings of Providence, who has always assisted us when we have assisted ourselves, the whole situation will be changed by winter." [24]

The fall of Atlanta on September 1 and Early's defeats in the Valley assured not only a second term for Lincoln but also further years of war for the embattled Confederacy. Faced with the specter of an extended conflict and realizing that "we are probably about to be more closely pressed than ever before," Pegram neither questioned the assumptions with which he had grown up nor feared that the South had permanently fallen into God's disfavor. Defeats were temporary setbacks, inspired by God in order to test the resolve and moral courage of Southerners. Although those outside the army may well have seen a crumbling Confederacy, Pegram's faith prevented his acknowledging the demise of the new nation. This was an outlook he shared with many others in the army—perhaps most strikingly with other younger officers. After the disaster at Third Winchester, for example, Dodson Ramseur wrote a friend that in a time of great trial Southerners must "show that we are made of true metal. Let us then be brave cheerful and trustful." A just God, avowed Ramseur, would order all things for the good of his people. Similarly, during the wretched winter encampment in east Tennessee, James D. Nance wrote that "God often tries our faith and patience, in withdrawing His Spirit from us, and happy is he who can endure hardness as a faithful soldier of Christ." Though "slow to anger and plentious in mercy," Nance added, "He will not always chide; neither will he keep His anger forever." [25]

Because there had been little activity along Pegram's front during the last week of September, he visited the Petersburg library. After paying a dollar to this "very useful institution," he could check out any books he wished to read in camp. "Instead of wasting my spare time," he noted, "I try to carry out Longfellow's idea of 'learning to labour and to wait, with a heart for any fate.'" At the same time, gossip and rumors flourished in camp. "The enemy will make vigorous efforts to cut us off [from] the South," Pegram correctly predicted, "and besiege Richmond on all sides." The recent triumphs of Generals William T. Sherman in Georgia and Philip H. Sheridan in the Shenandoah Valley might well force Grant "to do something" to salvage his reputation, leading Pegram to anticipate that the Union general "will push for our right." [26] Indeed, the Boydton Plank Road and the highly coveted Southside Railroad—which together constituted the last links between Petersburg and the rest of the South—became the Army of the Potomac's new fixation.

After Sheridan's victories over Early, Grant was eager to prevent Lee from sending reinforcements into the Valley. Believing the defenses of Richmond and Petersburg to be dangerously overextended, he instructed General Benjamin F. Butler to take 26,000 men north of the James and strike the lightly held trenches outside Richmond. With any luck, Grant reasoned, this might prevent Lee from strengthening Early, force him to draw troops from Petersburg, and leave his supply lines south of town in a precarious situation. At the same time, Meade could exploit any opportunity below Petersburg with his 25,000 men. Grant began his Fifth Offensive of the siege on September 29 hoping this would be the final stroke of the campaign. [27]

Grant determined that a two-pronged assault north and south of the James would throw Lee off balance, allowing at least one of the Union wings to locate an opening and achieve a decisive victory. Butler's troops delivered the first blow of the Fifth Offensive south of Richmond; Meade's forces waited in reserve, enabling Confederate soldiers to leave Petersburg for Richmond. Butler successfully carried Fort Harrison, a major Confederate bastion, and a serious loss for Lee. The Southern commander then called for reinforcements from the Cockade City, eventually stripping more than 5,000 men from the line that protected the Boydton Plank Road and the Southside Railroad. Only one Confederate for every three paces remained behind the trenches on Hill's right flank. Grant's ploy had worked.[28]

Meade tested Hill's paper-thin lines on September 30. The bulk of Warren's Fifth Corps, accompanied by the white divisions of General John G. Parke's Ninth Corps, spearheaded the drive toward the junction of the Poplar Spring Church Road and the Squirrel Level Road. Late in the afternoon Parke's leading division smashed through the Confederate outer defensive line at Peeble's farm. The Federals continued pushing northward up the Church Road, arriving at a point only a mile from the Boydton Plank Road before news of the impending danger reached Cadmus Wilcox. He instantly forwarded two of his brigades and the Crenshaw, the Letcher, and probably the Purcell Artillery to Heth, who had stationed two brigades near the breakthrough. The advancing Southern footsoldiers stopped the Northerners at the Jones house, forcing Parke's men to retreat down the Church Road, with Heth's and Wilcox's soldiers in pursuit.[29]

McGowan's South Carolina brigade rode the crest of the Confederate counterattack. Passing the Jones house, though, his troops suddenly ran into stiff resistance in the fields north of the Pegram house. Wilcox realized that if the momentum of the assault were maintained, they would retake the ground west of the Squirrel Level Road lost earlier in the day. This opportunity could not be squandered, and Pegram quickly received his call to the front with orders to soften the Union line so that McGowan could continue forward. Unlimbering his cannon to the left of the Pegram House Road, Willy spurred his horse toward the infantry "with an eye to pushing forward his artillery should occasion offer." The Federal fire grew more intense. Ultimately, McGowan's men could not sustain their forward drive and gradually retired toward Pegram's cannon.[30]

The sight of retreating infantry made Pegram anxious, especially when they were the soldiers supporting his batteries. Unable to restrain himself, he wrested a flag away from one of the retreating Confederate standard-bearers. He then placed the staff on his stirrup and galloped straight for the enemy's line. Wheeling his horse around forty or fifty yards in front of the South Carolinians, he "shouted out in tones that rang clear above the iron storm, *Follow me, men!*" "It was a scene," Gordon McCabe recalled, "never to be forgotten."

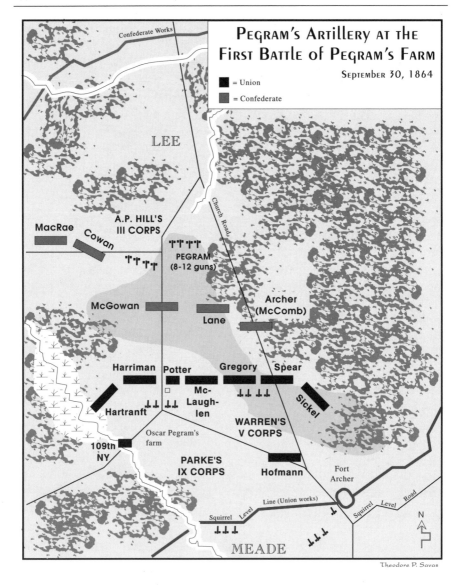

Map 13.

Pegram's "boyish form . . . cut against the crimson western sky," vanishing for a moment behind a veil of "billowing smoke." With a "rousing yell," McGowan's brigade closed up its ranks and held its ground for the rest of the day. Chagrined, the flag-bearer humbly asked Pegram to "give me back my colors, Colonel," promising to "carry them wherever you say!" As Willy handed the banner over, he soothed the soldier's wounded pride, saying that because "it was necessary to let the whole line see the colors, that's the only reason I took them." [31]

Night closed the fighting with Confederates still in control of the Boydton Plank Road. Still, Meade had made significant progress by extending his lines further west, past the Squirrel Level Road. "I took three battys with Gen. Heth, & we attacked them in the afternoon," Willy reported to his sister Mary, "driving them a mile into the entrenchments, killing many, & capturing over a thousand prisoners." The "disparity in number," he explained, prevented the infantry from charging the Union works.[32] That evening the Federals constructed an impressive set of fortifications facing northwest, with Peeble's farm marking the center of the line. Fort Bratton (formerly Fort McCrae) anchored the Union right, which connected with the Weldon Railroad works. Dislodging the Federals from their trenches along the Squirrel Level Road would not be an easy task.

Wilcox remained on the battlefield with two brigades and the Letcher Artillery, while Pegram and the Crenshaw and Purcell Batteries accompanied Heth's division on a night march. As rain whipped across the sky, the column moved in the direction of Petersburg before turning down the Squirrel Level Road. Halting at the Davis house, Hill faced his bedraggled veterans toward Meade's right flank. "The object of this movement," Pegram told Mary, "was to break our old line on that road which the enemy occupied, & sweep down on either side to Fort McCrae." In the meantime Wilcox had prepared his troops for battle behind some heavy woods and a field of sorghum. He would press the enemy's center when he heard Heth's guns.[33]

Close to seven in the morning of October 1, skirmish fire filtered through the woods on the Federal right. Heth's picket line had pushed beyond the enemy's outer works, but the Northerners had retired to their main line astride the Squirrel Level Road, where they checked the Confederate advance. Heth immediately called on Pegram, who put his batteries at a gallop. Unlimbering his cannon, he groped ineffectually for the range of the Union fortifications. Federal guns soon replied, and a heated exchange developed between the opposing pieces. For thirty minutes Pegram's cannon dueled with Fifth Corps batteries.[34]

Although Heth refused to launch his main assault, Wilcox handled his troops energetically during the morning. At the first sounds of fighting on his left, he ordered his brigades forward, while the Letcher Artillery delivered an enfilading fire at the enemy near the Pegram house. The Confederates bagged two hundred Northern prisoners, and Wilcox continued to probe the Federal line. Not until nine o'clock did Heth finally commit MacCrae's brigade to a strong reconnaissance. But instead of facing Meade's flank, the Confederates found themselves engaged in a frontal assault. Torrents of rain swept down on them

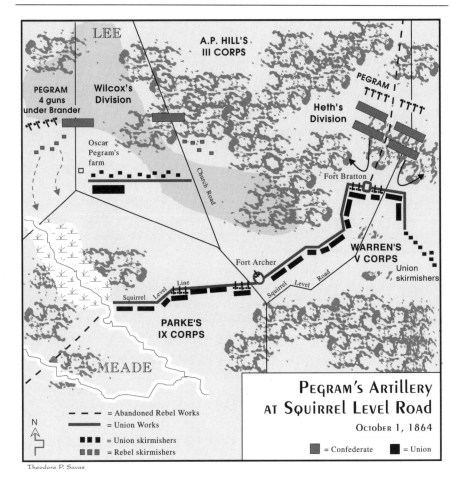

LEE

A.P. HILL'S
III CORPS

Wilcox's
Division

PEGRAM
4 guns
under Brander

PEGRAM

Heth's
Division

Oscar
Pegram's
farm

Church Road

Fort Bratton

Fort Archer

WARREN'S
V CORPS
Union
skirmishers

Squirrel   Level
Line

Squirrel Level Road

Squirrel   Level   Road

PARKE'S
IX CORPS

MEADE

N

- - - = Abandoned Rebel Works
——— = Union Works
■ ■ ■ = Union skirmishers
■ ■ ■ = Rebel skirmishers

**Pegram's Artillery
at Squirrel Level Road**
October 1, 1864

■ = Confederate   ■ = Union

Theodore P. Savas

Map 14.

as they charged across the field into a series of well-directed Federal volleys. Smoke hung close to the ground in the moist air. Out of this acrid mist bands of demoralized Confederates soon ran toward the rear. Seeing the infantry falter, Pegram spurred his horse forward and tried in vain to rally them. A bullet struck his leg, leaving Willy "lame" for several days, yet he "did not have to leave the field." [35]

The brigades of Davis and Archer reinforced MacCrae but broke forty yards short of the Federal earthworks. After losing close to four hundred men, Heth was forced to concede the futility of his assaults, retiring to some old trenches near the W. W. Davis house. Minor skirmishing continued the next day, during which Pegram lost "my good old horse, who has carried me safely through so many hard fought battles." Significant fighting had now ended along the Squirrel Level Road, and Hill's troops had prevented a Federal lodgement on the

Boydton Plank Road during the combat on the twenty-ninth and the first. The Northerners had extended their lines another three miles west of the Weldon Railroad, however, stretching the Army of Northern Virginia to its virtual breaking point. Armed with only 50,000 muskets, Lee now faced the task of occupying thirty-five miles of trenches.[36]

Three days after the battle at Pegram's farm, Pegram caught wind of "one of those old lusty yells," sweeping like a rainstorm "from one end of the line to the other." This legendary cry did Pegram's "ears good." The men's jubilation, he explained, "was caused by the fact that the troops had gotten out of the trenches around the City." Seeing trees and smelling "fresh country air" invigorated their weary bodies. On October 5, Pegram also informed Mary and the rest of the family that "God had extended his usual merciful protection to me." Exposed to "more infantry fire" during the last week than ever before, Pegram reported, he had sustained a slight injury, but he added that "today I am well." The swelling had gone down, and "the place on my leg has healed up."[37]

During this lull in the fighting in early October, Pegram also reflected on the military situation. The enemy was "strengthening their position," he wrote—but only briefly as they "will endeavour to push out again shortly." Heth had told him just a few minutes earlier that "we must all be ready to attack them whenever" they presented themselves outside their works. Willy felt little apprehension, though, over the safety of the Southside Railroad. "Our position here is so strong," he asserted, "that Grant might mass his whole army against it and I do not think we would have anything to fear." Moreover, he rated the spirits of the men as "remarkably fine," although he regretted that "we have not enough of them."

Pegram considered the recent campaign "the most remarkable in the annals of history." In fact, he declared, "it would be impossible for the best writer in the world to do justice to this noble army." Whereas Grant possessed a vast reservoir of manpower, Pegram lamented the absence of Confederate resources "from which to supply the places of those who have fallen." "In addition to the hard fighting," Lee's veterans had to endure "*hard* marches & work—work similar to, and as hard as, the labourers on a railroad or plantation." "And yet," Willy remarked with amazement, "the morale of the army, with few exceptions, has been preserved intact."

Pegram tried to explain to Mary the absence of a recent victory equal to the army's earlier triumphs. "The reason why the men do not charge the enemy out of their works as they did in 1862," he wrote, "is not from the want of courage, but from the want of physical strength." Willy hoped his sister would not conclude that "I feel dispirited." "I merely mention these facts in justice to this noble army, to shew you the reason why it does not achieve the brilliant feats that characterized it in '62." "A month's rest in the country" and "a little reorganization," he believed, "would allow the army to shew itself to be equal to more than it has ever done." Because his sister retained notions of courage that were popular at the beginning of the war, Pegram worried that she might think the soldiers had simply lost their will to fight. His concern reflected the gulf between the civilian and army experience that had emerged by 1864. While Willy still believed men should disregard personal safety in battle, he now realized that noble gestures in front of enemy trenches resulted in nothing more than death. Civilians, however, might not understand how the nature of the war had changed.

In the same letter of October 5, Pegram reported that "news from all quarters this morning is very encouraging." Impressed by General Nathan B. Forrest's daring raids in Alabama, Pegram considered the Tennessean "one of the greatest Cavalry officers who ever lived." The repulse of the Federals at Saltville during the first week of October demonstrated the worth of Virginia's reserves, and renewed activity on Hood's and Early's fronts also looked promising. Pegram admitted that he felt "the greatest anxiety" over the future of the Army of Tennessee and the Army of the Valley, adding that a "re-enactment of Atlanta & Fisher's Hill" would be disastrous. But news about the family remained bright, as John had received command of Robert Rodes's division, although he remained a senior brigadier. Willy thought it a blessing that John "did not get the Cavalry." He was, however, distressed by rising prices and the "unsettled state of affairs in Richmond," which led Pegram to fear that his mother and sisters would receive few applications for the fall term. In these trying times, he sympathized with Mary "in your labours."

Pegram and his men enjoyed a respite from significant combat through the middle of October. Writing again to Mary on October 24, Pegram reported that "there is nothing new on the lines around Petersburg." He considered fall "the most pleasant season of the year" yet found camp life distasteful because the brisk weather made his men "feel so unsettled." Although the weather was too cold to permit comfortable sleeping in tents, it was still too early to construct winter quarters. Willy and his cannoneers slept around smoke-filled campfires to stay warm at night. Even so, he made the best of the situation and "passed the evenings very pleasantly" by reading near the fire. During the day, Pegram was "kept so busy on the lines and so far from Petersburg" that he rarely visited his relatives in the city.[38]

On one excursion into town Pegram heard gossip to the effect that he had fallen in love with and been discarded by a woman named Betty Eppes. Outraged by this rumor, he traced it to Miss Eppes herself, who admitted she had spread the story throughout the city. "You know what a very slight acquaintance I had with this *young lady*," he pleaded to Mary, "and that such an idea never once occurred to me." Although he had always known that "war was exceedingly demoralizing to all classes," he could not understand why "it would bring a young lady to this." Another rumor had surfaced about his being "very much in love with Miss Tabb." "I have about as much idea of being in love with her," he declared sarcastically, "as with any other large piece of statuary." Drawing again on his reserves of humor, Willy also commented to his sister that all the idle talk surrounding his personal life made him "wish that rumor would at least let me make my own selection." Pegram could not imagine, he averred, "that there is a man in the army who has less idea of falling in love with anybody, than myself." Even though he was "a great advocate for matrimony," he told Mary, "it is useless for me to think of it for number of years yet, and therefore [I] do not do so."

Quite apart from the gossip surrounding Pegram's private affairs, recent developments in the Shenandoah Valley also troubled him. Jubal Early suffered a tremendous defeat at Cedar Creek on October 19 that shook the morale of the Army of Northern Virginia. "I have been feeling anxious about Brother since Early's last disaster," Pegram wrote. Because John's name had not been mentioned in the papers, Willy took "it for granted that he is safe," although it unsettled him that he had "heard nothing from him directly or through you all at home, for a long time." Concerning his family's situation, Pegram expressed his relief that "good teachers" had been secured. But he admitted to distress at learning "that the boarding department promises so unfavorable." He considered it "very bad to have to take families with school girls."

Pegram expected Grant to reopen active operations in time to help Lincoln win the presidential election. On the one hand, if Grant failed in his "attempt to extend their lines further to our right," he believed "the Northern people will not have time to be undeceived, before the election comes off." "On the other hand," he reasoned, Grant might be "satisfied with Sheridan's brilliant victories, and will not wish another defeat here." Because political considerations dictated the course of Grant's campaign, Pegram "would not be surprised if the first of these suppositions proved correct." Whenever the Federals resumed the offensive, they would find Lee's army prepared. The men were "in good condition," Willy claimed, and the ranks were expanding "every day," on top of which "Longstreet's return to duty causes very great satisfaction."

As Pegram predicted, Grant tried to capture the Boydton Plank Road. On October 27 Parke's Ninth Corps received orders to press the western end of Hill's line, allowing Warren's Fifth Corps and a part of Hancock's Second Corps, supported by General David M. Gregg's cavalry, to sweep around the flank. Federal officers bungled the plan from the beginning. Their troops became inextricably confused in the swamps surrounding Hatcher's Run; black skies and a spitting rain made it seem as if they were fighting with blinders. Mahone knocked back a series of uncoordinated assaults and organized a counterattack that punched a hole in the middle of the enemy's line. Even so, Federals soon swarmed around the isolated Confederate command. "It was like one man getting in between four," Pegram observed. Although Pegram desperately wanted to assist Mahone with his thirty guns, "the nature of ground" prevented his doing so. Willy could do no more than lob a few shells at the enemy.[39]

Even without Pegram's assistance, Mahone managed to "cut his way out in a very handsome manner." If not for an "impassible marsh," he thought, Mahone "could have captured all of the force he had cut off." Gunfire flared up and down the line from Hatcher's Run to the Boydton Plank Road until dark, and the next day all three Federal corps withdrew to their old positions, with the loss of more than 1,500 men. "Back at the old spot again, and nothing accomplished!" a Union artillerist wrote with disgust. "Nothing save a few hundred more men laid under the sod, and a thousand or two carried off with a ball in their body or minus a leg or arm."[40]

On October 28 Pegram moved a few of his batteries with the only available infantry toward the Federal left flank. Instead of an enemy crouched behind entrenchments near the Boydton Plank Road, they found that the Federals "had withdrawn, leaving their dead and wounded in our possession." If the enemy "held the road," Pegram observed, "they would have gained a foothold several miles further to the right," with the Southside Railroad within reach. Writing his mother at the close of the day, he exclaimed: "God be praised that he has again spared my life, and has given us a fine victory." Although Meade's troops maintained their original position, they had failed in the object of their attack. According to Pegram, the Northerners had made "a hasty retreat leaving their dead & wounded in our hands," proof that they "must be much demoralized." Believing that Grant's failure to control the Southside Railroad before the Northern elections might prove disastrous to the Lincoln campaign, Pegram evaluated the "results of this victory" as "the most important since we have been here." He concluded that "we cannot, as a people, be too grateful to Providence for his mercy in granting us this victory at all points on the 27th."[41]

Pegram also passed along some confidential information to his mother "which I do not wish to go outside of our immediate family." With the death of General James J. Archer, Heth and Hill suggested that Pegram take over his brigade and receive a brigadier general's commission. "*No officer in the Army of Northern Virginia,*" Heth stated on Willy's recommendation, "*has done more to deserve this promotion than Lieutenant-Colonel Pegram.*" But even with such accolades from his superiors, Pegram predicted that Lee would not approve such a move "on account of my age, and on account of his objection to irregular promotions, i.e., promoting an officer from one branch of the service into another."[42]

Pegram urged his mother not to mention a word of this "to a soul" because Lee "will do whatever is for the good of the service, and I had rather be in the ranks, than have him do otherwise." He hoped she would not be "disappointed if Gen. Lee refuses to have me promoted." If the promotion did come, Pegram vowed that his "unexpected favour of Providence" would not make him conceited. He planned to follow the maxim given him by General Dabney Maury: "Never to seek promotion, & never to refuse it; but leave it to your superiors to judge of you." If he received the position, he would "constantly seek the guidance of that Merciful God, who has been so merciful to me, a sinner." Pegram knew that God would settle the issue, as "He orders all things for the best." [43].

Pegram's prospective brigade was "in a very bad state of discipline and organization, having been so long without a permanent commander." Heth told him that "if anybody could bring it out, I would." "You see how much is expected of me," Willy remarked, "and how well I will have to do, to merit their good opinion." He knew that his combat record made him a favorable candidate for promotion. If this were not the case, he "should be afraid to go again on the battle field." Pegram strongly implied that zeal in battle had saved him from death, whereas passiveness in the face of the Federals would leave him vulnerable to enemy bullets. Worst of all, unsoldierly behavior might jeopardize his relationship with God. Courage ensured divine protection both in combat and in the afterlife. Rather than see the wreath and stars of a brigadier general sewn to his own collar, Pegram hoped for John's promotion. He had no doubt that John, who "has as much military, & all other sense, in one minute, as I have in a year," richly deserved a major generalship. Pegram concluded by asking his mother to send this missive to John "as I wish to give him an account of the proceeding here; but do not wish to write it over again." "I had rather fight a battle," he declared, "than write an account of one." [44]

As Pegram anticipated, Lee did not approve his candidacy for promotion, a decision that must have shocked many inside and outside the army, especially since rumors confirming Pegram's promotion to brigadier general had already surfaced in the Richmond papers. When Heth personally asked that Willy command Archer's brigade, Lee answered: "He is too young . . . I think a man of twenty-five is as good as he ever will be; what he acquires after that age is from experience." Furthermore, Lee could not understand why Pegram would want to transfer from the artillery when he "is doing excellent service." "But General," Heth interrupted, "your officers have nothing to look forward to but promotion"—to which Lee responded that he "would be delighted if Mr. Davis would find someone to command and relieve me. I would gladly command a regiment or a brigade." On the subject of Pegram, Lee subsequently informed Gordon McCabe that "no one in the army had a higher opinion of his gallantry & worth than myself." Colonel Pegram had the command of "a fine battalion of Artillery, a service in which he was signally skillful, in which he delighted & in which I understood that he preferred to remain." [45]

The fighting near Hatcher's Run and the Boydton Plank Road essentially marked the end of Grant's flanking maneuvers for the rest of year. During the winter of 1864–65, Pegram's gunners manned the trenches that ran along the

Figure 13. Robert E. Lee
(1807–1870). Lee wrote of
Pegram after the war that
"no one in the army had
a higher opinion of his
gallantry and worth than
myself." (Photograph
courtesy of the Library
of Congress)

Boydton Plank Road from Burgess's Mill on the extreme right of the army to
Fort Gregg, a redoubt resting slightly above the Dupree Road on the west side
of the city. Most of Pegram's artillerists constructed their winter quarters near
Burgess's Mill. "We are done [with] our quarters and in them," one of Willy's
men wrote on December 2, so "I have a little more time." He wished only that
"they will let us stay where we are for the winter and if they do we can be
comfortable." "We are still looking for a fight," he added, "and I wish that if it
has to come off it would come off and then stop for I am sick and tired of it."
If hostilities suddenly erupted, though, Pegram's battalion contained sufficient
armaments. William N. Pendleton reported at the end of December that the
Purcell and Letcher Artillery each had four Napoleons on the firing line while
the Crenshaw Battery worked four three-inch rifles. The entire battalion also
served two eight-inch mortars and two twenty-four-pounder mortars.[46]

Pegram's quarters near Burgess's Mill kept his men behind the lines and beyond the range of the Federal sharpshooters. "We are on the line where they
don't sharp shoot any," the same member of the Crenshaw Artillery observed,
"and I don't want them to get at it either, for I love fresh air." The respite from

the enemy's bullets offered little comfort to men flirting with starvation. Another of Pegram's soldiers recalled that "this was, indeed, a severe winter on both horses and men, and the suffering caused by the scarcity of food cannot be expressed." As if to make matters worse, the scenery around Burgess's Mill presented a dreary picture to Pegram and his cannoneers. "Conceive a ragged half demolished mill," wrote a third artillerist, "where the busy clack of the clapper is replaced by the weary whistling wind." Waxing poetic, he added that "a ghostly dead pine forest" rotted "in squalid sadness," encircling the "desolate mud" shore around the pond.[47]

Because the battalion's winter encampment was "such a long distance" from the commissary department, the cannoneers often missed the standard ration of "one pint of corn meal and an eighth of a pound of pork." They supplemented their diet with fresh fish from a nearby pond. After chiseling a hole through the ice, several men spent an entire night on the frozen lake in order to catch a catfish, a delicacy that created "great joy among their messmates." Pegram's men also scavenged the countryside for "the Dinwiddie persimmon," a "very delightful fruit." Creative methods of foraging, however, yielded less than enough food to sustain life. Delirious from hunger, one soldier in the Crenshaw Artillery made out a wish list of edibles in December, asking his mother to forward the provisions to Burgess's Mill: "Send me some apples that is nice and send me some applebutter and about a gallon of it and 5 or 6 pounds of cow butter and pyes, and make them good and short, and some nice biscuits and a plenty of them, and you may send me two nice loaves of light bread and some beans that is hulled if you will, and if you want you may send me some bacon to season them with and then if you have anything more to put in it, it is alright." "I will tell you the truth," he wrote in conclusion, "they don't give us enough to eat. One pound of cornmeal and ½ pound of meat and that is not good. I am hungry now and I have nothing to eat."[48]

The coming of the new year found the Army of Northern Virginia deployed precariously around Petersburg and Richmond. Bands of disaffected Confederates slipped away from the trenches every day. Just over a thousand soldiers deserted during the last two weeks of February alone. On February 24 Lee called the secretary of war's attention "to the alarming number of desertions that are now occurring in the army." This development, the general maintained, has "a very bad effect upon the troops who remain and give rise to painful apprehension." According to Lee, soldiers received letters from family and friends advising them to "take care of themselves, assuring them that if they will return the bands of deserters so far outnumber the home guards that they will be in no danger of arrest." "Unless some change can be wrought in the state of public sentiment," Lee did not know what else could be done "to prevent this evil."[49]

The cannoneers who remained in the trenches frequently saw Pegram and

Figure 14. John Pegram
(1832–1865), Willy's oldest
brother, "Whenever I meet
anyone of Brother's friends,"
Willy wrote after John's
death, "my grief breaks
out afresh." (Photograph
courtesy of the Virginia
Historical Society)

his brother John riding the lines together. On January 12 a bilious fever incapacitated Willy, forcing him to return home and remain in bed. This must have been especially difficult for Pegram because the long-awaited wedding of John and Hetty Cary was only a week away. Unable to return to active duty, Willy almost certainly missed the service at Saint Paul's Episcopal Church on January 19.

Not surprisingly, the marriage of John Pegram to the most celebrated belle in the South drew the attention of Richmond's social elite. President and Mrs. Davis sent their personal carriage to take the bride and groom to the chapel, where guests waited "an unusually long time" in an overcrowded gallery because the horses attached to the Davis's coach refused to move. There was a small reception after the ceremony, followed by a honeymoon at John's head-

Figure 15. Hetty Cary (1836–1892). Willy was slightly smitten by his brother's wife, who was considered by many the South's most beautiful woman. She was one of the "greatest" attractions "in the world" to him. (Photograph courtesy of the Virginia Historical Society)

quarters in a pleasant farmhouse nine miles south of Petersburg and not far from his lines at Hatcher's Run.[50]

The Pegram household keenly felt the crippling food shortages that had led to wide social unrest in Richmond. John regretted his inability to help the family in "the breadstuff line" but hoped to send some pork or bacon from the army's quartermaster. He suggested that his mother buy a large quantity of meat and then let one their slaves use the pork to bargain for other needed products. "Some of the most luxurious farmers" maintain themselves by bartering their goods, he noted. The oldest Pegram also wondered how his little brother was feeling. He trusted that Willy had recovered from his sickness, "but if he is not, do not let him come back to the Army, for nothing is doing just at this time." A day earlier Lee had informed John that he "sent Willy's name up for promotion in the Artillery." The general also "expressed an earnest wish that Willy's health might soon be restored." In fact, John S. Wise recalled that Lee, who appeared emotionally "undemonstrative in most things," regarded Pegram "with undisguised affection and pride."[51]

A mere three days after telling his family how much he looked forward to entertaining them "at my house," John received a fatal wound at Hatcher's Run.

A bullet "struck him in the side just above the lower rib" as he rode in front of his division. He toppled from his saddle with the words "I am wounded badly. Get me off at once, if you are going to do so." "He said no more," recorded a nearby witness, "but died so calmly that those around him knew not to the moment he ceased to breathe." William Pegram's guns participated in the fight at Hatcher's Run. "Fortunately," Gordon McCabe noted, the artillerist "happened to be at home on sick leave." While John's body was carried to Lee's headquarters, his wife received word that "she might safely return to their quarters . . . for it *would be late before he could get back.*" She was informed of his death the next day and escorted John's body to Richmond. Hetty's cousin, Burton Harrison, recalled that "no one of us is likely to forget the days that followed." Willy's friend, Ham Chamberlayne, wrote that when it came to John Pegram, he could name no home where "anyone fill[s] so large a place as he did," adding that he well knew the Pegram family "must suffer immense grief." He had heard that Hetty was "prostrated by the horrour of it," but Pegram's mother appeared the most embittered.[52]

John's lifeless body rested in state in Saint Paul's Church. The same minister who had performed the wedding ceremony also conducted the funeral service. Pegram's hearse and "his war charger," with his "boots in the stirrups," waited outside the sanctuary. Hetty led the procession on the "slow pilgrimage" to Hollywood Cemetery. The party ascended a steep bluff to the Pegram plot, which overlooked the James River. The Pegram family gathered behind the widow, as Willy said good-bye to the man he admired most in the world. John's death left Willy unable to "express the grief this blow has brought upon us all." Yet he was thankful that God "did not take him from this world, until he had learned to look above it." Willy also expressed his relief that John's death had come instantly because his brother had "always wished" to pass away in this manner. Willy could not "but feel grateful for the belief that he is enjoying eternal rest & happiness now, and for the hope that we may be united with him hereafter." Though the trauma of his brother's death must have set back his own recovery, Pegram informed Gordon McCabe on February 15 that "I am getting much better, and hope to return to camp next week."[53]

A week later Pegram did indeed join his battalion south of Petersburg. The color had returned to his face, he felt stronger, and he asked his family not to feel any "further anxiety with regard to my health." Everyone in camp, in fact, told him "that I am looking like myself again." He had been worried about his mother and two sisters, especially after he had received a gloomy letter from Jennie. Reminding his youngest sibling on March 10 to "fight against everything like despondency," Pegram reasoned that hope would be lost "if all things were ordered by our enemy, and the present state of affairs was placed upon us by human agency." Pegram knew "this is not the case," as "'God reigneth,' and 'all things work together for good, to those that love God.'"[54]

Pegram saw his family's misfortunes and the dark future of the Confederacy as part of Providence's plan. "He has his good purpose in chastising us now," he told Jennie, "which, I doubt not, when it is revealed to us, we will find to have been to *our good*." It was impossible for Willy even to consider the possibility of a Southern defeat. Unwavering faith in God assured him of the righteousness of the Confederate cause. Pegram believed that Providence would not allow a noble crusade to fail—a view seconded by many others, such as Dodson Ramseur, who had assured his wife in May 1864 that God would soon "cause this cruel war to end & reunite us in peace & safety, happiness and independence." [55]

Now that Pegram had returned to the army, he saw "our affairs . . . growing brighter each day." Recent showers had made the roads impassable, forcing Grant to postpone his drive on the Southside Railroad. While the Federal soldiers huddled in their water-filled trenches, Pegram thought Lee would have the chance to reorganize his forces. He also hoped that the family were "cheered by Bragg's victory." (Willy was probably referring to the battle of Kinston, in North Carolina, which occurred on March 8 and 9, although it scarcely could be considered a Confederate triumph.) In fact, Pegram had a hunch it resembled similar victories Bragg supposedly had achieved "in the South-west." Almost casually, he also noted that his "commission of Colonel of Artillery has arrived at Army Hd. Qrs.," guessing he would "probably receive it tomorrow." [56]

Pegram added a third star to his collar in March, although his commission was dated February 18. The well-earned promotion did little, however, to fill the emptiness Pegram felt over his brother's loss. It is a testimony to his strength of character, as McCabe recalled, that Pegram managed to "put aside his own grief to speak cheering words to those about him." In Richmond, Willy had heard people speculating that the Army of Northern Virginia might have to abandon the Old Dominion. "I would rather die than see Virginia given up, even for three months," he calmly told his comrades, "but we'll all follow the battle-flag *anywhere*." [57]

When Pegram inspected his lines during the middle of the month, memories of his brother overwhelmed him. Incapable of riding "in any direction from here" without being "reminded most painfully of Brother," Willy confided to Mary on March 14 that he "had quite a trying day," for he had talked about John with John B. Gordon, Henry Heth, and his wife. At moments like these, when he met "Brother's friends whom I have not seen," Pegram wrote, his sorrow broke "out afresh." "I do not like to annoy anyone here with expressions of my grief," he admitted to Mary, "& it is such a relief to be able to give utterance to someone who sympathizes with it." Even though he knew this subject "will distress you," he could not help mentioning it. "Whenever I take up my pen to write home," he added, "the picture of your sad & anxious faces presents itself to my mind, and I cannot refrain from the topic." [58]

Turning to a "more cheerful subject"—the military situation—Pegram thanked "God that this is growing brighter each day" and hoped Mary could "see this as clearly as I, and everyone in this army, do." He considered Robert F. Hoke's defense of Fort Fisher and Wade Hampton's victories in South Carolina "worth a great deal to us." "I trust, & believe," he added, "they are forerunners of greater success." Although Union armies were relentlessly driving through North Carolina against light opposition, Pegram remained convinced that "Sherman has lost his opportunity to do us any serious injury," believing instead that "his situation is becoming daily more critical." He offered the outlook of Lee's veterans as the strongest evidence of the Confederacy's promising future: the "spirit & opinion of the army is worth more than that of the people of Richmond, or of people out of it."

Indeed, Pegram had lost all faith in Southerners outside the military, including his own family. Only a veteran, in his view, could evaluate the progress of the war. "You are so completely surrounded by croakers & cowards," he told his sister, that it was not surprising "the mind is so excited with rumours, conceived in their craven hearts, and spread by every idle tongue." Because of disloyal people, Pegram warned Mary, "that you cannot look coolly or dispassionately on anything." He blamed the nation's troubles on those who failed to discharge their duty to the Confederacy and to God. Providence would not reject the South, Pegram maintained, because Southerners were God's chosen people, embarked upon a holy crusade to free themselves from the immoral North. If Willy harbored any anxieties about the Confederacy's future, they stemmed from a fear that certain elements of the South had betrayed the dominant worldview of the planter class.

Three days after he sent his letter to Mary, Pegram informed his brother James West that neither of their sisters had recovered from the shock of John's death. On a happier note, though, Willy told Jimmy that he recently had learned from General Gordon of his great success at "raising your negro regiment": Pegram's brother "had already gotten a large number [of blacks], & had marched them through Richmond to the entrenchments." The Confederate Congress had indeed approved the incorporation of blacks into the army on March 13, but emancipation became part of the plan only when President Davis issued General Order No. 14 ten days later. This gave bondsmen the rights of freemen if they entered the Confederate army—an act, according to one historian, that "transformed an ambiguous public law into a radical public policy."[59]

Before the president broadened the scope of the congressional plan, Pegram expressed his full support for raising black troops. He complimented James West on March 17 for "being the first to make the start." Pegram sensed that the recruitment of slaves met "with general approbation" in the entire army. Some of the best officers under Lee, the artillerist discovered, "are trying to get commands in the Corps D'Afrique."[60] Pegram's approval of arming slaves—

an apparent reversal of his earlier attitude toward the sight of blacks carrying weapons—reflected his overriding commitment to Confederate nationhood. His willingness to tamper with the system that supported his class position and defined the South's political economy attested to his overriding desire to form a nation independent of the North. But at the same time Pegram understood the enlistment of slaves in the army as a temporary war measure, one that implied no final rejection of the peculiar institution.

By the end of March Grant had prepared yet another strike against the Southside Railroad. To secure the vital lifeline, Lee ordered George E. Pickett to deploy 6,000 men at Five Forks, where the White Oak Road intersected the Ford Road. Pegram accompanied Pickett's force with four cannon from the Crenshaw Artillery and two pieces from Carpenter's Battery, the remainder of the battalion's guns filling the line near Burgess's Mill. Before Pickett's column began its journey on March 30, Pegram and McCabe reported to General Richard H. Anderson's headquarters. There they saw Heth and Lee, who appeared to be in a foul humor, riding down the lines. While the young officers waited for orders, they "went into an abandoned cabin and read our Bible." The previous fall Pegram had written of his adjutant: "I don't know any young man whom I admire altogether as much as Gordon McCabe. He has more information than anyone of his age I ever saw. He is my ordnance officer, but in order to go into battle, does the duties of adjutant also; and is excessively gallant." "We study the Bible together a great deal," he added, and "I enjoy his company very much."[61]

After Pegram and McCabe discussed the scripture, Willy rode with Lee "toward the enemy to reconnoiter." Orders for Pegram to accompany Pickett's division to the extreme right of the army arrived at 11:00 A.M. According to McCabe, everyone knew that Fitzhugh Lee's cavalry "needed us badly" and that "the utmost rapidity of march was demanded of us." Moving at once, Pegram and his adjutant left their blankets and rations near Burgess's Mill, expecting to return before nightfall. Pegram could have stayed with the bulk of his command at the mill, but McCabe recalled that Willy "would always go where there was the likeliest chance of fighting: so he elected to go with these six guns."[62]

The men managed to maintain high spirits despite a heavy rain. Sheridan's cavalry harassed Pickett's exposed flank for most of the day. Instead of pushing on, Pickett repeatedly stopped the column and formed lines of battle, halts that annoyed Pegram greatly because his cannon inevitably sank into the sloppy road. While his teamsters whipped their horses in an attempt to pry the guns loose from the mud during one of the halts, Willy and McCabe galloped toward the sound of rattling carbines. Union troopers swarmed on all sides of Pickett's force, but fortunately their inaccurate fire missed Pegram and McCabe. Pegram's six pieces and the rest of Pickett's infantry reached the Forks around

Figure 16. William Gordon McCabe (1841–1920), Pegram's trusted adjutant. "I don't know any young man whom I admire altogether as much as Gordon McCabe," Pegram wrote in 1865. "His Christian character is beautiful" and "I enjoy his company very much." (Photograph from *Memories and Memorials of William Gordon McCabe,* by Armistead Gordon, Old Dominion Press, 1925)

4:30 in the afternoon. "Wet, hungry, cold and sleepy," Pegram and McCabe lay next to their campfire without an oilcloth or blanket.[63]

A cold rain awakened Pegram and his cannoneers about three o'clock the next morning. A hungry Willy stood with McCabe near their men's fire until the sun glimmered above the trees. By eight o'clock Pickett started his men toward Dinwiddie Court House. Along the way Pegram passed his father's childhood home, Bonneville. Sheridan's cavalry contested the advance most of the day, but Pegram was given little opportunity to employ his artillery. As twilight faded and blackness enveloped the pine forests of Dinwiddie County, Pickett's command lay within half a mile of the courthouse. "While still in full flush of pursuit orders came to halt" the Confederate advance, which prompted "unspeakable amazement" in Pegram and McCabe. Both artillerists agreed that Pickett should push Sheridan past the courthouse, seize the Boydton Plank Road, and assume a position "squarely in the rear of Grant's troops."[64]

Unlike his excessively ardent subordinates, Pickett was worried, and perhaps prudently enough, about the location of the Union Fifth Corps. Finding himself eight miles south of Five Forks and fearing the enemy might cut off his retreat, Pickett ordered his sleepy soldiers back on the road at two in the morning. They passed over ground gained the previous day and arrived at the Forks near sunrise. "Regret exceedingly your forced withdrawal," Lee informed Pickett on April 1, "and your inability to hold the advantage you had gained." He sternly warned his subordinate to *"hold Five Forks at all hazards."* The Southside Railroad must be protected.[65]

Unfortunately, the terrain around the Forks offered few defensive advantages to Pickett. Lacking high ground for artillery, Pegram reluctantly posted the two guns from Carpenter's Battery and one from the Crenshaw Artillery in some woods at the Forks. McCabe asserted that his pieces *"commanded nothing* but the *intervening* road[s]" at the junction, and begged Willy to protest to Pickett. But Pegram's "rigid creed was, 'always obey orders.'" Still bitter about the placement of the guns after the war, McCabe claimed that Pickett "knew far more about brands of whisky than he did about the uses of artillery."[66]

The Confederates strengthened their position with some light breastworks. A soldier who spotted Pegram placing his cannon at the Forks thought he "looked like the god of war" mounted on his white horse, his gold spectacles on his nose. After making final adjustments, Pegram took his three other cannon to Pickett's right near the Gilliam field. The surrounding area resembled the bucolic South before the war. A broad meadow lay before them, with an "old-fashioned Virginia mansion that gleamed white" through the pines. Apple and peach trees, in full bloom, emerged through the "delicious haze so common in lowland Virginia." It was close to ten o'clock, and Pegram and McCabe had located no food except some parched corn stolen from the horses' feed. Luckily, though, they soon received some bread and meat from Henry Lee, an old friend from the University of Virginia.[67]

Their feast abruptly ended when Sheridan's cavalry appeared at the edge of the Gilliam field, only eight hundred yards away from Pegram's pieces. One Confederate gunner "made a splendid shot, bursting a shell just in front of the colours." Before the Northern troopers darted back into the woods, Captain James Knox of the Thirtieth Virginia warned Willy: "You cannot do any good there now, get off your horse, you are too good a mark & come here with us." "I am not going to stay here long," Pegram replied, "I have other artillery elsewhere." As soon as the fighting ended at the Gilliam field, blasts of musketry sounded from the center of the line. Pegram and McCabe rode back toward the Forks. Amid heavy firing, Willy demanded that McCabe dismount, but the latter refused, offering the comment that he would stay on his horse as long as Pegram remained mounted. But then, just as the muzzles of his three cannon grew warm, the Federal troopers disengaged.[68]

Infantrymen at the Forks began singing "Dixie" and "Bonnie Blue Flag" as

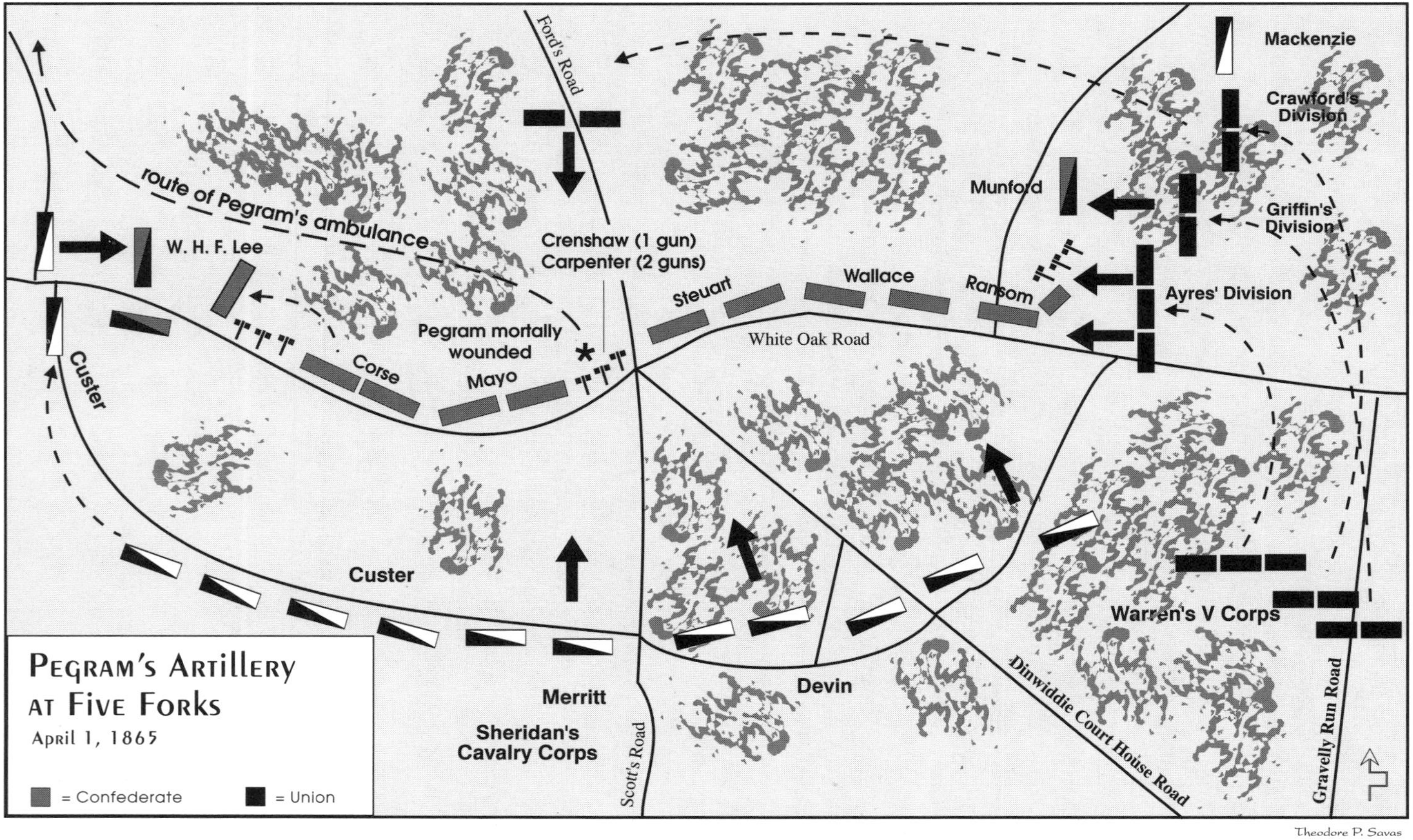
Pegram's Artillery at Five Forks
April 1, 1865
= Confederate
= Union
Ford's Road
route of Pegram's ambulance
W. H. F. Lee
Crenshaw (1 gun)
Carpenter (2 guns)
Pegram mortally wounded
Steuart
Wallace
Ransom
Munford
Mackenzie
Crawford's Division
Griffin's Division
Ayres' Division
White Oak Road
Corse
Mayo
Custer
Custer
Merritt
Sheridan's Cavalry Corps
Scott's Road
Devin
Dinwiddie Court House Road
Warren's V Corps
Gravelly Run Road
Theodore P. Savas

Map 15.

Pegram and Gordon returned to their section near the Gilliam field. Exhausted from being in the saddle for three straight days, Willy slept on ground granted in 1665 to his ancestor Robert Coleman. McCabe occupied his time with a copy of the *Richmond Examiner*. Some of Pegram's cannoneers cooked their food, others sprawled in the grass, talking and laughing. A bright April sun cast a warm peacefulness over the field until an eruption of musketry at four o'clock shattered the deceptively tranquil afternoon. Some 17,000 men of Warren's Fifth Corps had crossed the White Oak Road and overrun the exposed Confederate left flank. Even as his line collapsed and Confederate soldiers fled to the northwest, Pickett was enjoying a shad bake with Generals Fitzhugh Lee and Thomas L. Rosser just above Hatcher's Run. Not until Pickett saw one of his couriers captured by the Federals on the Ford Road did the festivities come to an end. Bending low on the right flank of his horse for protection from the enemy's muskets, Pickett miraculously ran the gauntlet of fire to the Forks.[69]

As soon as Pegram and McCabe heard the explosion of gunfire, they leapt onto their horses and hurried "at full speed" to the sound of firing. Sheridan's dismounted cavalrymen had pressed to within thirty yards of the Forks by the time the officers reached their men and were laying down a withering fire with Spencer carbines. Pegram's gunners responded by hurling double rounds of canister three times a minute at the Northerners. "Our officers were as cool as if on parade," McCabe wrote, "and the men were serving their guns with a precision and rapidity beyond all praise." He grimly added that the "enemy would pay dearly for every inch they gained there."[70]

Pegram and McCabe remained the only mounted officers in the area. Willy typically exposed himself to enemy fire. "Never shall I forget," McCabe wrote six days later, "the sweet serenity of his face as he rode erect to the very front of the line." The young colonel remained motionless between two of his guns as his cannoneers worked their pieces with mechanical rhythm. "Fire your canister low, men," he shouted above the din of battle. Suddenly, Pegram reeled from his saddle and collapsed on the ground. "Oh! Gordon, I am mortally wounded," he cried out, "take me off the field."[71] A bullet had pierced his left arm and passed through his side. McCabe dismounted immediately and rushed to Pegram's aid. The musketry had intensified, converging on the Forks from the front, left, and rear. Bullets thudded into the trees around the wounded colonel and his adjutant, as a few cannoneers and battery horses fell to the ground around them.

McCabe called for a litter corps. The firing had become so heavy that the two stretcher-bearers cowered on the ground until Pegram's adjutant threatened "to hurt them if they did not take Colonel Pegram up and carry him off." As McCabe ushered Willy behind the lines, he caught sight of Pickett and thought him "thoroughly 'rattled.'" The general was yelling to his officers in "disarrayed tones to get out the best way they could." Retaining his own com-

Figure 17. Five Forks. Pegram was mortally wounded near the modern sign marking route 613. His cannon were facing the postbellum house. (Author's photograph.)

posure, McCabe returned to his cannoneers and reiterated the need to fire their canister low. He then returned to Pegram, who pressed his adjutant's hand and said: "Tell mother & both my sisters that I commend them to God's protection." McCabe had Pegram placed in an ambulance that traversed the quarter mile between two parallel lines of battle before turning off the Ford Road and heading west through a grove of pines. By the time the wounded colonel departed the field, Warren's soldiers had swung around the Confederate rear and cleared a path to the Southside Railroad. The capital of the Confederacy was doomed.[72]

Amid the tide of fugitives, McCabe cradled his dying comrade to prevent the jolting wagon from "hurting his wounds." Willy could hear the salvos of his artillery pounding in the background. That he could not be with his cannon must have been as excruciating to him as his wound. He had once promised that he never would lose a single cannon to the enemy unless his dead body lay in front of it. Now, as life drained from Pegram's body, Federals swarmed

Figure 18. Lithograph depicting the mortal wounding of William Pegram at Five Forks. (From *Christ in Camp,* by J. William Jones, B. F. Johnson & Co., 1887)

around his three fieldpieces at the Forks, capturing men and ordnance, although the three guns at the Gilliam field were spared. McCabe and Pegram prayed and exchanged a few words in the ambulance. "Gordon," said Willy, "I am perfectly resigned, if it is God's will to take me, but it will be such a blow to them at home." "My God," McCabe cried out, "why hast Thou forsaken me!" "Don't say that Gordon, it is not right," Pegram quickly replied. Bending to kiss his friend "over and over again," McCabe called Pegram by his given name for the first time: "Oh! Willie, I did not know how much I loved you until now." "But I did, Gordon," Willy said.[73]

Pegram's ambulance covered the ten miles from the Forks before creaking into Ford's Depot around ten o'clock that night. Obtaining the only available room with a bed, Pegram rested above Colonel Joshua H. Hudson of the Twenty-sixth South Carolina, who also had received a grievous wound that day. Hudson begged for the morphine that McCabe had reserved for Pegram. But Pegram's suffering was so severe, McCabe told the South Carolinian that he considered it his duty to reserve the small supply for Willy. Word then spread inside the house that Federal cavalry had approached the area, whereupon McCabe sent the colonel's horse, overcoat, spurs, and spectacles off to prevent their capture. All the able-bodied men fled the building except McCabe, who stayed with Willy for his final ordeal.[74]

Pegram had fallen asleep about an hour after being placed in bed. A stupor followed, from which he never emerged. McCabe "could only sit by him & smooth his hair & kiss him over & over again & call him a thousand fond names." As best he could, McCabe "bound up his wounds" and "moistened his lips with water." Falling on his knees, he prayed that God might "spare his life to me." At eight o'clock on April 2, a Sunday morning, Willy "died as gently as an infant." A desolate McCabe dug his friend's grave behind the house with the help of some black servants. He then laid Pegram "out in his uniform and read the burial service over him." "Oh! what a splendid soldier he looked," wrote McCabe to Willy's sister Mary.[75]

Advancing Northern cavalry shortened McCabe's final moments with his comrade. Forced to leave Willy and mount his horse, he "made his escape" as Federal pickets "shot at me repeatedly." Amid the shattered fragments of the Army of Northern Virginia, McCabe became infuriated at the sight of "the crowd of stragglers" streaming toward the Blue Ridge Mountains. He could not "give up this beloved Virginia because of the faint-heartedness & cowardice of these men, who have deserted their colours." "If the men will only remain at their posts & trust in God," he asserted, "everything would go right." McCabe added bitterly that "if we lose our country, it is our own fault"—a sentiment Pegram surely would have shared.[76]

McCabe sympathized with the soldiers "who have followed for four years the shining sabre of my peerless Colonel. Hungry, wet, with blistered feet, without sleep, they have stood by their guns & fought with a desperation, a superb courage that I never dreamed of." McCabe believed he remained in close communion with Pegram during the retreat. "Day by day, night after night, on this terrible retreat," he wrote, "I have talked fondly to his spirit, & I know that he has been with me, & that he would rather have died than lived to have seen this day." McCabe sensed that his own life might end soon and that he would be reunited with Willy. But if he survived, McCabe promised to "follow the 'Battle Flag' to the gulf, even as he would have done." [77]

HE FELL IN THE DISCHARGE OF HIS DUTY,

AND DIED WITH THE PHILOSOPHY OF A CHRISTIAN

CLOSE TO TEN O'CLOCK ON THE MORNING OF DECEMBER 6, 1865, FRIENDS and relatives of Virginia Pegram filed into her home on Linden Row. The remains of her youngest son had arrived in Richmond earlier in the morning from his humble grave in Dinwiddie County for reinterment in Hollywood Cemetery. "While in the press of momentous events, and the general grief with which the whole community is stricken by the losses of the great strife through which we have p[assed]," the *Richmond Whig* had written of Willy Pegram a day earlier, "we cannot pass by the occasion without adding our tribute of respect to the memory of this gallant soldier and Christian gentleman." As the paper went on to say: "No man has left behind him a more spotless record or a fairer name. Exposing himself almost recklessly in every battle, and promoted often for courage and skill, he went through unscathed, until he fell at last, with the cause he had struggled so gallantly to maintain." A Norfolk correspondent echoed the sentiments of the Richmond paper, writing that Pegram "fell in the discharge of his duty, and died with the philosophy of a Christian and dignity of a soldier. . . . Peace to his ashes."[1]

At the time of his death, Pegram ranked as one of the army's most prominent artillerists. Fellow battalion commander John Cheves Haskell believed that many shared his view of Pegram as "the best officer of artillery in the Army of Northern Virginia."[2] Sheer hard fighting and fearlessness under fire had earned Willy respect from his men as well as accolades from his superiors. His swift rise from sergeant to full colonel stands as an impressive achievement, especially in an army that was filled with officers who demonstrated a remarkable capacity to lead men in battle.

Pegram distinguished himself in Lee's army by his ability to deploy his cannon as an offensive weapon. "As commander of an artillery battalion he built up a reputation second to none for effective handling of his guns," a veteran of the Army of Northern Virginia, Robert Stiles, wrote of Pegram, "his favorite method, where practicable, being to rush to close quarters with the enemy and open at the shortest possible range." While Willy well understood the decisive role that his guns could play by charging them into the enemy, he "admitted that it seemed deadly, but insisted that it saved life in the end." When Pegram initially employed this tactic—at Mechanicsville, Malvern Hill, and Cedar Mountain—he almost destroyed his battery, while at the same time inflicting little damage against the Federals. Willy, however, learned from these setbacks, even as his superiors, the newspapers, and his men were giving his performance during these early battles high marks.[3]

Figure 19. William Pegram's grave at Hollywood Cemetery, Richmond. (Photograph courtesy of Tara M. Carmichael)

By 1863, though, Pegram had matured into a reliable battalion commander who tempered his aggressiveness with sound tactical judgement. At Chancellorsville, Gettysburg, the Weldon Railroad on August 21, and Second Reams Station, Pegram carefully pushed his batteries forward with adequate infantry support, allowing his men to punish the Federals without jeopardizing his entire command. At the Crater, Pegram took a more circuitous route to the battlefield because Union fire raked the most direct road, a decision that he might not have made earlier in the war.

While Pegram showed increasing prudence in handling his batteries as the war progressed, this never detracted from his enthusiasm for combat. He almost always requested that superiors place his battalion in positions where it could see the most fighting. On the first day of Gettysburg, for example, Pegram literally begged Hill to take his battalion out of reserve and allow him to accompany Heth into town. In another instance, Willy rushed into Hill's tent the day after he had virtually annihilated his battery at Mechanicsville. "I am Pegram of Pegram's battalion. I bring you a message from my men," he boldly reported. "In recognition of service done on yesterday, what is left of Pegram's battalion claims as its right the most exposed position on the firing line this morning."[4]

Renowned throughout the army for his eagerness to engage the enemy, Pegram sometimes elicited remarks from Lee's infantrymen such as "there's going to be fight, for her comes that damn little man with the 'specs.'"[5] It was true that Pegram enjoyed battle, but he also believed it a soldier's responsibility to seek the most dangerous post. Shirking combat constituted a serious transgression, one that violated duty to God, nation, community, and family. Devotion to and love for these people and these ideas propelled Willy into battle.

Pegram combined his fondness for battle with the gifts of a natural leader. He gained the devotion of his men by exhibiting utter contempt for the enemy under fire. In a war where personal actions often had a decisive impact on the outcome of events, Pegram realized that his behavior could inspire his men to similar feats. "There was a certain magnetism about Willie Pegram that impressed all who came into his presence," observed one of his cannoneers. "Never excited, possessing at all times that perfect equipoise so much prized in a commander, he embodied all the qualities of a soldier. While a strict disciplinarian, he was ever thoughtful of his men."[6] In virtually every battle he performed conspicuously. At Mechanicsville, Malvern Hill, Cedar Mountain, Fredericksburg, and Chancellorsville he led by example, cheering on his men, running among his cannon, and assisting his gunners when the crews became depleted.

Although by 1863 many Northern and Southern officers had begun to question the value of recklessly exposing themselves to the enemy, yet Pegram articulated in words and demonstrated in action the same notions of courage that he had espoused at the beginning of the war. When many people outside the army considered the Southern cause doomed by the fall of 1864, Pegram fought on with a burning intensity. At Pegram's farm on September 30, for example, Willy spurred his horse in front of his cannon and tried to rally the disorganized infantry who were supporting his batteries. The next day at the Squirrel Level Road he again left his guns and rushed into the thick of fighting to restore the morale of some infantry regiments. Following these two battles, he informed his sister Mary that he had "never been under more infantry fire than in these fights." Indeed, Gordon McCabe believed that, next to Jeb Stuart, Willy had probably been under fire more than "any man in the Army of Northern Virginia." His cannoneers often remarked that there was not a bullet "moulded that could hit him."[7]

Pegram himself was little concerned whether such a bullet existed. His unshakable faith in God strengthened his resolve in battle, for it assured him that heaven awaited any man who died in this holy cause. Even during the later stages of the war, when it appeared the Confederacy had little chance of achieving victory, he did not despair. Religion did not prompt Willy to evaluate critically the morality or righteousness of either the Confederacy or his accustomed way of life. In his case, as in that of countless other young Southern officers, his religious convictions worked to form him into an ardent nationalist, whose commitment to the Confederacy never waned.

It is in fact unusual for people to step outside their own experience and critically judge the assumptions and values with which they grew up—even if they were intimately associated with an institution as intrinsically abhorrent as slavery. Because Pegram believed that God had ordained Southerners his chosen people before the war, he also reasoned that Providence would never abandon the Confederacy, a nation that embodied the home of Christian civilization. Willy could thus interpret military reverses as temporary setbacks that were simply part of God's plan to test the faith of Southerners. Similarly, he pointed to civilians who abandoned God or tried to profit from the war and challenge the antebellum social order as the source of divine wrath. It never entered Pegram's mind that the support of slavery, or some other moral sin, could possibly explain Confederate defeat on the battlefield. Simple faith and trust in God, Pegram maintained, would bring independence and the halcyon days of the antebellum era.

Pegram was neither a zealot nor a fanatic. Rather, he resembled many other Southerners who went to war in 1861 believing the South had embarked on a mission to preserve a superior way of life that had been endangered by the godless North. Whether one accepts that real differences existed between the two regions is beside the point. The fact remains that, from the perspective of men like Willy, the Republican party—with its attacks against the expansion of slavery and its emphasis on social mobility—threatened the South. Once the Republicans had gained control of the White House, Pegram feared, his community, home, and family would be at their mercy. The election of Lincoln thus placed more than personal honor at risk. Were the new president's ideas to win general acceptance, the traditions, values, and way of life that had been part of Pegram's family for generations and gave meaning to his own life would face a precarious existence. The South's antebellum class structure and social relations might eventually unravel. As Reconstruction demonstrated, Pegram's fears were not without merit. In the end, William Pegram gave his life in defense of a nation that upheld a social order that he cherished, respected, and, most of all, believed to have been ordained by God. Pegram's letters testify to his devotion to the Confederacy and its principles, but his actions in battle provide the most powerful evidence of his commitment to Southern independence.

Less than a year after the death of John Pegram, Willy's mother, sisters, and one surviving brother gathered again at the family plot above the waters of the

James River. There, buried next to his oldest brother, lay the young man who had entered the war an inconspicuous student from the University of Virginia and had left the world as a man renowned for his force of character, piety, and courage. Writing to Willy's sister Mary on April 7, 1865, about the death of her brother, William Gordon McCabe captured the feelings of loss and despair that must have gripped Willy's comrades, family, and friends. "He died as he had lived, without fear or reproach—the truest Christian, the best friend, the most splendid soldier in all the world!"[8]

NOTES

BIBLIOGRAPHY

INDEX

NOTES

ABBREVIATIONS USED IN NOTES

AL	Alderman Library, Manuscript Department, University of Virginia, Charlottesville, Va.
Compiled Service Records of Confederate Generals	Compiled Service Records of Confederate Generals and Officers and Nonregimental Men, National Archives, Washington, D.C.
Compiled Service Records of Confederate Soldiers	Compiled Service Records of Confederate Soldiers Who Served in Organizations from the State of Virginia, National Archives, Washington, D.C.
DU	William R. Perkins Library, Manuscript Department, Duke University, Durham, N.C.
EBL	Eleanor Brockenbrough Library, Museum of the Confederacy, Richmond
Munford-Ellis Papers (GWM)	Munford-Ellis Papers, George W. Munford Division, William R. Perkins Library, Duke University, Durham, N.C.
Munford-Ellis Papers (TTM)	Munford-Ellis Papers, Thomas T. Munford Division, William R. Perkins Library, Duke University, Durham, N.C.
NA	National Archives, Washington, D.C.
OR	*The War of the Rebellion: A Compilation of the Official Records of the Union and Confederate Armies.* U.S. War Department, Washington, D.C.
ORN	*Official Records of the Union and Confederate Navies in the War of the Rebellion.* U.S. War Department, Washington, D.C.
P-J-M Papers	Pegram-Johnson-McIntosh Papers, Virginia Historical Society, Richmond
Ridley Papers	The Ridley Family of Southampton County, Va., Papers, 1776–1897, Virginia Historical Society, Richmond
SCL	South Caroliniana Library, University of South Carolina, Columbia, S.C.
SHC	Southern Historical Collection, Wilson Library, University of North Carolina, Chapel Hill, N.C.

VHS	Virginia Historical Society, Richmond
VSL	Virginia State Library, Richmond
WCL	William L. Clements Library, University of Michigan, Ann Arbor

INTRODUCTION

1. See Mathews, *Religion in the Old South*, p. 129. I also accept Mathews's definition of evangelicalism as "a personal relationship with God in Christ, established through the direct action of the Holy Spirit, an action which elicits in the believer a profoundly emotional conversion experience" (p. xvi). According to Mathews, evangelical preaching has as its focus "a direct, psychological assault upon sin and the equally direct and much more comforting offer of personal salvation" (p. 129).

2. This overarching sense of unity explains why the Presbyterian James Henley Thornwell's ideas found acceptance throughout the South, among Christians of various denominations. Even Pegram's own minister, Charles F. E. Minnigerode, preached at Methodist and Presbyterian churches despite his official position as a priest in an Episcopal parish. See Farmer, *Metaphysical Confederacy*; Henry Lee Curry, "Confederate Careers of James Armstrong Duncan, Moses Drury Hoge, and Charles Frederic Ernest Minnigerode" (Ph.D. diss., Emory University, 1971). On interdenominational agreement on proslavery Christian doctrine, see Mathews, *Religion in the Old South*, p. 130; Loveland, *Southern Evangelicals and the Social Order, 1800–1860*, pp. ix–x, 201–2; Maddex, "'The Southern Apostasy' Revisited: The Significance of Proslavery Christianity," p. 139; Genovese and Fox-Genovese, "Religious Ideals of Southern Slave Society," p. 12.

3. Mathews, *Religion in the Old South*, p. 130.

4. See ibid., p. 167.

5. In conceptualizing generation, I have been informed by the work of Marvin Rintala and Alan B. Spitzer, who argue that between the ages of seventeen and twenty-five a political outlook is basically formed and a group consciousness established. Generational consciousness must demonstrate a relationship between the historical-social process and the cohort's formative years. I consider Southern men born between 1833 and 1843 to be part of the same generation because they became "political beings" during the 1850s. Political turmoil over slavery, the emphasis on a Southern education for Southern youth, and rapid modernization provided Pegram and his generation with a distinct perspective on their society's place within a world that generally embraced free labor. See Spitzer, "Historical Problem of Generations;" Rintala, "Generation." See also Genovese and Fox-Genovese, "Religious Ideals of Southern Slave Society," pp. 5–6.

6. Although Charles F. E. Minnigerode does not rank as one of the South's leading religious thinkers, he offered an interpretation of the South, the Confederacy, and Northern reformers consistent with the dominant system of thought in the Old South. See Curry, "Confederate Careers of James Armstrong Duncan, Moses Drury Hoge, and Charles Frederic Ernest Minnigerode," pp. 124–26; Charles F. E. Minnigerode, "The Great Victory," *Daily Richmond Examiner*, July 29, 1861, p. 3; "Dr. Minnigerode's Sermon," *Southern Churchman*, Feb. 22, 1865, p. 1. While Pegram spent most of his time at the University of Virginia in James P. Holcombe's classroom, he must also have heard the lectures or read the works of Albert T. Bledsoe. On Holcombe's view of slavery and the evils of "progress," see Holcombe, *An Address, On the Right of the State to Institute Slavery*; for Bledsoe's contribution to the proslavery debate, see Elliott, ed., *Cotton is King and Pro-slavery Arguments*, pp. 271–458.

7. William Pegram to Mary Evens Pegram Anderson, Feb. 11, 1864; William Pegram to Virginia Johnson Pegram McIntosh, July 14, 1864, P-J-M Papers.

8. For Pegram's views on the North and secession, see William Pegram to Virginia Johnson Pegram McIntosh, Nov. 10, 1860; William Pegram to Mary Evans Pegram Anderson, Feb. 18, 1861; William Pegram to John Pegram, Feb. 11,

1862, P-J-M Papers; William Pegram to Charles Ellis Munford, April 18, 1861, Munford-Ellis Papers (GWM). On Pegram's perception of cultural differences with the North as typical of most Southerners, see Wiley, *Life of Johnny Reb,* pp. 15–16; Jimerson, *Private Civil War,* pp. 124–27.

9. Foner, *Free Soil, Free Labor, Free Men,* pp. 300, 313–17.

10. William Pegram to Mary Evans Pegram Anderson, Feb. 18, 1861; William Pegram to Virginia Johnson Pegram McIntosh, Nov. 10, 1860, P-J-M Papers; William Pegram to Charles Ellis Munford, April 18, 1861, Munford-Ellis Papers (GWM).

11. On the Whigs' support of economic development and their belief in social inequality, see Oakes, *Slavery and Freedom,* pp. 122–23; Cole, *Whig Party in the South,* pp. 58, 62. See also Samuel Bassett French, "A Biographical Sketch of General James West Pegram," Samuel Bassett French Biographical Sketches, VSL. On the fears of slaveholders, see Genovese, *Slaveholders' Dilemma,* pp. 4, 7.

12. Faust, *Creation of Confederate Nationalism,* p. 28. There are countless examples of Pegram's zeal in battle and his reasons for fighting so desperately. For one of the best, see William Pegram to Virginia Johnson Pegram McIntosh, Aug. 14, 1862, P-J-M Papers. On notions of courage in the Civil War and how these were related to religion, see Linderman, *Embattled Courage,* pp. 158–60.

13. Secondary works on weak Confederate morale and nationalism tend to generalize about white Southerners without accounting for class and regional differences, whereas in my view Pegram represents but one slice of Southern society: Virginia slaveholders born between 1833 and 1843. Given that most of the extant secondary sources examine the disaffection felt among yeomen and poor whites, we need more studies that explore the varied reactions of specific segments of the slaveholding class to the exigencies of war. For example, many slaveholders expressed dissent over the Confederate government's prosecution of the war. It is thus a mistake to assume that all slaveholders supported the Confederacy to the end. Studies that emphasize weak Confederate morale and nationalism include Escott, *After Secession;* Owens and Cooke, eds., *Old South in the Crucible of War;* Wiley, *Road to Appomattox.*

14. As George B. Forgie has noted, Americans socialized in the early republic possessed a strong physical and psychological attachment to the revolutionary generation and to the Union. In contrast, Southerners of Pegram's generation were not intimately familiar with the founding fathers, with the result that their loyalty to Union lacked the emotional commitment characteristic of previous generations. See Forgie, *Patricide in the House Divided,* pp. 3–7; see also McCardell, *Idea of a Southern Nation,* p. 178.

15. William Pegram to Mary Evans Pegram Anderson, Aug. 1, 1864; William Pegram to Mary Evans Pegram Anderson, Oct. 5, 1864; William Pegram to Virginia Johnson Pegram, Oct. 28, 1864; William Pegram to Mary Evans Pegram Anderson, March 14, 1865, P-J-M Papers.

16. Mitchell, "Creation of Confederate Loyalties," p. 100.

17. William Pegram to Mary Evans Pegram Anderson, July 21, 1864, P-J-M Papers.

18. Stephen Dodson Ramseur to David Schenck, Oct. 10, 1864, Stephen Dodson Ramseur Papers, SHC.

19. William Pegram to Virginia Johnson Pegram, Oct. 28, 1864, P-J-M Papers.

20. On weak Confederate morale and guilt over slavery, see in particular Coulter, *Confederate States of America, 1861–1865,* p. 566; Stampp, *Imperiled Union,* pp. 252, 255, 264; Oakes, *Ruling Race,* pp. 102, 119; Beringer et al., *Why the South Lost the Civil War,* pp. 360–61; Faust, *Creation of Confederate Nationalism,* pp. 41–42; Mohr, *On the Threshold of Freedom,* pp. 235–71; Shattuck, *A Shield and Hiding Place,* p. 9. In contrast, Eugene D. Genovese has vigorously argued that by 1860 few slaveholders felt guilt over slavery: see his *World the Slaveholders Made,* pp. 146–47.

ONE: "THE GOD OF ALL NATIONS"
WILL DIRECT ALL THINGS FOR THE BEST

1. Kulikoff, *Tobacco and Slaves*, pp. 47–48; Jones, *Dinwiddie County*, p. 46.

2. Jones, *Dinwiddie County*, pp. 49–52; Simmons, *Pegrams of Virginia*, pp. 29–32, 43–44, 47–49. Dinwiddie County tax records from the late 1820s confirm John Pegram's status as a well-to-do planter. He owned thirty slaves in 1825–26 and twenty-nine the next two years. Taxes on his personal property were exceptionally high during his period—an average of $16.80 per year, although his tax records for the years between 1829 and 1831 could not be located (entries for John Pegram, "Personal Property Taxes for Dinwiddie County, Virginia, 1825–1828," VSL).

3. Mary Evans Pegram Anderson, "113 West Franklin Street," p. 2, manuscript in the P-J-M Papers; Samuel Bassett French, "A Biographical Sketch of General James West Pegram," Samuel Bassett French Biographical Sketches, VSL.

4. French, "A Biographical Sketch of General James West Pegram."

5. Simmons, *Pegrams of Virginia*, p. 56; see also Hervey, *Racing in America, 1665–1865*, 2:78, 79, 80, 85, 86.

6. Anderson, "113 West Franklin Street," p. 2; Hervey, *Racing in America*, 2:78; entries for James West Pegram, "Personal Property Taxes for the City of Richmond, 1840–1844," VSL. Marriage between planters and financiers occurred frequently in the antebellum South. As Eugene D. Genovese has effectively argued, merchant capital, far from undermining or revolutionizing an existing regime, was inherently conservative in nature and thus often buttressed the old ruling order. Although Pegram's financial and particularly his commercial interests might have clashed with those of his father and relatives because of his position in the bank, he still worked within a system where political power and capital rested in slaves and land. In most cases Southern bankers only granted loans for socially acceptable goals, namely for the purchase of slaves or land, and for other agrarian pursuits. See Genovese, *Political Economy of Slavery*, pp. 20–21. On the role of merchant capital in Southern society, see also the prologue and chap. 3 in Fox-Genovese and Genovese, *Fruits of Merchant Capital*.

7. Christian, *Richmond: Her Past and Present*, pp. 141–42; Anderson, "113 West Franklin Street," p. 3; Virginia Pegram's family Bible, now in the private possession of the estate of J. Rieman McIntosh.

8. Christian, *Richmond: Her Past and Present*, p. 146; "The Fighting Pegrams," unidentified and anonymous newspaper clipping, P-J-M Papers. Personal property tax records for the city of Richmond from 1840 to 1844 reveal a significant increase in the material prosperity of the Pegram household. After James West accepted the position of head banker in 1843, he purchased two additional slaves, making eight altogether, and an additional four-wheel carriage and two-wheel carriage. His taxes in 1843–44 averaged $42.07, an exceptionally high figure in comparison to the sums paid by most Richmonders.

9. Anderson, "113 West Franklin Street," pp. 3–4.

10. Unidentified author, "Eulogy to Virginia Johnson Pegram," p. 6; Henry Clay to William R. Johnson, Oct. 27, 1844, P-J-M Papers.

11. "Terrible Steamboat Disaster . . . ," *Richmond Whig and Public Advertiser*, Nov. 1, 1844, p. 1; "From New Albany, Indiana," *Richmond Daily Whig*, Nov. 1, 1844, p. 1; Anderson, "113 West Franklin Street," p. 4.

12. "Death of Gen. Pegram," *Richmond Whig and Public Advertiser*, Nov. 1, 1844, p. 1; "Death of Gen. Pegram," *Daily Richmond Enquirer*, Nov. 2, 1844, p. 1; "Resolution of Bank of Virginia," *Daily Richmond Enquirer*, Nov. 5, 1844, p. 1; Henry Clay to William Johnson, Oct. 27, 1844, P-J-M Papers; unidentified author, "Eulogy to Virginia Johnson Pegram," p. 7.

13. Unidentified author, "Eulogy to Virginia Pegram," pp. 3, 6; "Materials Relating to the Estate of James W. Pegram," Johnson Family Papers, VHS; Eliza Wilkins Bruce to James Coles Bruce, March 13, 1845, Berry Hill Bruce Papers, AL; Anderson, "113 West Franklin Street," p. 4.

14. The two letters written from Oakland by Virginia Pegram—the one dated Dec. 11, 1848, the other July 27, 1850, and both now located in the Johnson Family Papers, VHS—are the only record of the family's stay at William Johnson's

plantation; Meagher, *History of Education in Richmond*, p. 72.

15. Hervey, *Racing in America*, 2:79; Haskell, *Haskell Memoirs*, p. 83.

16. Heitman, *Historical Register and Dictionary of the United States Army*, 1:780; James West Pegram Jr. to Charles Ellis Munford, April 26, 1860, Munford-Ellis Papers (GWM).

17. T. C. DeLeon, *Belles, Beaux and Brains of the 60's*, pp. 125, 169; James West Pegram, Jr., to Charles Ellis Munford, May, 21, 1860, Munford-Ellis Papers (GWM).

18. Arthur Scrivenor, "Sketch of General James West Pegram and Descendants," Pegram Family Papers, SHC; Yeary, ed. and comp., *Reminiscences of the Boys in Gray*, p. 198.

19. Unidentified author, "Eulogy to Virginia Pegram," pp. 7–8; Haskell, *Haskell Memoirs*, p. 83; Stiles, *Four Years under Marse Robert*, p. 110.

20. Shattuck, *A Shield and Hiding Place*, pp. 2, 6. Pegram's faith in the Southern way of life and its stewardship under God is revealed time and time again in his wartime correspondence. One of the best examples is William Ransom Johnson Pegram to Virginia Johnson Pegram, Oct. 28, 1864, P-J-M Papers. On Southern religion generally, see Mathews, *Religion in the Old South*.

21. Samuel Bassett French, "Sketch of William Ransom Johnson Pegram," Samuel Bassett French Biographical Sketches, VSL; Yeary, ed. and comp., *Reminiscences of the Boys in Gray*, p. 198; Haskell, *Haskell Memoirs*, p. 83; Stiles, *Four Years under Marse Robert*, p. 110.

22. Hervey, *Racing in America*, 2:86–87; "Amount of Debts of the Estate of W. R. Johnson," April 15, 1850; "Estimate of W. R. Johnson's Estate, April 15, 1850," Johnson Family Papers, VHS. The public sale of most of his slaves and implements at Oakland in 1845, which yielded him more than $17,000, and the precipitous decline of his personal property taxes in Chesterfield County from $24.90 in 1836 to $6.37 in 1847 reflect a sharp reduction in Johnson's material possessions: see "Public Sales of Negroes, Stocks &c at Oakland," Johnson Family Papers, VHS; entries for William R. Johnson, "Personal Property Taxes for Chesterfield County, 1836–1847," VSL.

23. Meagher, *History of Education in Richmond*, pp. 72–73; unidentified author, "Eulogy to Virginia Pegram," pp. 8–9. According to the entries for Virginia Johnson Pegram in "Personal Property Taxes for the City of Richmond, 1851–1860," the Pegram family never really lacked for material comforts. Even before Virginia started her school in 1855 the family fared extremely well, even if they were not able to maintain the lifestyle typical of members of the planter class. Between 1851 and 1860 Virginia Pegram owned between seven to nine slaves, although none were males over the age of twenty-one. In 1854 the Pegrams' possessions were taxed at $8.80, an average sum for most middle-class families. Six years later, however, the tax collector appraised their personal property at $3,735 and levied a tax of $20.94, a dramatic increase that attests to the success of the Pegram school.

24. Meagher, *History of Education in Richmond*, pp. 72–73; Louisa B. Ridley Drewry to Elizabeth Norfleet Goodwyn Ridley, May 2, 1863, Ridley Papers, VHS; Eliza B. Sims Timberlake to Maria C. Sims, Nov. 17, 1863, Bailey Family Papers, VHS.

25. Unidentified author, "Eulogy to Virginia Pegram," p. 7; James West Pegram, Jr., to Charles Ellis Munford, Oct. 25, 1859, Munford-Ellis Papers (GWM); William Pegram to John Pegram, Jan. 25, 1860, P-J-M Papers. Willy commented that his mother had received so many applications that his Aunt Lelia would have to share a room with a girl named Lucy May, further noting that "they have scarcely a corner" in which to put additional guests.

26. Christian, *Richmond: Her Past and Present*, p. 167; Thomas, *Confederate State of Richmond*, pp. 20–21; DeLeon, *Four Years in Rebel Capitals*, p. 85.

27. Thomas, *Confederate State of Richmond*, p. 25; Mordecai, *Richmond in By-Gone Days*, pp. 214, 219–20; unidentified author, "Eulogy to Virginia Pegram," p. 9.

28. Johnson, *University Memorial*, p. 715; Worsham, *One of Jackson's Foot Cavalry*, pp. 1–2.

29. Heitman, *Historical Register and Dictionary of the United States Army*, 1:780; Samuel Bassett French, "Sketch of John Pegram," Samuel Bassett French Biographical Sketches, VSL; James West Pegram, Jr., to Charles Ellis Munford, May 21, 1860, Munford-Ellis Papers (GWM).

30. For a discussion of Republican party ideology, see Foner, *Free Soil, Free Labor, Free Men*.

On Pegram's fears over the Republican party, see William Pegram to Virginia Johnson Pegram McIntosh, Nov. 10, 1860, P-J-M Papers.

31. Christian, *Richmond: Her Past and Present,* pp. 201–3; "Speech of Governor Wise," *Daily Richmond Enquirer,* Oct. 25, 1859, p. 1; Manarin and Wallace, *Richmond Volunteers,* p. 231; William Pegram to John Pegram, Jan. 23, 1860, P-J-M Papers.

32. William Pegram to John Pegram, Jan. 23, 1860, P-J-M Papers.

33. See Genovese, *Political Economy of Slavery,* pp. 17–18. On Pegram's views regarding secession, see William Pegram to Virginia Johnson Pegram McIntosh, Nov. 10, 1860, P-J-M Papers.

34. Ferslew, comp., *Second Annual Directory for the City of Richmond* (Richmond, 1860), p. 177; McDowell, "Military Career of Colonel William Ransom Johnson Pegram, C.S.A." M.A. thesis, University of Richmond, 1964, pp. 6–7; "Parade of the 22d," semi-weekly *Richmond Enquirer,* Feb. 24, 1860, p. 1; William Pegram to John Combe Pegram, March 8, 1860, P-J-M Papers; James West Pegram, Jr., to Charles Ellis Munford, April 26, 1860, Munford-Ellis Papers (GWM).

35. William Pegram to John Pegram, Jan. 23, 1860, P-J-M Papers; James West Pegram, Jr., to Charles Ellis Munford, May 21, 1860, Munford-Ellis Papers (GWM)

36. Jordan, *Charlottesville and the University of Virginia,* pp. 3–4.

37. William Pegram to Virginia Johnson Pegram McIntosh, Nov. 10, 1860, P-J-M Papers; Johnson, *University Memorial,* p. 715.

38. Jordan, *Charlottesville and the University of Virginia,* p. 5; "University of Virginia Matriculation Register, 1856–1868," AL; *Catalogue of the University of Virginia, Session of 1860–'61,* pp. 36–37, 42–43; Patton, *Jefferson, Cabell, and the University of Virginia,* p. 199.

39. William Pegram to Mary Evans Pegram Anderson, Feb. 18, 1861, P-J-M Papers.

40. *Catalogue of the University of Virginia, Session of 1860–'61,* p. 22; Jordan, *Charlottesville and the University of Virginia,* pp. 6–7; Bruce, *History of the University of Virginia, 1819–1919,* 3:160–65.

41. Henry Lenoir to Fred [?], Nov. 9, 1860, Lenoir Family Papers, SHC.

42. Shanks, *Secession Movement in Virginia,* p. 115; William Pegram to Virginia Johnson Pegram McIntosh, Nov. 10, 1860, P-J-M Papers.

43. William Pegram to Virginia Johnson Pegram McIntosh, Nov. 10, 1860, P-J-M Papers.

44. Ibid.

45. Henry Lenoir to his mother, Jan. 20, 1860, Lenoir Family Papers, SHC; Johnson, *University Memorial,* p. 715; Bruce, *History of the University of Virginia,* 3:267; Patton, *Jefferson, Cabell, and the University of Virginia,* p. 204.

46. Patton, *Jefferson, Cabell, and the University of Virginia,* pp. 267–69; William Pegram to Mary Evans Pegram Anderson, Feb. 18, 1861, P-J-M Papers.

47. Patton, *Jefferson, Cabell, and the University of Virginia,* p. 207.

TWO: WE ARE GOING TO HAVE A TERRIBLE WAR

1. William Pegram to Charles Ellis Munford, April 18, 1861, Munford-Ellis Papers (GWM).

2. Ibid.

3. Ibid.; Jones quoted in Myers, *Children of Pride* (abr. ed.), p. 48. In his outrage over Carlile's prounion position, Pegram was overly optimistic about the unpleasant fate presumably awaiting this Northern sympathizer. Carlile not only escaped the noose but never even found himself behind bars: see *Dictionary of American Biography,* 3:493–94.

4. Worsham, *One of Jackson's Foot Cavalry,* pp. 2–3.

5. Ibid., p. 3–4.

6. *Fredericksburg News,* May 3, 1861, p. 2.

7. Compiled Service Records of Confederate Generals, roll 195; Worsham, *One of Jackson's Foot Cavalry,* p. 4.

8. William Pegram to Mary Evans Pegram Anderson, May 3, 1861, P-J-M Papers.

9. *Richmond Dispatch,* May 23, 1861, p. 2; *OR,* 2:867.

10. Ibid.

11. *Richmond Dispatch,* June 3, 1861, p. 2.

12. *ORN,* 4:490; *OR,* 2:56, 898.

13. *Fredericksburg News,* June 4, 1861, p. 2.

14. *ORN,* 4:501, 493; *Richmond Dispatch,* June 3, 1861, p. 2.

15. *OR,* 2:134.

16. See Freeman, *Lee's Lieutenants,* 1:27–34, 36; Chesnut, *Mary Chesnut's Civil War,* p. 476.

17. *OR,* 2:565.

18. Ibid.

19. Ibid., 2:565, 499, 476.

20. Howard, *Recollections and Opinions Concerning the Events,* pp. 40–41.

21. *OR,* 5:114–15.

22. "Caption of Events for Capt. Cayce's Company Virginia Light Artillery," Compiled Service Records of Confederate Soldiers (Cayce's Artillery), roll 276.

23. William Pegram to John Pegram, Feb. 11, 1862; William Pegram to Virginia Johnson Pegram McIntosh, April 3, 1862, P-J-M Papers.

24. William Pegram to John Pegram, Feb. 11, 1862, P-J-M Papers.

25. Stephen Dodson Ramseur to Ellen Richmond Ramseur, April 24, 1864, Stephen Dodson Ramseur Papers, SHC.

26. Carmichael, *Purcell, Crenshaw and Letcher Artillery,* pp. 8–9; William Pegram to Virginia Johnson Pegram McIntosh, April 3, 1862, P-J-M Papers.

27. William Pegram to Virginia Johnson Pegram McIntosh, April 3, 1862, P-J-M Papers.

28. Chamberlayne, *Ham Chamberlayne—Virginian,* p. 75.

29. Ibid., p. 79.

30. Ibid., pp. 77–78; John Tyler, diary entry, May 20, 1862, AL; Maggie Tucker to Charles E. Munford, May 5, 1862, Munford-Ellis Papers (GWM).

31. Johnston and Williams, eds. and comps., *Hard Times, 1861–1865,* 1:69.

32. For the Southern side of the Seven Days campaign, see Dowdey, *Seven Days;* Freeman, *Lee's Lieutenants,* 1:489–669.

33. Editorial writer in the *Southern Churchman;* "Col. William Johnson Pegram," *Confederate Veteran* 38:113; Fulton, "Picketing on the Potomac," *Confederate Veteran* 32:428.

34. *OR,* 11, pt. 2:841; "The Purcell Battery," *Daily Richmond Examiner,* July 15, 1862, p. 1.

35. "The Purcell Battery," *Daily Richmond Examiner,* July 15, 1862, p. 1.; *OR,* 11, pt. 2:899; Dawson, *Reminiscences of Confederate Service,* p. 49.

36. Dawson, *Reminiscences of Confederate Service,* pp. 185, 49.

37. "The Purcell Battery," *Daily Richmond Examiner,* July 15, 1862, p. 1; Dawson, *Reminiscences of Confederate Service,* p. 185.

38. Carmichael, *Purcell, Crenshaw and Letcher Artillery,* pp. 15–16; "The Purcell Battery," *Daily Richmond Examiner,* July 15, 1862, p. 1; Dawson, *Reminiscences of Confederate Service,* p. 185; William Ellis Jones, diary entry, June 26, 1862, WCL.

39. Dawson, *Reminiscences of Confederate Service,* p. 48; Wise, *Long Arm of Lee,* 1:208.

40. "The Purcell Battery," *Daily Richmond Examiner,* July 15, 1862, p. 1; *OR,* 11, pt. 2:837. Hill's casualty figure for the Purcell Artillery is slightly inaccurate: the company lost forty-six men, not forty-seven.

41. "The Purcell Battery," *Daily Richmond Examiner,* July 15, 1862, p. 1.

42. Ibid.

43. Wise, *Long Arm of Lee,* 1:221–24.

44. Dowdey, *Seven Days,* pp. 320–31; *OR,* 11, pt. 2:812–13.

45. *OR,* 11, pt. 2:813; "The Purcell Battery," *Daily Richmond Examiner,* July 15, 1862, p. 1; Carmichael, *Purcell, Crenshaw and Letcher Artillery,* p. 18.

46. *OR.* 11, pt. 2:813, 819; Wise, *Long Arm of Lee,* 1:231.

47. *OR,* 11, pt. 2:813; William Pegram to Charles Ellis Munford, April 18, 1861; John H. Munford to Sallie Munford, July 6, 1862, Munford-Ellis Papers (GWM).

48. "The Purcell Battery," *Daily Richmond Examiner*, July 15, 1862, p. 1; *OR*, 11, pt. 2:818–19.

49. Dowdey, *Seven Days*, pp. 339–44; Carmichael, *Purcell, Crenshaw and Letcher Artillery*, p. 18. The *Daily Richmond Examiner* stated on July 15 that the Purcell Artillery had had twenty men "cut down," but the Compiled Service Records and the *OR* do not substantiate this claim.

50. "The Purcell Battery," *Daily Richmond Examiner*, July 15, 1862, p. 1; *OR*, 11, pt. 2:983; Carmichael, *Purcell, Crenshaw and Letcher Artillery*, p. 41.

According to the *Examiner*, sixty-five members of the Purcell Artillery had been either killed or wounded. *OR* tabulates the battery's losses at sixty, while the Compiled Service Records for the Purcell Artillery at the National Archives place the company's casualties at fifty-seven.

51. Pender. *The General to His Lady*, p. 191; Davidson, *Captain Greenlee Davidson, C.S.A.*, p. 45.

52. *OR*, 11, pt. 2:843. For a further discussion of the concept of courage among Civil War soldiers, see Linderman, *Embattled Courage*, chap. 1.

THREE: WHAT HAVE I TO FEAR FROM YANKEE BULLETS AND SHELLS?

1. "The Purcell Battery," *Daily Richmond Examiner*, July 15, 1862, p. 1; McCabe, "Reunion of Pegram Battalion," p. 12.

2. McCabe, "Reunion of Pegram Battalion," p. 12; Bruce, *History of the University of Virginia*, 3:307.

3. Chamberlayne, *Ham Chamberlayne—Virginian*, pp. 85–86.

4. On the Southern side of the Second Manassas campaign, see Hennessy, *Return to Bull Run*, pp. 1–95; Allan, *Army of Northern Virginia in 1862*, pp. 150–243; Freeman, *Lee's Lieutenants*, 2:1–95.

5. Chamberlayne, *Ham Chamberlayne—Virginian*, p. 87; William Pegram to Mary Evans Pegram Anderson, Aug. 8, 1862, P-J-M Papers.

6. William Ellis Jones, diary entry, June 26, 1862, WCL; Chamberlayne, *Ham Chamberlayne—Virginian*, p. 87.

7. William Pegram to Mary Evans Pegram Anderson, Aug. 8, 1862, P-J-M Papers.

8. Ibid.

9. For the definitive study of Cedar Mountain and Pegram's role in the engagement, see Krick, *Stonewall Jackson at Cedar Mountain*.

10. *OR*, 12, pt. 2:226.

11. William Pegram to Virginia Johnson Pegram McIntosh, Aug. 14, 1862, P-J-M Papers.

12. Ibid.; Yeary, ed. and comp., *Reminiscences of the Boys in Gray*, p. 198; John W. D. Farrar in "Our Confederate Column," *Richmond Times Dispatch*, October 19, 1902.

13. Yeary, ed. and comp., *Reminiscences of the Boys in Gray*, p. 198; *OR*, 12, pt. 2:226; Farrar, "Our Confederate Column," *Richmond Times Dispatch*, Oct. 19, 1902.

14. Yeary, ed. and comp., *Reminiscences of the Boys in Gray*, p. 198; Farrar, "Our Confederate Column," *Richmond Times Dispatch*, Oct. 19, 1902; William Pegram to Virginia Johnson Pegram McIntosh, Aug. 14, 1862, P-J-M Papers.

15. Krick, *Stonewall Jackson at Cedar Mountain*, pp. 299–302; *OR*, 12, pt. 2:187.

16. William Pegram to Virginia Johnson Pegram McIntosh, Aug. 14, 1862, P-J-M Papers; Johnson, *University Memorial*, p. 717. For a more thorough examination of Pegram's role on the night of August 9 at Cedar Mountain, see Krick, *Stonewall Jackson at Cedar Mountain*, pp. 306–14.

17. Odell, "Pegram's Strategy at Cedar Mountain," *Confederate Veteran* 26:488; Johnson, *University Memorial*, p. 717; Krick, *Stonewall Jackson at Cedar Mountain*, p. 306.

18. William Pegram to Virginia Johnson Pegram McIntosh, Aug. 14, 1862, P-J-M Papers; *OR*, 12, pt. 2:184; Krick, *Stonewall Jackson at Cedar Mountain*, pp. 306–8.

19. Farrar, "Our Confederate Column," *Richmond Times Dispatch*, Oct. 19, 1902; Gilmor, *Four Years in the Saddle*, p. 54; William Pegram to Virginia Johnson Pegram McIntosh, Aug. 14, 1862, P-J-M Papers.

20. Krick, *Stonewall Jackson at Cedar Mountain*, pp. 310–13; William Pegram to Virginia Johnson Pegram McIntosh, Aug. 14, 1862, P-J-M Papers.

21. *OR*, 12, pt. 2:226, 218; Chamberlayne, *Ham Chamberlayne—Virginian*, p. 91.

22. William Pegram to Virginia Johnson Pegram McIntosh, Aug. 14, 1862, P-J-M Papers.

23. Linderman, *Embattled Courage*, p. 103; James Drayton Nance to Laura Nance, Nov. 20, 1863, James Drayton Nance Collection, SCL; Stephen Dodson Ramseur to Ellen Richmond Ramseur, July 7, 1863, Stephen Dodson Ramseur Papers, SHC; James Drayton Nance to Laura Nance, Aug. 18, 1863, James Drayton Nance Collection, SCL.

24. William Pegram to Virginia Johnson Pegram McIntosh, Aug. 14, 1862, P-J-M Papers.

25. On the preliminary movements of the Second Manassas campaign, see Allan's *Army of Northern Virginia in 1862*, pp. 181–96.

26. William Pegram to Virginia Johnson Pegram McIntosh, Sept. 7, 1862, P-J-M Papers; William Jones, diary entry, Aug. 17, 1862, WCL. On the views of soldiers toward military executions, see Linderman. *Embattled Courage*, pp. 174–77.

27. Allan, *Army of Northern Virginia in 1862*, pp. 184–85; William Pegram to Virginia Johnson Pegram, Sept. 7, 1862, P-J-M Papers.

28. Allan, *Army of Northern Virginia in 1862*, pp. 187–88; William Pegram to Virginia Johnson Pegram, Sept. 7, 1862, P-J-M Papers.

29. Allan, *Army of Northern Virginia in 1862*, pp. 195–96; Douglas, *I Rode with Stonewall*, p. 130; William Pegram to Virginia Johnson Pegram, Sept. 7, 1862, P-J-M Papers. The best account of the role of the Confederate artillery at Fauquier Springs can be found in Davidson, *Captain Greenlee Davidson*, pp. 42–44.

30. For a discussion of Jackson's flanking movement around Pope, see Hennessy, *Return to Bull Run*, pp. 96–137; Freeman, *Lee's Lieutenants*, 2:81–104.

31. William Ellis Jones, diary entry, Aug. 25, 1862, WCL; William Pegram to Virginia Johnson Pegram, Sept. 7, 1862, P-J-M Papers.

32. William Pegram to Virginia Johnson Pegram, Sept. 7, 1862, P-J-M Papers; Chamberlayne, *Ham Chamberlayne—Virginian*, p. 100.

33. William Pegram to Virginia Johnson Pegram, Sept. 7, 1862, P-J-M Papers.

34. *OR*, 12, pt. 2:674; William Pegram to Virginia Johnson Pegram, Sept. 7, 1862, P-J-M Papers.

35. William Pegram to Virginia Johnson Pegram, Sept. 7, 1862, P-J-M Papers. Pegram's short-term memory must have been fading when he wrote his mother: he told her that he lost "three men severely wounded" on August 28, yet there is no question that the batteries in Hill's division did not participate in the fight at Groveton. See Lindsay Walker's report in *OR*, 12, pt. 2:674. For an exhaustive treatment of the battle of Second Manassas, see Hennessy's *Historical Report on the Troop Movements for the Second Battle of Manassas* and his *Return to Bull Run*.

36. Hennessy, *Historical Report on the Troop Movements for the Second Battle of Manassas*, p. 189; *OR*, 12, pt. 2:674; William Pegram to Virginia Johnson Pegram, Sept. 7, 1862, P-J-M Papers.

37. Hennessy, *Historical Report on the Troop Movements for the Second Battle of Manassas*, pp. 261–427; *OR*, 12, pt. 2:674.

38. William Pegram to Virginia Johnson Pegram, Sept. 7, 1862, P-J-M Papers; Hennessy, *Historical Report on the Troop Movements for the Second Battle of Manassas*, pp. 536, 545.

FOUR: YOU WILL PRONOUNCE THIS A PRETTY BATTERY

1. Yeary, ed. and comp., *Reminiscences of the Boys in Gray*, p. 198.

2. William E. Jones, diary entry, Aug. 31, 1862, WCL. On the Southern side of Chantilly and the movements leading up to the engagement, see Freeman, *Lee's Lieutenants*, 2:128–35.

3. William E. Jones, diary entry, Sept. 1, 1862, WCL; William Pegram to Virginia Johnson Pegram, Sept. 7, 1862, P-J-M Papers.

4. William Pegram to Virginia Johnson Pegram, Sept. 7, 1862, P-J-M Papers. On the 1862 Maryland campaign in general, see Sears, *Landscape Turned Red*; Murfin, *Gleam of Bayonets*. On the attitudes of Marylanders toward the Confederacy, see Fields, *Slavery and Freedom on the Middle Ground*, pp. 90–130.

5. William Pegram to Virginia Johnson Pegram, Sept. 7, 1862, P-J-M Papers.

6. Davidson, *Captain Greenlee Davidson*, p. 50. On the condition of the Army of Northern Virginia, see Krick, "Army of Northern Virginia in September 1862," pp. 35–55.

7. William Pegram to Virginia Johnson Pegram, Sept. 7, 1862, P-J-M Papers.

8. Davidson, *Captain Greenlee Davidson*, p. 49.

9. On Jackson's capture of the Union garrison at Harpers Ferry, see Frye, "Drama between the Rivers," pp. 14–34.

10. *OR*, 19, pt. 1:980.

11. Ibid.; Yeary, ed. and comp., *Reminiscences of the Boys in Gray*, pp. 198–99.

12. Yeary, ed. and comp., *Reminiscences of the Boys in Gray*, p. 199; Davidson, *Captain Greenlee Davidson*, p. 52; *OR*, 19, pt. 1:980.

13. Yeary, ed. and comp., *Reminiscences of the Boys in Gray*, p. 199.

14. Davidson, *Captain Greenlee Davidson*, pp. 52–53; Douglas, *I Rode with Stonewall*, p. 161.

15. *OR*, 19, pt. 1:980, 984; Davidson, *Captain Greenlee Davidson*, p. 53.

16. *OR*, 19, pt. 1:981. On the battle of Antietam generally, see Sears, *Landscape Turned Red*.

17. *OR*, 19, pt. 1:981, 985; Chamberlayne, *Ham Chamberlayne—Virginian*, p. 112.

18. Douglas, *I Rode with Stonewall*, p. 174; Sears, *Landscape Turned Red*, p. 295–96.

19. Douglas, *I Rode with Stonewall*, p. 186; William Pegram to Virginia Johnson Pegram McIntosh, Oct. 7, 1862, P-J-M Papers.

20. William Pegram to Virginia Johnson Pegram McIntosh, Oct. 7, 1862, P-J-M Papers. On soldiers' attitudes toward civilians, see Linderman, *Embattled Courage*, pp. 216–39.

21. William Pegram to Virginia Johnson Pegram McIntosh, Oct. 7, 1862, P-J-M Papers.

22. *OR*, 19, pt. 2:642; see also p. 647. On the reorganization of Lee's artillery in the fall of 1862, see Wise, *Long Arm of Lee*, 1:327–56. Hill was apparently concerned that the Purcell Artillery would be disbanded immediately after the battle of Sharpsburg, and he asked Lee on September 23 not to violate the integrity of Pegram's company. See *OR*, 19, pt. 2:623; Robertson, *General A. P. Hill*, pp. 155–56.

23. *OR*, 19, pt. 2:652; Carmichael, *Purcell, Crenshaw and Letcher Artillery*, pp. 31–32; William Pegram to Virginia Johnson Pegram McIntosh, Oct. 7, 1862, P-J-M Papers.

24. John H. Munford to Sallie Munford, Oct. 24, 1862, Munford-Ellis Papers (GWM).

25. Davidson, *Captain Greenlee Davidson*, pp. 56–57.

26. William Pegram to Virginia Johnson Pegram McIntosh, Oct. 24, 1862, P-J-M Papers.

27. John H. Munford to Sallie Munford, Oct. 24, 1862, Munford-Ellis Papers (GWM); William Pegram to Virginia Johnson Pegram McIntosh, Oct. 24, 1862, P-J-M Papers.

28. William Pegram to Virginia Johnson Pegram McIntosh, Oct. 24, 1862, P-J-M Papers.

29. Davidson, *Captain Greenlee Davidson*, pp. 58–59, *OR*, 19, pt. 2:983.

30. William Ellis Jones, diary entry, Nov. 12, 1862, WCL; Davidson, *Captain Greenlee Davidson*, p. 58.

31. William Ellis Jones, diary entries, Nov. 23 and 24, 1862, WCL.

32. William Pegram to Virginia Johnson Pegram McIntosh, Nov. 29, 1862, P-J-M Papers.

33. Whan, *Fiasco at Fredericksburg*, pp. 59–62; Hotchkiss, *Make Me a Map of the Valley*, p. 97. An excellent source on the campaign and battle of Fredericksburg generally is Freeman, *Lee's Lieutenants*, 2: 317–76.

34. Whan, *Fiasco at Fredericksburg*, pp. 37–46, 59–62.

35. *OR*, 21:636–37.

36. Von Borcke, *Memoirs of the Confederate War for Independence*, 1:117; Freeman, *Lee's Lieutenants*, 2:341–43.

37. Whan, *Fiasco at Fredericksburg*, pp. 62–63; Hotchkiss, *Make Me a Map of the Valley*, p. 100.

38. Whan, *Fiasco at Fredericksburg*, pp. 63–65; McCabe, "Reunion of Pegram Battalion," p. 14.

39. *OR*, 21: 637–38; William Ellis Jones, diary entry, Dec. 13, 1862, WCL; Poague, *Gunner with Stonewall*, p. 55.

40. *OR*, 21: 636; Whan, *Fiasco at Fredericksburg*, pp. 65–67; "A Letter from the Battlefield," *Charleston Daily Courier*, Dec. 30, 1862, p. 4.

41. *OR*, 21:649, 638.

42. "From Fredericksburg," *Richmond Daily Dispatch*, Dec. 25, 1862, p. 1.; "A Letter from the Battlefield," *Charleston Daily Courier*, Dec. 30, 1862, p. 4.

43. *OR*, 21:649.

44. Faust, ed., *Historical Times Illustrated Encyclopedia of the Civil War*, pp. 289–90.

45. *OR*, 21:650, 648; "Sketches on the Battlefield," *Richmond Examiner*, Dec. 18, 1862, p. 1.

FIVE: FORTUNATELY WITH US, THE SOLDIERS MAKE THE OFFICERS

1. William Pegram to Virginia Johnson Pegram McIntosh, Jan. 8, 1863, P-J-M Papers. On the condition of Lee's army in the winter of 1862–63, see Freeman, *Lee's Lieutenants*, 2:430–31.

2. Louisa B. Ridley Drewry to her mother, Feb. 28, 1863; Elizabeth Norfleet Goodwyn Ridley to her mother, April 11, 1863; Louisa B. Ridley Drewry to Elizabeth Norfleet Goodwyn Ridley, March 3, 1863, Ridley Papers.

3. Goolsby, "Crenshaw Battery," *Southern Historical Society Papers*, 28:350; William Pegram to Virginia Johnson Pegram McIntosh, Jan. 8, 1863, P-J-M Papers

4. William Pegram to Virginia Johnson Pegram McIntosh, Jan. 8, 1863, P-J-M Papers; Myers, *Children of Pride* (abr. ed.), p. 265.

5. *OR*, 25, pt. 2:614; Alexander, *Fighting for the Confederacy*, p. 104. On the reorganization of the artillery during the winter of 1862–63, see Wise, *Long Arm of Lee*, 1:412–25.

6. *OR*, 25, pt. 2:616.

7. *OR*, 25, pt. 2:635, 636; Wise, *Long Arm of Lee*, 1:426–27; McCabe "Reunion of Pegram Battalion," p. 15.

8. John H. Munford to Sallie Munford, Feb. 24, 1862, Munford-Ellis Papers (GWM).

9. Goolsby, "Crenshaw Battery," p. 350; John O. Farrell, diary entry, March 1, 1863, EBL; John H. Munford to Sallie Munford, April 24, 1863, Munford-Ellis Papers (GWM).

10. Hotchkiss and Allan, *The Battle-Fields of Virginia: Chancellorsville*, pp. 25–28. On the Chancellorsville campaign and battle, see Bigelow,

Campaign of Chancellorsville; Freeman, *Lee's Lieutenants*, 2:524–643.

11. Chamberlayne, *Ham Chamberlayne—Virginian*, pp. 171–72.

12. *OR*, 25, pt. 1:796–97; Hotchkiss, *Make Me a Map of the Valley*, p. 137; Alexander, *Fighting for the Confederacy*, pp. 197–98.

13. *OR*, 25, pt. 1:797, 937.

14. *OR*, 25, pt. 1:937; John O. Farrell, diary entry, May 2, 1863, EBL.

15. Freeman, *Lee's Lieutenants*, 2:538–47.

16. *OR*, 25, pt. 1:937–938; Brunson, *Pee Dee Light Artillery*, p. 25.

17. John O. Farrell, diary entry, May 2, 1863, EBL.

18. Alexander, *Fighting for the Confederacy*, pp. 202–4.

19. *OR*, 25, pt. 2:885–86.

20. Alexander, *Fighting for the Confederacy*, pp. 206–7.

21. Ibid., pp. 207–8; *OR*, 25, pt. 1:938.

22. *OR*, 25, pt. 1:938, 823.

23. Ibid.

24. Klein, *Edward Porter Alexander*, pp. 65–66; Fulton, *Family Record and War Reminiscences*, p. 91; *OR*, 25, pt. 1:938; Wise, *Long Arm of Lee*, 2:507.

25. *OR*, 25, pt. 1:938; Johnson, *University Memorial*, p. 362; Alexander, *Fighting for the Confederacy*, p. 209; *OR*, 25, pt. 1:938.

26. Wise, *Long Arm of Lee*, pp. 510–12; *OR*, 25, pt. 1:938.

27. *OR*, 25, pt. 1:938; Chamberlayne, *Ham Chamberlayne—Virginian*, p. 176.

28. Pegram quoted in Colston, "In the Battle of Chancellorsville," *Confederate Veteran* 5:287; Wise, *Long Arm of Lee*, 2:512–13; Alexander, *Fighting for the Confederacy*, p. 210; *OR*, 25, pt. 1:938.

29. Wise, *Long Arm of Lee*, 2:513–14; Johnston and Williams, eds. and comps., *Hard Times, 1861–1865*, 1:19; *OR*, 25, pt. 1:938; John O. Farrell, diary entry, May 3, 1863, EBL.

30. Freeman, *Lee's Lieutenants*, 2:603–35.

31. Faust, ed., *Historical Times Illustrated Encyclopedia of the Civil War*, p. 127; Chamberlayne, *Ham Chamberlayne—Virginian*, p. 176; *OR*, 25, pt. 1:938–39.

32. Chamberlayne, *Ham Chamberlayne—Virginian*, p. 176; John H. Munford to Sallie Munford, May 14, 1863, Munford-Ellis Papers (GWM); *OR*, 25, pt. 1:939.

33. *OR*, 25, pt. 1:945, 824; Compiled Service Records of Confederate Generals, roll 196 (William Nelson Pendleton's CSR); John H. Munford to Sallie Munford, May 14, 1863, Munford-Ellis Papers (GWM).

34. William Pegram to Mary Evans Pegram Anderson, May 11, 1863, P-J-M Papers

35. Ibid.

36. Ibid.

37. Ibid.

38. Ibid.

39. John Munford to Sallie Munford, May 14, 1863, Munford-Ellis Papers (GWM); Chamberlayne, *Ham Chamberlayne—Virginian*, pp. 180–81.

40. Wise, *Long Arm of Lee*, 2:565–72.

41. William Pegram to Mary Evans Pegram Anderson, May 12, 1863, P-J-M Papers; Chamberlayne, *Ham Chamberlayne—Virginian*, p. 182; Freeman, *R. E. Lee*, 3:18–19.

42. Chamberlayne, *Ham Chamberlayne—Virginian*, p. 184; John Munford to Sallie Munford, June 12, 1863, Munford-Ellis Papers (GWM). According to McCabe's "Reunion of Pegram Battalion Association" (p. 15), Pegram became ill while on leave in Richmond, but this account can be dismissed in light of John Munford's wartime letter.

43. Johnson, *University Memorial*, p. 721; Chamberlayne, *Ham Chamberlayne—Virginian*, p. 189; *OR*, 27, pt. 2:610.

44. *OR*, 27, pt. 2:677; Chamberlayne, *Ham Chamberlayne—Virginian*, pp. 191–92.

45. Marye, "First Gun at Gettysburg," *American Historical Register*, 2:1228.

46. Member of the Crenshaw Battery, "From Gen. Lee's Army," *Richmond Daily Enquirer*, July 15, 1863, p. 2. On Gettysburg more generally, see Coddington, *Gettysburg Campaign*.

47. Coddington, *Gettysburg Campaign*, pp. 192–95.

48. Member of the Crenshaw Battery, "From Gen. Lee's Army," *Richmond Daily Enquirer*, July 15, 1863, p. 2; *OR*, 27, pt. 2:677.

49. Fleet, *Green Mount*, p. 262.

50. On the changing views of Civil War soldiers regarding courage, see Linderman, *Embattled Courage*, pp. 134–35.

51. Marye, "First Gun at Gettysburg," pp. 1228–29; *OR*, 27, pt. 2:637.

52. Marye, "First Gun at Gettysburg," pp. 1228–29.

53. *OR*, 27, pt. 2:637; Wise, *Long Arm of Lee*, 2:616–17.

54. Coddington, *Gettysburg Campaign*, p. 267; Johnson, *University Memorial*, pp. 424, 430.

55. Coddington, *Gettysburg Campaign*, p. 268.

56. Fleet, *C. B. Fleet*, p. 53; *OR*, 27, pt. 2:678.

57. Coddington, *Gettysburg Campaign*, pp. 271–72; *OR*, 27, pt. 2:678.

58. Coddington, *Gettysburg Campaign*, pp. 279–80; McCabe, "Reunion of Pegram Battalion," p. 6; *OR*, 27, pt. 2:638, 674–75.

59. Coddington, *Gettysburg Campaign*, pp. 286, 287; *OR*, 27, pt. 2:349, 639.

60. *OR*, 27, pt. 2:675; Wainwright, *A Diary of Battle*, pp. 235–36.

61. Coddington, *Gettysburg Campaign*, pp. 293–94; Marye, "First Gun at Gettysburg," p.

1230. It is difficult to determine Pegram's exact actions on the night of July 1, but Alexander lists the responsibilities of a battalion commander after a battle in *Fighting for the Confederacy*, p. 243.

62. *OR*, 27, pt. 2:678; Member of the Crenshaw Artillery, "From Gen. Lee's Army," July 15, 1863, *Richmond Daily Enquirer*, p. 2; Alexander, *Fighting for the Confederacy*, p. 252.

63. Marye, "First Gun at Gettysburg," p. 1230; Alexander, *Fighting for the Confederacy*, pp. 250–51.

64. Member of the Crenshaw Artillery, "From Gen. Lee's Army," *Richmond Daily Enquirer*, July 15, 1863, p. 2; unidentified newspaper clipping in scrapbook, George S. Bernard Papers, DU.

65. Wainwright, *A Diary of Battle*, p. 249; Member of the Crenshaw Artillery, "From Gen. Lee's Army," July 15, 1863, *Richmond Daily Enquirer*, p. 2; Marye, "First Gun at Gettysburg," p. 1231.

66. Alexander, *Fighting for the Confederacy*, pp. 259, 248.

67. Marye, "First Gun at Gettysburg," p. 1231; unidentified newspaper clipping in scrapbook, George S. Bernard Papers, DU.

68. John O. Farrell, diary entry, July 4, 1863, EBL; *OR*, 27, pt 2:678–79, 612, 355–56, 346.

69. John O. Farrell, diary entry, July 4, 1863, EBL; Marye, "First Gun at Gettysburg," p. 1232.

70. Member of the Crenshaw Artillery, "From Gen. Lee's Army," *Richmond Daily Enquirer*, July 15, 1863, p. 2; *OR*, 27, pt. 2:679.

SIX: THE MUSIC OF A SHELL WOULD BE DELIGHTFUL

1. James M. Hart to his uncle, Aug. 31, 1863, James Malcolm Hart Collection, AL; Fleet, *Green Mount*, p. 261.

2. Fleet, *Green Mount*, pp. 261–62; Compiled Service Records of Confederate Soldiers, Record group no. M324; Krick, *Fredericksburg Artillery*, pp. 97–111.

3. William Pegram to Mary Evans Pegram Anderson, Sept. 10, 18[63], P-J-M Papers.

4. Ibid.

5. Freeman, *Lee's Lieutenants*, 3:238–41.

6. Freeman, *Lee's Lieutenants*, 3:241–47; Carmichael, *Purcell, Crenshaw and Letcher Artillery*, p. 193; E. G. Gwathmey to Nannie, Nov. 7, 1863, E. G. Gwathmey Papers, 1809–1971, VHS.

7. Krick, *Fredericksburg Artillery*, pp. 69–70; Freeman, *Lee's Lieutenants*, 3:269–74. For a more detailed discussion of the Mine Run campaign, see Graham and Skoch, *Mine Run*.

8. Freeman, *Lee's Lieutenants*, 3:274–75; John M. Hart to his mother, Dec. 4, 1863, James Malcolm Hart Collection, AL.

9. James M. Hart to [?], n.d., James Malcolm Hart Collection, AL. Although the recipient of this letter is unknown, its content leaves no doubt that it was written during the Mine Run campaign.

10. James M. Hart to his mother, Dec. 1, 1863, James Malcolm Hart Collection, AL.

11. Freeman, *Lee's Lieutenants*, 3:275–76; James M. Hart to his mother, Dec. 4, 1863, James Malcolm Hart Collection, AL; William Pegram to Mary Evans Pegram Anderson, Dec. 16, 1863, P-J-M Papers; James M. Hart to his mother, Dec. 16, 1863, James Malcolm Hart Collection, AL.

12. William Pegram to Mary Evans Pegram Anderson, Dec. 16, 1863, P-J-M Papers.

13. Ibid. See also Warner and Yearns, *Biographical Register of the Confederate Congress*, pp. 86–87.

14. William Pegram to Mary Evans Pegram Anderson, Dec. 16, 1863, P-J-M Papers.

15. Yearns, *Confederate Congress*, pp. 86–88; Thomas, *Confederate Nation*, p. 260; William Pegram to Mary Evans Pegram Anderson, Dec. 16, 1863, P-J-M Papers; Franklin Gaillard to Maria Gaillard, Nov. 10, 1863, Franklin Gaillard's Civil War Letters, SHC.

16. William Pegram to Mary Evans Pegram Anderson, Dec. 16, 1863, P-J-M Papers.

17. Ibid.

18. William Pegram to Mary Evans Pegram Anderson, Feb. 11, 1864, P-J-M Papers.

19. Ibid.

20. Ibid.; Stephen Dodson Ramseur to David Schenck, n.d., Stephen Dodson Ramseur Papers, SHC.

21. Goff, *Confederate Supply*, pp. 198–200; Johnston and Williams, eds. and comps., *Hard Times, 1861–1865*, 1:92; Lee, *Wartime Papers*, pp. 659, 660.

22. William Pegram to Mary Evans Pegram Anderson, Feb. 11, 1864, P-J-M Papers; *OR*, 33:1173.

23 William Pegram to Mary Evans Pegram Anderson, Feb. 11, 1864, P-J-M Papers.

24. Inspection Reports and Related Records, record group no. M935, NA.

25. Compiled Service Records of Confederate Generals, Record group no. M331; *OR*, 33:1269.

26. William Pegram to Edward and Lucy Pegram, May 2, 1864, P-J-M Papers.

27. Porter, *Campaigning with Grant*, p. 37. For a discussion of the Wilderness campaign, see Steere, *Wilderness Campaign*, and Trudeau, *Bloody Roads South*.

28. *OR*, 36, pt. 1:1070, 318.

29. Trudeau, *Bloody Roads South*, pp. 40–53; Grant, *Personal Memoirs*, 2:193; Chamberlayne, *Ham Chamberlayne—Virginian*, p. 219; Young, "A Campaign with Sharpshooters," *Annals of the War*, p. 271; *OR*, 36, pt. 1:1028.

30. *OR*, 36, pt. 1:1071; Grant, *Personal Memoirs*, 2:196–200.

31. *OR*, 31, pt. 1:1071; Gallagher, *Stephen Dodson Ramseur*, pp. 101–3.

32. *OR*, 36, pt. 1:1040; Krick, *Fredericksburg Artillery*, p. 73; Clark, "History of My Life," typescript given to Robert K. Krick by J. Roger Mansfield, Robert K. Krick Private Collection, Fredericksburg (hereafter Clark, "History of My Life").

33. Faust, ed., *Historical Times Illustrated Encyclopedia of the Civil War*, p. 827; Freeman, *R. E. Lee*, 3:297–98.

34. Lee, *Wartime Papers*, p. 723; *OR*, 36, pt. 1:1056, 1071; Freeman, *R. E. Lee*, 3:302–3.

35. *OR*, 36, pt. 1:1071; Hotchkiss, *Make Me a Map of the Valley*, p. 202; Freeman, *R. E. Lee*, 3:306–7.

36. *OR*, 36, pt. 1:1042–43; Freeman, *R. E. Lee*, 3:309–12. For a more detailed discussion of the Spotsylvania campaign, see Matter, *If It Takes All Summer*.

37. Matter, *If It Takes All Summer*, pp. 156–58, 167, 183–222.

38. Johnson, *University Memorial*, p. 722; McCabe, "Reunion of Pegram Battalion," p. 7.

39. McCabe, "Reunion of Pegram Battalion," p. 7; Lee, Jr., *Recollections and Letters of General Robert E. Lee*, pp. 124, 125.

40. Chamberlayne, *Ham Chamberlayne—Virginian*, pp. 221–22; Clark, "History of My Life," p. 2.

41. Matter, *If It Takes All Summer*, p. 308; Wainwright, *A Diary of Battle*, p. 377; Chamberlayne, *Ham Chamberlayne—Virginian*, p. 222; M. S., "Pegram's Battalion," *Richmond Whig*, June 21, 1864, p. 1.

42. Freeman, *R. E. Lee*, 3:341–42; Miller, *North Anna Campaign*, pp. 5, 7–8.

43. Miller, *North Anna Campaign*, p. 37; Hotchkiss, *Make Me a Map of the Valley*, p. 206; Freeman, *R. E. Lee*, 3:351–52.

44. Miller, *North Anna Campaign*, pp. 69–70; McCabe, "Reunion of Pegram Battalion," p. 7.

45. Wise, *Long Arm of Lee*, 2:804–5; *OR*, 36, pt. 1:1047; Miller, *North Anna Campaign*, pp. 70, 82; Alex M. Musser, diary entry, May 23, 1864 (typescript located at Fredericksburg and Spotsylvania Military Park, Fredericksburg); Wainwright, *A Diary of Battle*, pp. 385–86.

46. Freeman, *R. E. Lee*, 3:355–60.

47. *OR*, 36, pt. 1:1050; Edwin C. Bearss, Troop Movement Maps for the Battle of Cold Harbor, located at Richmond National Battlefield Park, Richmond.

48. Hotchkiss, *Make Me a Map of the Valley*, p. 209; Catton, *A Stillness at Appomattox*, p. 159; *OR*, 36, pt. 1:369.

49. *OR*, 36, pt. 1:369; Wise, *Long Arm of Lee*, 2:822; Lyman, *Meade's Headquarters, 1861–1863*, pp. 147, 148; Catton, *A Stillness at Appomattox*, p. 163.

50. M. S., "Pegram's Battalion," *Richmond Whig*, June 21, 1864, p. 1.

51. *OR*, 36, pt. 1:1051–52; Swinton, *Campaigns of the Army of the Potomac*, p. 499; Alexander, *Fighting for the Confederacy*, p. 419.

52. Alexander, *Fighting for the Confederacy*, pp. 421–22, 424; Lee, *Wartime Papers*, p. 788; Alexander, *Fighting for the Confederacy*, pp. 430–31.

53. Howe, *Petersburg Campaign*, p. 133; Caldwell, *History of a Brigade of South Carolinians*, pp. 213–14.

54. William Pegram to Virginia Johnson Pegram McIntosh, June 28, 1864, P-J-M Papers.

55. Ibid.

56. Swinton, *Campaigns of the Army of the Potomac*, pp. 511–13.

57. William Gordon McCabe, "Defense of Petersburg," *Southern Historical Society Papers*, 2:275–76.

58. Goolsby, "Crenshaw Battery," p. 364.

59. William Pegram to Virginia Johnson Pegram McIntosh, July 14, 1864, P-J-M Papers.

60. Ibid.

61. Ibid.

62. Douglas, *I Rode with Stonewall*, pp. 295–96; William Pegram to Virginia Johnson Pegram McIntosh, July 14, 1864, P-J-M Papers.

63. William Pegram to Mary Evans Pegram Anderson, July 21, 1864, P-J-M Papers

64. Ibid.

65. Ibid.

66. Chamberlayne, *Ham Chamberlayne—Virginian*, p. 102.

67. Faust, ed., *Historical Times Illustrated Encyclopedia of the Civil War*, p. 190; Grant, *Personal Memoirs*, 2:311–15.

68. Bernard, ed. and comp., *War Talks of Confederate Veterans*, p. 178.

69. Ibid.; William Pegram to Virginia Johnson Pegram McIntosh, Aug. 1, 1864, P-J-M Papers.

70. Bernard, ed. and comp., *War Talks of Confederate Veterans*, p. 178; William Pegram to Virginia Johnson Pegram McIntosh, Aug. 1, 1864, P-J-M Papers.

71. William Pegram to Virginia Johnson Pegram McIntosh, Aug. 1, 1864, P-J-M Papers.

72. Ibid.

73. Ibid.

74. Ibid.

SEVEN: TELL MOTHER & BOTH MY SISTERS THAT I COMMEND THEM TO GOD'S PROTECTION

1. Goolsby, "Crenshaw Battery," pp. 362–63.

2. Powell, *Fifth Army Corps*, pp. 710–11; Horn, *Petersburg Campaign*, pp. 61–62.

3. Henry Heth, "Report of Operations of Heth's Command from May 4, 1864, to December 4, 1864," pp. 10–11, EBL (hereafter Heth, "Report of Operations"); *OR*, 42, pt. 1:540.

4. Heth, "Report of Operations," p. 11; Horn, *Petersburg Campaign*, pp. 67–68; *OR*, 42, pt. 2:1187.

5. Heth, "Report of Operations," pp. 11–12; *OR*, 42, pt. 1:541.

6. Heth, "Report of Operations," p. 12; *OR*, 42, pt. 1:541; Horn, *Petersburg Campaign*, p. 88.

7. Horn, *Petersburg Campaign*, p. 96; Wainwright, *A Diary of Battle*, pp. 453–54; Judson, *History of the Eighty-Third Regiment Pennsylvania Volunteers*, p. 106.

8. Horn, *Petersburg Campaign*, pp. 96, 97.

9. "The Battle on the Weldon Rail Road," *Southern Records (Milledgeville, Ga.)*, Sept. 13, 1864, p. 1 (originally printed in the *Richmond Dispatch*, Aug. 26, 1864); Wainwright, *A Diary of Battle*, pp. 454; Judson, *History of the Eighty-Third Regiment Pennsylvania Volunteers*, p. 106.

10. Judson, *History of the Eighty-Third Regiment Pennsylvania Volunteers*, p. 107; Wainwright, *A Diary of Battle*, pp. 454–55.

11. Judson, *History of the Eighty-Third Regiment Pennsylvania Volunteers*, p. 107; Horn, *Petersburg Campaign*, p. 111; "The Battle on the Weldon Rail Road," *Southern Records (Milledgeville, Ga.)*, Sept. 13, 1864, p. 1.

12. Horn, *Petersburg Campaign*, p. 112; *OR*, 42, pt. 2:1194–95; Jones, *A Rebel War Clerk's Diary*, p. 267.

13. *OR*, 42, pt. 2:391; Grant, *Personal Memoirs*, 2:324; Horn, *Petersburg Campaign*, pp. 117, 120.

14. See Horn, *Petersburg Campaign*, pp. 123, 131–32, 137.

15. Horn, *Petersburg Campaign*, p. 154; Stedman, "Battle at Ream's Station," *Southern Historical Society Papers*, 19:117–18.

16. Dunlop, *Lee's Sharpshooters*, p. 195; Gibbon, *Personal Recollections of the Civil War*, p. 257.

17. *OR*, 42, pt. 2:226, 227; Bruce, *Twentieth Regiment of Massachusetts Volunteer Infantry*, p. 422; Edwin C. Bearss, "Ream's Station," p. 52 (typescript located at Petersburg National Military Park, Petersburg); Gibbon, *Personal Recollections of the Civil War*, p. 259; Grant, *Personal Memoirs*, 2:324.

18. Horn, *Petersburg Campaign*, p. 171; Heth, *Memoirs of Henry Heth*, p. 195; *OR*, 42, pt. 1: 858; Chamberlayne, *Ham Chamberlayne—Virginian*, p. 264.

19. William Pegram to Mary Evans Pegram Anderson, Sept. 1, 1864, P-J-M Papers.

20. Ibid.

21. Ibid.

22. Carmichael, *Purcell, Crenshaw and Letcher Artillery*, p. 215; William Pegram to Mary Evans Pegram Anderson, Sept. 24, 1864, P-J-M Papers.

23. William Pegram to Mary Evans Pegram Anderson, Sept. 24, 1864, P-J-M Papers.

24. Ibid.

25. Stephen Dodson Ramseur to David Schenck, Oct. 10, 1864, Stephen Dodson Ramseur Papers, SHC; James D. Nance to Mr. Brantly, Jan. 12, 1864, James D. Nance Papers, SCL.

26. William Pegram to Mary Evans Pegram Anderson, Sept. 24, 1864, P-J-M Papers.

27. Sommers, *Richmond Redeemed*, p. 5. This volume offers the most comprehensive examination of Grant's Fifth Offensive currently available.

28. Ibid., pp. 110, 207–8.

29. Ibid., pp. 222–23, 274.

30. Ibid., pp. 296–97; McCabe, "Reunion of Pegram Battalion," pp. 16–17.

31. McCabe, "Reunion of Pegram Battalion," p. 17.

32. William Pegram to Mary Evans Pegram Anderson, Oct. 5, 1864, P-J-M Papers.

33. Ibid.; Sommers, *Richmond Redeemed*, p. 326.

34. Sommers, *Richmond Redeemed*, pp. 329–30.

35. Ibid., pp. 329–36; William Pegram to Mary Evans Pegram Anderson, Oct. 5, 1864, P-J-M Papers.

36. William Pegram to Mary Evans Pegram Anderson, Oct. 5, 1864, P-J-M Papers.

37. Ibid. All the quoted material in the following four paragraphs has been taken from this letter.

38. William Pegram to Mary Evans Pegram Anderson, Oct. 24, 1864, P-J-M Papers. Again, the quotations in the following three paragraphs are all from this letter.

39. William Pegram to Virginia Johnson Pegram, Oct. 28, 1864, P-J-M Papers.

40. Ibid.; Wainwright, *A Diary of Battle*, p. 477.

41. William Pegram to Virginia Johnson Pegram, Oct. 28, 1864, P-J-M Papers.

42. Ibid.; McCabe, "Reunion of Pegram Battalion," p. 17.

43. William Pegram to Virginia Johnson Pegram, Oct. 28, 1864, P-J-M Papers.

44. Ibid.

45. *Richmond Daily Whig*, Nov. 5, 1864; Heth, *Memoirs of Henry Heth*, p. 195; Robert E. Lee to Gordon McCabe, Feb. 9, 1870, Gordon McCabe Collection, AL.

46. Goolsby, "Crenshaw Battery," p. 367; Johnston and Williams, eds. and comps., *Hard Times, 1861–1865*, 1:88; *OR*, 42, pt. 3:1341.

47. Johnston and Williams, eds. and comps., *Hard Times, 1861–1865*, 1:88–89; Chamberlayne, *Ham Chamberlayne—Virginian*, p. 314; *OR*, 42, pt. 3:1341.

48. Goolsby, "Crenshaw Battery," p. 367; Johnston and Williams, eds. and comps., *Hard Times, 1861–1865*, 1:89.

49. Wise, *Long Arm of Lee*, 2:924; Lee, *Wartime Papers*, p. 910.

50. William Pegram to Mary Evans Pegram Anderson, March 14, 1865, P-J-M Papers; Harrison, *Recollections Grave and Gay*, pp. 201–5.

51. John Pegram to Virginia Johnson Pegram, Feb. 3, 1865, P-J-M Papers; Wise quoted in Scrivenor, "Sketch of General James West Pegram," Pegram Family Papers, SHC.

52. R. Travers to Virginia Johnson Pegram, Feb. 10, 1865, P-J-M Papers; Johnson, *University Memorial*, p. 724; Harrison, *Recollections Grave and Gay*, pp. 203–5; Chamberlayne, *Ham Chamberlayne—Virginian*, p. 309.

53. Harrison, *Recollections Grave and Gay*, p. 203; William Pegram to William Gordon McCabe, Feb. 15, 1865, P-J-M Papers.

54. William Pegram to Virginia Johnson Pegram McIntosh, March 10, 1865, P-J-M Papers.

55. Ibid.; Stephen D. Ramseur to Ellen Richmond Ramseur, May 31, 1864, Stephen Dodson Ramseur Papers, SHC.

56. William Pegram to Virginia Johnson Pegram McIntosh, March 10, 1865, P-J-M Papers.

57. Johnson, *University Memorial*, p. 725.

58. William Pegram to Mary Evans Pegram Anderson, March 14, 1865, P-J-M Papers, from which the quotations in the following two paragraphs have also been drawn.

59. William Pegram to James West Pegram, Jr., March 17, 1865, P-J-M Papers; Thomas, *Confederate Nation*, pp. 296–97.

60. William Pegram to James West Pegram, Jr., March 17, 1865, P-J-M Papers.

61. Pickett, *Pickett and His Men*, pp. 385–87; Gordon, *Memories and Memorials of William Gordon McCabe*, 1:163; William Pegram to Mary Evans Pegram Anderson, Oct. 5, 1864, P-J-M Papers.

62. Gordon, *Memories and Memorials of William Gordon McCabe*, 1:163; William Gordon McCabe to Thomas T. Munford, Oct. 1, 1905, Munford-Ellis Papers (TTM).

63. Gordon, *Memories and Memorials of William Gordon McCabe*, 1:163.

64. Gordon, *Memories and Memorials of William Gordon McCabe*, 1:164; Stern, *An End to Valor*, p. 125; William Gordon McCabe to Thomas T. Munford, Oct. 1, 1905, Munford-Ellis Papers (TTM).

65. Pickett, *Pickett and His Men*, pp. 386–87.

66. Ibid.; "Thomas T. Munford's Narrative on Five Forks with Marginalia Notes by W. Gordon McCabe," miscellany—box 2, Munford-Ellis Papers (TTM).

67. Cardwell, "Battle of Five Forks," *Confederate Veteran*, 22:117; Gordon, *Memories and Memorials of William Gordon McCabe*, 1:168, 164.

68. Gordon, *Memories and Memorials of William Gordon McCabe*, 1:164–65; Captain Robert Knox to Robert W. Hunter, Aug. 3, 1906, Department of Military Affairs, box 47, VSL.

69. Pickett, *Pickett and His Men*, p. 388; Scrivenor, "Sketch of General James West Pegram," p. 49; Gordon, *Memories and Memorials of William Gordon McCabe*, 1:165; Freeman, *Lee's Lieutenants*, 3:668–69. The best study on Five Forks to date is undoubtedly Calkins and Bearss, *Battle of Five Forks*.

70. William Gordon McCabe to Mary Evans Pegram Anderson, April 7, 1865, P-J-M Papers; Gordon, *Memories and Memorials of William Gordon McCabe*, 1:169.

71. William Gordon McCabe to Mary Evans Pegram Anderson, April 7, 1865, P-J-M Papers.

72. "Testimony of W. Gordon McCabe adj. in Pegram's light artillery C.S.A., June 7, 1880," in *Proceedings, Findings and Opinions of the Court of Inquiry in the Case of Gouverneur K. Warren* (1883), 1:513, U.S. War Department, Washington, D.C.; "Munford Narrative on Five Forks," Munford-Ellis Papers (TTM); William Gordon McCabe to Mary Evans Pegram Anderson, April 7, 1865, P-J-M Papers.

73. William Gordon McCabe to Mary Evans Pegram Anderson, April 7, 1865, P-J-M Papers.

74. Ibid. and see also Hudson, *Sketches and Reminiscences,* pp. 68–69.

75. William Gordon McCabe to Mary Evans Pegram Anderson, April 7, 1865, P-J-M Papers.

76. William Gordon McCabe to Mary Early, April 7, 1865, Early Family Papers, 1764–1956,

VHS; William Gordon McCabe to Mary Evans Pegram Anderson, April 7, 1865, P-J-M Papers.

77. William Gordon McCabe to Mary Evans Pegram Anderson, April 7, 1865, P-J-M Papers.

CONCLUSION: HE FELL IN THE DISCHARGE OF HIS DUTY, AND DIED WITH THE PHILOSOPHY OF A CHRISTIAN

1. "Colonel William J. Pegram," *Richmond Whig,* Dec. 5, 1865, p. 1; *Richmond Daily Dispatch,* Dec. 9, 1865, p. 1 (originally printed in the *Norfolk Virginian,* n.d.).

2. Haskell, *Haskell Memoirs,* p. 83.

3. Stiles, *Four Years under Marse Robert,* p. 110.

4. Goolsby, "Col. William Johnson Pegram," *Confederate Veteran* 38:271.

5. Wise, "Boy Gunners of Lee," *Southern Historical Society Papers,* 42:156.

6. Goolsby, "Col. William Johnson Pegram," p. 271.

7. William Pegram to Mary Evans Pegram Anderson, Oct. 5, 1864, P-J-M Papers; Gordon, *Memories and Memorials of William Gordon McCabe,* 2:170.

8. William Gordon McCabe to Mary Evans Pegram Anderson, April 7, 1865, P-J-M Papers.

BIBLIOGRAPHY

MANUSCRIPT COLLECTIONS

Ann Arbor, Michigan
William L. Clements Library, University of
Michigan
Diary of William Ellis Jones.

Carlisle, Pennsylvania
United States Army Military History
Institute, Carlisle Barracks
David Gregg McIntosh Memoirs.

Chapel Hill, North Carolina
Southern Historical Collection, Wilson
Library, University of North Carolina
Franklin Gaillard's Civil War Letters.
Lenoir Family Papers.
Pegram Family Papers.
Stephen Dodson Ramseur Papers.

Charlottesville, Virginia
Alderman Library, Manuscript Department,
University of Virginia
Berry Hill Bruce Papers.
Gordon McCabe Collection.
James Malcolm Hart Collection.
Diary of John Tyler.
University of Virginia Matriculation
Register, 1856–1868.

Columbia, South Carolina
South Caroliniana Library, University of
South Carolina
James Drayton Nance Collection.

Durham, North Carolina
William R. Perkins Library, Manuscript
Department, Duke University
George S. Bernard Papers.
Munford-Ellis Papers, George W.
Munford Division and Thomas T.
Munford Division.

Fredericksburg, Virginia
Fredericksburg and Spotsylvania National
Military Park
Diary of Alex M. Musser.
Robert K. Krick Private Collection
Clark, George W. "The History of My
Life."

Petersburg, Virginia
Petersburg National Military Park
Bearss, Edwin C. "Reams' Station."
Petersburg National Battlefield
Historical Report on Troop
Movements. Petersburg: N.d.
Bearss, Edwin C. "The Battle of Weldon
Railroad."
Petersburg National Battlefield Historical
Report on Troop Movements.
Petersburg: N.d.

Richmond, Virginia
Eleanor Brockenbrough Library, Museum of
the Confederacy
Henry Heth. "Report of Operations of
Heth's Command from May 4, 1864 to
December 4, 1864."
Diary of John O. Farrell.
Richmond National Military Park
Bearss, Edwin C. Troop Movement Maps
for the Battle of Cold Harbor, N.d.
Virginia Historical Society
Bailey Family Papers, 1802–1980.
Early Family Papers, 1764–1956.
E. G. Gwathmey Papers, 1809–1971.
Johnson Family Papers.
Pegram-Johnson-McIntosh Collection.
The Ridley Family of Southampton
County, Va., Papers, 1776–1897.
Virginia State Library
Purcell Artillery and Thirtieth Infantry
file in Department of Military Affairs.
Samuel Bassett French Biographical
Sketches.
Personal Property Taxes for Chesterfield
County, Virginia, 1836–1847.
Personal Property Taxes for Dinwiddie
County, Virginia, 1825–1828.
Personal Property Taxes for the City of
Richmond, 1840–1844, 1851–1860.

Washington, D.C.
National Archives
Adjutant and Inspector General's Office,
C.S.A. Inspection Reports and Related
Records Received by the Inspection
Branch. Record group no. M935.

Compiled Service Records of
Confederate Generals and Staff
Officers and Nonregimental Enlisted
Men. Record group no. M331.

Compiled Service Records of
Confederate Soldiers Who Served in
Organizations from the State of
Virginia, Brander, Cayce, and Ellett's
Companies of Artillery. Record group
no. M324.

Population Schedules of the Eighth
Census of the United States, 1860.
Record group no. M653.

Population Schedules of the Seventh
Census of the United States, 1850.
Record group no. M432.

Population Schedules of the Sixth Census
of the United States, 1840. Record
group no. M704.

NEWSPAPERS

Charleston Daily Courier (South Carolina)
Daily Richmond Examiner
Daily Richmond Enquirer
Fredericksburg News
Richmond Daily Dispatch
Richmond Enquirer (semi-weekly)
Richmond Whig

Richmond Times Dispatch
Richmond Whig and Public Advertiser
Richmond Examiner
Richmond Daily Whig
Richmond Dispatch
Southern Records (Milledgeville, Georgia)
Southern Churchman (Richmond)

PRIMARY SOURCES

Alexander, Edward Porter. *Fighting for the Confederacy: The Personal Recollections of General Edward Porter Alexander*. Ed. Gary W. Gallagher. Chapel Hill, N.C., 1989.

Allan, William. *The Army of Northern Virginia in 1862*. 1892. Repr., Dayton, Oh., 1984.

Bernard, George S., ed. and comp. *War Talks of Confederate Veterans*. 1892. Repr., Dayton, Oh., 1981.

Brunson, Joseph W. *The Pee Dee Light Artillery: A Historical Sketch*. Ed. William Stanley Hoole. Dayton, Oh., 1983.

Caldwell, J. F. J. *The History of a Brigade of South Carolinians, Known First as "Gregg's," and Subsequently as "McGowan's Brigade."* 1866. Repr., Dayton, Oh., 1974.

Cardwell, David. "The Battle of Five Forks." *Confederate Veteran* 22:117–20.

Catalogue of the University of Virginia, Session of 1860–'61. Richmond, 1861.

Chamberlayne, John Hampden. *Ham Chamberlayne—Virginian: Letters and Papers of an Artillery Officer in the War for Southern Independence, 1861–1865*. Ed. by C. G. Chamberlayne. Richmond, 1932.

Chesnut, Mary. *Mary Chesnut's Civil War*. Ed. C. Vann Woodward. New Haven, Conn., 1981.

Colston, F. M. "In the Battle of Chancellorsville," *Confederate Veteran* 5:287–89.

Davidson, Greenlee. *Captain Greenlee Davidson, C.S.A.: Diary and Letters, 1851–1863*. Ed. Charles W. Turner. Verona, Va., 1975.

Dawson, Francis W. *Reminiscences of Confederate Service, 1861–1865*. Ed. Bell I. Wiley. Baton Rouge, La., 1980.

DeLeon, T. C. *Belles, Beaux and Brains of the 60's*. New York, 1907.

———. *Four Years in Rebel Capitals: An Inside View of Life in the Southern Confederacy from Birth to Death*. Mobile, 1890.

Douglas, Henry Kyd. *I Rode With Stonewall*. 1940. Repr., Chapel Hill, N.C., 1968.

Dunlop, W. S. *Lee's Sharpshooters; or, The Forefront of Battle*. Little Rock, Ark., 1899.

Editorial writer in the *Southern Churchman*. "Col. William Johnson Pegram." *Confederate Veteran* 38:113, 125.

Elliott, E. N., ed. *Cotton Is King and Pro-slavery Arguments: Comprising the Writings of Hammond, Harper, Christy, Stringfellow, Hodge, Bledsoe, and Cartwright*. 3d ed. Augusta, Ga., 1860.

Ferslew, W. Eugene, comp. *Second Annual Directory for the City of Richmond, to Which Is Added a Business Directory for 1860*. Richmond, 1860.

Fleet, Benjamin Robert. *Green Mount*. Ed. Betsy Fleet and John D. P. Fuller. Lexington, Ky., 1962.

Fleet, Charles B. *C. B. Fleet: The Man and the Company.* Ed. by Elizabeth M. Hodges. Lynchburg[?], Va., 1985[?].

Fulton, William Frierson. *Family Record and War Reminiscences.* N.p., n.d.

Fulton, W. R. "Picketing on the Potomac." *Confederate Veteran* 32:427–28.

Gibbon, John. *Personal Recollections of the Civil War.* 1928. Repr., Dayton, Oh., 1978.

Gilmor, Harry. *Four Years in the Saddle.* New York, 1866.

Goolsby, J. C. "Col. William Johnston Pegram." *Confederate Veteran* 6:270–71.

——. "Crenshaw Battery, Pegram's Battalion, Confederate States Artillery." In *Southern Historical Society Papers,* ed. J. William Jones et al., 28:336–77.

Gordon, Armistead Churchill. *Memories and Memorials of William Gordon McCabe.* 2 vols. Richmond, 1925.

Grant, Ulysses S. *Personal Memoirs of U. S. Grant.* 2 vols. New York, 1886.

Harrison, Constance Cary Burton. *Recollections Grave and Gay.* New York, 1916.

Haskell, John Cheves. *The Haskell Memoirs.* Ed. Gilbert E. Govan and James W. Livingood. New York, 1960.

Heth, Henry. *The Memoirs of Henry Heth.* Ed. James L. Morrison, Jr. Westport, Conn., 1974.

Holcombe, James P. *An Address, On the Right of the State to Institute Slavery.* Richmond, 1858.

Hotchkiss, Jedediah. *Make Me a Map of the Valley.* Ed. Archie P. McDonald. Dallas, 1973.

Hotchkiss, Jedediah, and William Allan. *The Battle-Fields of Virginia: Chancellorsville.* New York, 1867.

Howard, James McHenry. *Recollections and Opinions Concerning the Events Which Immediately Preceded and Followed the Outbreak of the War Between the Northern and Southern States.* Baltimore, 1922.

Hudson, Joshua Hilary. *Sketches and Reminiscences.* Columbia, S.C., 1903.

Johnson, John Lipscomb. *The University Memorial: Biographical Sketches of Alumni of the University of Virginia Who Fell in the Confederate War.* Baltimore, 1871.

Johnston, Jane Echols, and Brenda Lynn Williams, eds. and comps. *Hard Times, 1861–1865: A Collection of Confederate Letters, Court Minutes, Soldier Records and Local Lore from Craig County, Virginia.* 3 vols. Craig County, Va., 1986.

Jones, John B. *A Rebel War Clerk's Diary.* Ed. Earl Schenck Miers. New York, 1958.

Judson, Amos M. *History of the Eighty-Third Regiment Pennsylvania Volunteers.* Erie, Pa., 1865.

Lee, Robert E. *The Wartime Papers of R. E. Lee.* Ed. Clifford Dowdey and Louis H. Manarin. New York, 1961.

Lee, Robert E., Jr. *Recollections and Letters of General Robert E. Lee.* 1904. Repr., Wilmington, N.C., 1988.

Lyman, Theodore. *Meade's Headquarters, 1861–1863.* Ed. George R. Agassiz. 1922. Repr., Salem, N.H., 1970.

McCabe, William Gordon. *Annual Reunion of the Pegram Battalion Association.* Richmond, 1886.

——. "Defence of Petersburg." In *Southern Historical Society Papers,* ed. J. William Jones et al., 2:257–306.

Marye, John L. "The First Gun at Gettysburg, 'With the Confederate Advance Guard.'" *American Historical Register* 2:1225–32.

Myers, Robert Manson. *The Children of Pride: A True Story of Georgia and the Civil War.* Abr. ed. New Haven, Conn., 1984.

Odell, William S. "Pegram's Strategy at Cedar Mountain," *Confederate Veteran* 26:488.

Pender, William Dorsey. *The General to His Lady: The Civil War Letters of William Dorsey Pender to Fanny Pender.* Ed. William W. Hassler. 1962. Repr., Gaithersburg, Md., 1988.

Poague, William Thomas. *Gunner with Stonewall.* Ed. Monroe F. Cockrell. 1957. Repr., Wilmington, N.C., 1987.

Porter, Horace. *Campaigning with Grant.* 1897. Repr., Secaucus, N.J., 1984.

Stedman, Charles M. "Battle at Ream's Station." In *Southern Historical Society Papers,* ed. J. William Jones, et al., 19:113–20.

Stiles, Robert. *Four Years under Marse Robert.* 1903. Repr., Dayton, Oh., 1977.

U.S. War Department. *Official Records of the Union and Confederate Navies in the War of the Rebellion.* Washington D.C., 1896.

——. "Testimony of W. Gordon McCabe adj. in Pegram's light artillery C.S.A., June 7, 1880." In *Proceedings, Findings and Opinions in the Court of Inquiry in the Case of Gouverner K. Warren.* 3 vols. Washington D.C., 1883.

——. *The War of the Rebellion: A Compilation of the Official Records of the Union and Confederate Armies.* 127 vols., index, and atlas. Washington, D.C., 1880–1901.

Von Borcke, Heros. *Memoirs of the Confederate War for Independence.* 2 vols. New York, 1938.

Wainwright, Charles S. *A Diary of Battle: The Personal Journals of Charles S. Wainwright, 1861–1865*, ed. Allan Nevins. New York, 1962.

Wise, Jennings C. "The Boy Gunners of Lee." In *Southern Historical Society Papers*, ed. J. William Jones et al., 42: 152–73.

Worsham, John H. *One of Jackson's Foot Cavalry,*

ed. James I. Robertson, Jr., and Bell Irvin Wiley. 1912. Repr., Wilmington, N.C., 1987.

Yeary, Mamie, ed. and comp. *Reminiscences of the Boys in Gray, 1861–1865*. Dallas, 1912.

Young, John D. "A Campaign with Sharpshooters." *The Annals of the War: Written by Leading Participants North and South*. Philadelphia, 1879.

SECONDARY SOURCES

Bearss, Edwin C. *Historical Report on Troop Movements, Battle of First Manassas and Engagement at Blackburn's Ford*. Denver, 1981.

Beringer, Richard E., et al. *Why the South Lost the Civil War*. Athens, Ga., 1986.

Bigelow, John. *The Campaign of Chancellorsville: A Strategic and Tactical Study*. New Haven, 1910.

Bruce, George A. *The Twentieth Regiment of Massachusetts Volunteer Infantry, 1861–1865*. Boston, 1906.

Bruce, Philip Alexander. *History of the University of Virginia, 1819–1919*. 5 vols. New York, 1920–21.

Calkins, Chris, and Edwin C. Bearss. *The Battle of Five Forks*. Lynchburg, Va., 1985.

Carmichael, Peter S. *The Purcell, Crenshaw and Letcher Artillery*. Lynchburg, Va., 1990.

Catton, Bruce. *A Stillness at Appomattox*. New York, 1953.

Christian, W. Asbury. *Richmond: Her Past and Present*. Richmond, 1912.

Coddington, Edwin B. *The Gettysburg Campaign: A Study of Command*. New York, 1968.

Cole, Arthur Charles. *The Whig Party in the South*. Washington D.C., 1913.

Coulter, Ellis Merton. *The Confederate States of America, 1861–1865*. Baton Rouge, La., 1950.

Crofts, Daniel W. *Reluctant Confederates: Upper South Unionists in the Secession Crisis*. Chapel Hill, N.C., 1989.

Curry, Henry Lee. "The Confederate Careers of James Armstrong Duncan, Moses Drury Hoge, and Charles Frederick Ernest Minnigerode." Ph.D. diss., Emory University, 1971.

Dowdey, Clifford. *The Seven Days: The Emergence of Robert E. Lee*. 1964. Repr., New York, 1978.

Escott, Paul D. *After Secession: Jefferson Davis and the Failure of Confederate Nationalism*. Baton Rouge, La., 1979.

Farmer, James Oscar, Jr. *The Metaphysical Confederacy: James Henley Thornwell and the Synthesis of Southern Values*. Macon, Ga., 1986.

Faust, Drew Gilpin. *The Creation of Confederate Nationalism: Ideology and Identity in the Civil War South*. Baton Rouge, La., 1988.

Faust, Patricia L., ed. *Historical Times Illustrated Encyclopedia of the Civil War*. New York, 1986.

Fields, Barbara Jeanne. *Slavery and Freedom on the Middle Ground: Maryland during the Nineteenth Century*. New Haven, Conn., 1985.

Foner, Eric. *Free Soil, Free Labor, Free Men: The Ideology of the Republican Party before the Civil War*. New York, 1970.

Forgie, George B. *Patricide in the House Divided: A Psychological Interpretation of Lincoln and His Age*. New York, 1979.

Fox-Genovese, Elizabeth, and Eugene D. Genovese. *Fruits of Merchant Capital: Slavery and Bourgeois Property in the Rise and Expansion of Capitalism*. New York, 1983.

Freeman, Douglas Southall. *Lee's Lieutenants: A Study in Command*. 3 vols. New York, 1942–44.

——. *R. E. Lee*. 4 vols. New York, 1934–36.

Frye, Dennis E. "Drama between the Rivers: Harpers Ferry in the 1862 Maryland Campaign." In *Antietam: Essays on the 1862 Maryland Campaign*, ed. Gary W. Gallagher, pp. 14–34. Kent, Oh., 1989.

Gallagher, Gary W. *Stephen Dodson Ramseur: Lee's Gallant General*. Chapel Hill, N.C., 1985.

Genovese, Eugene D. *The Slaveholders' Dilemma: Freedom and Progress in Southern Conservative Thought, 1820–1860*. Columbia, S.C., 1992.

——. *The World the Slaveholders Made: Two Essays in Interpretation*. New York, 1969.

——. *The Political Economy of Slavery: Studies in the Economy and Society of the Slave South*. New York, 1965.

Genovese, Eugene D., and Elizabeth Fox-Genovese. "The Religious Ideals of Southern Slave Society," *Georgia Historical Quarterly*, no. 1 (Spring 1986): 1–16.

Goff, Richard D. *Confederate Supply*. Durham, N.C., 1969.

Graham, Martin and George Skoch. *Mine Run: A*

Campaign of Lost Opportunities. Lynchburg, Va., 1987.

Heitman, Francis B. *Historical Register and Dictionary of the United States Army.* 2 vols. Washington D.C., 1903.

Hennessy, John J. *Historical Report on the Troops Movements for the Second Battle of Manassas, August 28 through August 30, 1862.* Denver, 1985.

Hennessy, John J. *Return to Bull Run: The Campaign and Battle of Second Manassas.* New York, 1993.

Hervey, John. *Racing in America, 1665–1865.* 2 vols. New York, 1944.

Holt, Michael F. *The Political Crisis of the 1850s.* New York, 1978.

Horn, John. *The Petersburg Campaign: The Destruction of the Weldon Railroad: Deep Bottom, Globe Tavern, and Reams Station.* Lynchburg, Va., 1991.

Howe, Thomas J. *The Petersburg Campaign: Wasted Valor, June 15–18, 1864.* Lynchburg, Va., 1988.

Jimerson, Randall C. *The Private Civil War: Popular Thought during the Sectional Conflict.* Baton Rouge, La., 1988.

Johnson, Michael P. *Toward a Patriarchal Republic: The Secession of Georgia.* Baton Rouge, La., 1977.

Jones, Richard L. *Dinwiddie County: Carrefour of the Commonwealth.* Richmond, 1976.

Jordan, Ervin L., Jr. *Charlottesville and the University of Virginia in the Civil War.* Lynchburg, Va., 1988.

Klein, Maury. *Edward Porter Alexander.* Athens, Ga., 1971.

Krick, Robert K. *Stonewall Jackson at Cedar Mountain.* Chapel Hill, N.C., 1990.

——. "The Army of Northern Virginia in September 1862: Its Circumstances, Its Opportunities, and Why It Should Not Have Been at Sharpsburg." In *Antietam: Essays on the 1862 Maryland Campaign,* ed. Gary W. Gallagher, pp. 35–55. Kent, Oh., 1989.

——. *The Fredericksburg Artillery.* Lynchburg, Va., 1986.

——. *Lee's Colonels: A Biographical Register of the Field Officers of the Army of Northern Virginia.* Rev. ed. Dayton, Oh., 1984.

Kulikoff, Allan. *Tobacco and Slaves: The Development of Southern Cultures in the Chesapeake, 1680–1800.* Chapel Hill, N.C., 1986.

Linderman, Gerald F. *Embattled Courage: The Experience of Combat in the American Civil War.* New York, 1987.

Loveland, Anne C. *Southern Evangelicals and the Social Order, 1800–1860.* Baton Rouge, La., 1980.

McCardell, John. *The Idea of a Southern Nation: Southern Nationalists and Southern Nationalism, 1830–1860.* New York, 1979.

McDowell, Beverly Blair. "The Military Career of Colonel William Ransom Johnson Pegram, C.S.A." M.A. thesis, University of Richmond, 1964.

Maddex, Jack P., Jr. " 'The Southern Apostasy' Revisited: The Significance of Proslavery Christianity," *Marxist Perspectives* (Fall 1979): 132–41.

Manarin, Louis H., and Lee A. Wallace, Jr. *Richmond Volunteers: The Volunteer Companies of the City of Richmond and Henrico County, Virginia, 1861–1865.* Richmond, 1969.

Mathews, Donald G. *Religion in the Old South.* Chicago, 1977.

Matter, William D. *If It Takes All Summer: The Battle of Spotsylvania.* Chapel Hill, N.C., 1988.

Meagher, Margaret. *History of Education in Richmond.* Richmond, 1939.

Miller, J. Michael. *The North Anna Campaign: "Even to Hell Itself," May 21–26, 1864.* Lynchburg, Va., 1989.

Mitchell, Reid. "The Creation of Confederate Loyalties." In *New Perspectives on Race and Slavery in America: Essays in Honor of Kenneth M. Stampp,* ed. Robert H. Abzug and Stephen E. Maizlish, pp. 93–108. Lexington, Ky., 1986.

Mohr, Clarence L. *On the Threshold of Freedom: Masters and Slaves in Civil War Georgia.* Athens, Ga., 1986.

Mordecai, Samuel. *Richmond in By-Gone Days.* 1860. Repr., Richmond, 1946.

Murfin, James V. *The Gleam of Bayonets: The Battle of Antietam and the Maryland Campaign of 1862.* New York, 1965.

Oakes, James. *Slavery and Freedom: An Interpretation of the Old South.* New York, 1990.

——. *The Ruling Race: A History of American Slaveholders.* New York, 1982.

Owens, Harry P., and James J. Cooke, eds. *The Old South in the Crucible of War.* Jackson, Miss., 1983.

Patton, John S. *Jefferson, Cabell, and the University of Virginia.* New York, 1906.

Pfanz, Harry W. *Special History Report on Troop Movements Maps, 1862 Harpers Ferry National Historical Park.* Denver, 1976.

Pickett, LaSalle Corbell. *Pickett and His Men.* Atlanta, 1900.

Powell, William H. *The Fifth Army Corps.* New York, 1896.

Rintala, Marvin. "Generation." In *International Encyclopedia of the Social Sciences,* vol. 5, ed. David L. Sills.

Robertson, James I., Jr. *General A. P. Hill: The Story of a Confederate Warrior.* New York, 1987.

Sears, Stephen W. *Landscape Turned Red: The Battle of Antietam.* New York, 1983.

Shanks, Henry T. *The Secession Movement in Virginia, 1847–1861.* Richmond, 1934.

Shattuck, Gardiner H., Jr. *A Shield and Hiding Place: The Religious Life of the Civil War Armies.* Macon, Ga., 1987.

Simmons, Samuel William. *The Pegrams of Virginia and Descendants, 1688–1984.* Lakemont, Ga., 1985.

Sommers, Richard J. *Richmond Redeemed: The Siege at Petersburg.* Garden City, N.Y., 1981.

Spitzer, Alan B. "The Historical Problem of Generations." *American Historical Review* 78 (Dec. 1973): 1353–85.

Stampp, Kenneth. *The Imperiled Union: Essays on the Background of the Civil War.* New York, 1980.

Steere, Edward. *The Wilderness Campaign.* Harrisburg, Pa., 1960.

Stern, Philip Van Doren. *An End to Valor: The Last Days of the Civil War.* Cambridge, Mass., 1958.

Swinton, William. *Campaigns of the Army of the Potomac.* 1866. Repr., Secaucus, N.J., 1988.

Thomas, Emory M. *The Confederate Nation: 1861–1865.* New York, 1979.

———. *The Confederate State of Richmond: A Biography of the Capital.* Austin, Tex., 1971.

Trudeau, Noah A. *Bloody Roads South: The Wilderness to Cold Harbor, May–June 1864.* Boston, 1989.

Wallace, Lee A., Jr. *A Guide to Virginia Military Organizations, 1861–1865.* Rev. ed. Lynchburg, Va., 1986.

Warner, Ezra J., and Wilfred Buck Yearns. *Biographical Register of the Confederate Congress.* Baton Rouge, La., 1975.

Whan, Vorin E., Jr. *Fiasco at Fredericksburg.* University Park, Pa., 1961.

Wiley, Bell Irvin. *The Road to Appomattox.* Memphis, 1956.

———. *The Life of Johnny Reb: The Common Soldier of the Confederacy.* New York, 1943.

Wise, Jennings C. *The Long Arm of Lee, or The History of the Artillery of the Army of Northern Virginia.* 2 vols. Lynchburg, Va., 1915.

Yearns, Wilfred Buck. *The Confederate Congress.* Athens, Ga., 1960.

INDEX

A Nation Divided: New Studies in Civil War History